Active Platform Management Demystified

Unleashing the power of Intel® vPro™ Technology

Arvind Kumar
Purushottam Goel
Ylian Saint-Hilare

Intel
PRESS

ISBN 978-1-934053-19-5

This book is printed on acid-free paper. ∞

Publisher: Richard Bowles
Editor: David J. Clark
Managing Editor: Bruce Bartlett
Text Design & Composition: STI Certified
Graphic Art: PhoebusGroup (illustrations), Ron Bohart (cover)

Library of Congress Cataloging in Publication Data:

Printed in China

10 9 8 7 6 5 4 3 2 1

First printing, Version 1.0 June 2009

IMPORTANT

You can access the companion Web site for this book on the Internet at:

www.intel.com/intelpress/iamt

Use the serial number located in the upper-right hand corner of the last page to register your book and access additional material, including the Digital Edition of the book.

I dedicate this book to my wife Geetanjali, and my two lovely daughters, Arushi and Anika.

— A.K.

I dedicate this book to my father.

— P.G.

I dedicate this book to the contributors, reviewers, and Intel Press team who supported us through the development and completion of the project.

— Y. S-H..

Contents

Chapter 7 - The Components of Intel® Active Management Technology   95

Chapter 8 - Discovery of Platforms and Information   125

Foreword

It has been a long time coming...

In many product development cycles, platform management interfaces are an afterthought. Product managers concentrate solely on the core features of the product being developed and do not realize that additional features will not increase the value of the product if IT Administrators can not easily manage and integrate the product quickly into their existing data center management environment. IT organizations base purchasing decisions on the Total Cost of Ownership (TCO) of a product. TCO includes the purchase price of the product combined with the cost of power and cooling, maintenance, insurance, auditing, warranties, security as well as integration and testing.

As data center management continues to become more complex with new requirements for virtualization and now for green IT (measuring, monitoring and managing power consumption costs), integrating management into the original product designs is critical. Data centers have evolved from point management to managing services aligned with business goals. IT administrators manage a service that is provided by a set of interrelated systems and need to relate each of the services to their actual business goals and requirements. Platform management is no longer a differentiator, it is a requirement.

For data center management to be successful, industry standards are required. IT administrators must have a way to mix products in the data center without having to add special code for proprietary interfaces. The standards must be flexible enough to allow for a set of lowest common denominator management interfaces as well as allowing vendors to extend the interfaces for product-specific features and other added value. This combination enables IT administrators to manage products using a single method to get both standard interfaces and product-specific features and *Active Platform Management Demystified* is an excellent source of information on this precise subject.

Over the past five years, there has been a paradigm shift in the industry for standards-based management, as this book well attests. The Distributed Management Task Force (DMTF) has designed a set of standards and a model for how these standards fit together to address a vertical market. While the many management standards and related software already offer some combination of remote monitoring, security and management features, this book shows how Intel® vPro™ technology controlled by the Intel® Active Management Technology (Intel® AMT) takes platform management a giant step further. By making manageability part of the computer's actual silicon, Intel vPro technology delivers new possibilities for monitoring a computer while its power is turned off or repairing a computer remotely regardless of the state of the operating system—just what IT Administrators demand.

Intel is an active participant in defining both industry standards and Intel AMT extensions in such a way that it is easy for tools to interface with both operating system and hardware management interfaces. With the current version of Intel AMT, not only has the Desktop and mobile Architecture for System Hardware (DASH) Management Initiative been implemented, but support of the management profiles for Intel-specific features have been provided. This management approach enables IT administrators to manage all aspects of the platform following an industry standard.

Active Platform Management Demystified provides a history and background on the evolution of the standard technologies as well as detailed explanations of how IT administrators and developers can use the latest Intel platform technology.

IT administrators take notice! The future of standards-based desktop management is here.

Jim Davis
CEO/CTO
WBEM Solutions, Inc.

Preface

There is nothing more difficult to take in hand, more perilous to conduct or more uncertain in its success than to take the lead in the introduction of a new order of things.

—- Niccolo Machiavelli (1469–1527), *The Prince* (1532)

As with many other technologies, the development and advancement of computers has gone through distinct phases. In the early years of farm tractors, a single engine would be operated and maintained by a crew of many. The first computers were operated in much the same way, requiring many people to monitor and fix problems of a single computer.

As designs improved, tractors became smaller, more affordable, more reliable, and requiring less maintenance. There is a point after which it is cost effective to build proper diagnostic tools and maintenance right into a product. Modern tractors, like newer cars, have electronic diagnostic ports, service lights, along with sensors to monitor the proper functioning of the vehicle and warn of problems.

Another great example is large container and cruise ships running very large diesel engines. Proper functioning and monitoring of these engines is critical, so engine manufacturers offer real time satellite monitoring of these engines. It helps make sure the engine is running properly, keeps a real time log of what is going on and ultimately improves reliability and safety of the ship.

In the computer world, we face many problems and unexpected issues with computers and it should come as no surprise that similar strategies are being explored to keep computers up and running. Why not look into building manageability right into the computer itself?

As computers get more complex and run more complicated software, the amount of money spent on fixing problems and keeping them running grows quickly. With a limited budget, information technology (IT) departments are looking for better and smarter solutions at low cost.

In this book, we look at today's problem of maintaining computers and the broader topic of manageability: what is it and how can it help lower the cost of owning computers? We will also look at what areas are covered by manageability and examine solutions.

As the title of this book suggests, most of this book is dedicated to a unique Intel technology called Intel® Active Management Technology (Intel AMT) that builds manageability solutions right into the computer itself.

Who Should Read This Book

Since this book is rather technical, it's certainly not for everyone. People who have to manage a lot of computers, who are interested in manageability, or who participate in building management software are this book's intended audience. Trade experts interested in the details of Intel technologies will also be interested in peeking inside Intel Active Management Technology. People who are interested in computer manageability will hopefully learn as well from this book about the design choices and solutions built by Intel and other software developers.

Authors' Background

Arvind Kumar Arvind is a principal engineer and chief manageability architect at Intel and leads the definition and development of next-generation platform manageability architecture. He is an industry recognized expert in the area of systems and platform management and has been instrumental in development of various system management technologies such as Desktop Management Interface (DMI), Common Information Model (CIM), Web-Based Enterprise Management (WBEM), and WS-Management. Arvind has 22 years of experience in networking and systems management with active work in standards bodies such as the Distributed Management Task Force (DMTF) for over a decade. He currently represents Intel in the DMTF Technical Committee. At Intel, Arvind has been responsible for the architecture of Intel® Server Management products, BladeCenter† management and Intel Active Management Technology.

Arvind graduated from the Indian Institute of Technology, Roorkee in 1987 with a bachelor's degree in computer science and technology. He worked at Tata Consultancy Services, IBM, and Sequent Computer Systems prior to joining Intel in 1994.

Purushottam Goel Purushottam graduated from the Indian Institute of Technology, Roorkee, with a bachelor's degree in electrical engineering and later pursued his masters degree from the computer engineering department of BITS, Pilani, India. He was employed at the Bangalore R&D Center of Novell, Inc. from 1996 to 2000, working on various projects, primarily on the security components of the NetWare operating system. Subsequently he tried his luck in a couple of startups before joining Intel Corporation in 2002. Purushottam is one of the key architects of Intel AMT. He is responsible for designing the security features and aspects of Intel AMT. He also designed the configuration and setup mechanisms of Intel AMT.

Ylian Saint-Hilaire Fresh out of the University of Quebec in Montreal (UQAM) with a master's degree in computer sciences, Ylian moved to Oregon to work for Intel Corporation in 1998. His early work involved Internet Protocol security (IPsec) and network security. He later joined the digital home group at Intel and is known for his work on UPnP† and media adapters. In 2006, Ylian started work on a sample open source set of tools to facilitate using Intel AMT. These tools were made public on Intel's Web site as the Manageability Developer Tool Kit (DTK) in January 2007 and have been widely used ever since. Ylian also uses Intel AMT in his own home, allowing his home entertainment system to be managed remotely.

Acknowledgements

This book would not have been possible without the numerous contributions from a large number of people inside and outside of Intel.

The first and foremost credit goes to the various technical reviewers of the book, who have not only provided the suggestions and corrections on the text in the book, but also provided portions of the content. For that we are very grateful.

We are deeply indebted to Dori Eldar and Omer Levy, two of the brightest of the Intel AMT architects, for their detailed technical review of the entire book. We are grateful to the technical reviews from our Intel colleagues Sharon Smith, Shmuel Gershon, Aharon Robbins, Nitin Sarangdhar, Vedvyas Shanbhogue, Tom Propst, Jeff Marek, and Jeff Torello. Thanks also to Intel engineers David Hines, Michael Navon, Oren Shamir, and Dick Kleiman, who provided technical content and expert answers to our questions.

We are very thankful to the many contributions of the external reviewers: Winston Bumpus from VMWare, Max Sokolov and Steve Hand from Symantec, Jeff Hilland and Christoph Graham from Hewlett-Packard, Jim Davis from WBEM Solutions, Josh Cohen from Microsoft, Bob Blair from AMD, Hemal Shah from Broadcom, and Javier Andres Caceres Alvis from Aranda Software.

We would also like to extend our sincere thanks to our management, Mike Rhodehamel, Sanjay Vora, and Rob Crooke, who encouraged and allowed us to spend time on the book, and got us unstuck at times.

Support of Stephen S. Pawlowski, Intel Senior Fellow and CTO, and John Hengeveld from Intel Digital Enterprise Group has been essential in the creation and publishing of this book.

The support of Intel Press Publisher Richard Bowles throughout the project is greatly appreciated.

A special thanks to managing editor Bruce Bartlett who believed in us and kept the project on track and the authors motivated through the gentlest but persistent of nudges. Editor David Clark helped immensely to ensure we did not assault the English language too terribly and cleaned up after us diligently. The production team took the raw material and made a great looking book from it. We especially appreciate the work of Ron Bohart, the artist who created the intriguing cover art.

Kelly Sweeney and Kirti Devi performed a pivotal role in getting the word out about the book through their marketing efforts.

For anyone we may have missed, please accept our deepest apologies.

Arvind Kumar
Purushottam Goel
Ylian Saint-Hilare
March 2009

Chapter 1

Introduction to Platform Manageability

There are two kinds of people, those who finish what they start and so on.
—Robert Byrne

Too much coffee, premature loss of hair, late hours, and excessive stress are often symptoms of a network administrator facing a increasingly large network and difficult troubles. It's often after facing an endless stream of support issues that network administrators start asking: Isn't there another way to solve this? Computer software issues, hardware failures, software patches, network viruses, stolen hardware, and bad settings are just a few of the major headaches facing network administrators today and it's only getting worse as computers and operating systems become more complicated.

A long time ago, turning a computer off and on would solve just about any problem, but those days are long gone. With the interconnection of computers and the increasing complexity of software, the only solution is to deal with problems using increasingly smart network manageability software and hardware. On top of all of this, administrators are facing a scaling and cost problem. Organizations have thousands of computers that must run properly at all times and this with an increasingly reduced budget.

One could ask: if a computer is so smart, why can't it help trouble shoot problems, isolate viruses, and alert the administrator if something is going wrong and help in its own management tasks? This is where platform manageability comes into play.

In this book, we look at how a computer can best be managed; that is, the role of software manageability solutions and their limitations. Then we look at the Intel® vPro™ technology solution and how it can help with secure manageability features built right into the computer's hardware.

Platform Manageability

In this book, a platform is a computer system and all of its hardware components: motherboard, disk storage, network interface, and attached devices, as shown in Figure 1.1. In other words, it's everything that makes up the computer's hardware.

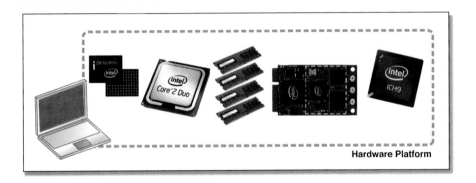

Figure 1.1   Hardware of a Modern Computer Platform

It is worth noting that the platform also includes the BIOS that boots up the computer. So if a BIOS setting is incorrect, and as a result the computer does not start up correctly, we can consider this to be a platform issue. Platforms have gotten significantly more powerful in the last few years, as illustrated in Figure 1.2. They can boot remote operating systems from the network, boot on RAID arrays, they have built-in security locks, and much more.

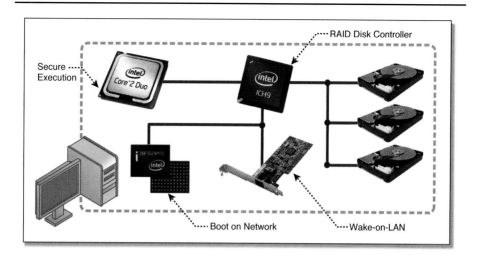

Figure 1.2   Advanced Features on Today's Computer Platforms

Platforms are much more powerful today; most platforms have limited manageability built in them. A buzzer may sound when the temperature is too high, or an error code is displayed when a disk fails. As we will see in this book, Intel vPro technology adds powerful new management features to the platform itself.

System Manageability

System manageability is broader; it includes both the software and hardware portions of a computer. The aim of system manageability is to take into account all of the components of a computer and ensure that they function correctly, as shown in Figure 1.3.

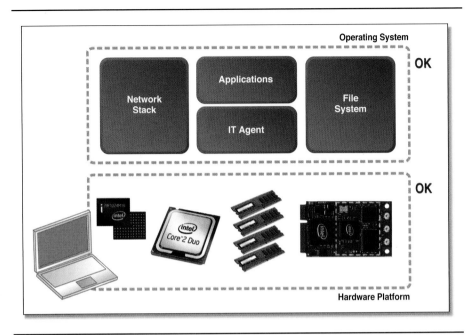

Figure 1.3 Both Platform and OS Software Running Correctly

One way to rate how effective a manageability solution works is to look at how much of the system is covered by the solution. Firewalls, anti-virus software, and remote control software all address, manage, and secure different portions of a system. The best solutions would of course be solutions that could monitor and address the widest array of possible platform and system problems. Network administrators may sometimes focus too much on one part of the system and forget others. For example: anti-virus software prevents a virus outbreak, but a bad driver patch stops all printers from working. For a manageability solution to work well, it must cover in the best way possible all of the components that make up a computer system, both the hardware platform and the software.

Since manageability software often runs within the computer's operating system it's trying to manage, it has limitations as to what it can monitor and fix. For example, if the BIOS settings are not set properly, software solutions can't easily change the BIOS. If a platform is not booting correctly, no manageability software is running at that time to investigate the problem. Software manageability solutions that run in the OS also run only then the computer is powered on and can't react when the computer is sleeping. While software solutions are powerful, they also have limitations because they run within the environment they are trying to manage.

Manageability Problems

In this section, we want to cover some of the problems network administrators are facing today and some of the same issues manageability solutions are trying to deal with.

Asset Inventory

Keeping tabs on the hardware and software inventory within an organization is probably the first problem administrators try to deal with. Where are the computers? Is there sufficient memory and disk space? Are hardware components being stolen? These questions are not only important, but in some organizations, computer asset tracking is required by law. Whether this information is used to understand when to upgrade computers or report theft to authorities, network administrators have to deal with this in one way or another.

Computer Repair

Keeping computers up and running is a difficult job. It can be costly if the downtime is significant or a technician has to make an on-site visit. Computers can break down because of hardware or software, and in both cases proper diagnostic is the first step to quick resolution. In some cases, repairs can be made by bringing a laptop to a repair desk for a few minutes, but in other cases, computers are critical or located in remote locations that don't allow for quick physical access.

Computer Security

Security is now a mainstream topic. Stolen disk drives, viruses, malware, and denial of service attacks sometimes get featured on the evening news. Increasingly, organizations are not only protecting their own data, but also the customer's data or patient information. Even if a computer is running correctly, it can still have severe security issues that need to be monitored and addressed quickly.

What makes security an especially difficult topic to address has to do with what software you can trust and what software you can't trust. Firewall software may be running on a computer, but other software may be able to turn it off. One could run software that would monitor the firewall, but who would monitor the monitoring software? Ultimately, what software can you trust when running in an environment where a user can run applications that are not trusted at any time?

Power Savings

Network administrators are now more and more frequently assigned the task of monitoring and finding ways to reduce power use. When computer resources are neatly arranged in server racks, this can be a simple task, but when computer resources are distributed across many sites, it is more difficult.

Many employees leave their computers on all the time resulting in a large waste of power. Network administrators can generally push operating system policies to place computers to sleep when idle, but this can have drawbacks when it's time to push urgent updates. It's also difficult to evaluate the efficiency of new power policies when there is no good way to know which computers are asleep. It may also be difficult to remotely tell if a computer is sleeping or disconnected from the network.

Possible Solutions

In most network environments, software agents and desktop remote control software are running on each computer along with a combination of anti-virus and firewall software. Since these management solutions are software running in the operating system, they are difficult to trust completely; they don't run unless the operating system is running correctly and they have various limitations in monitoring and controlling the computer and operating system on which they run.

One possible solution is to use a remote keyboard and mouse over network device (IP/KVM device) to fully control a computer remotely. These devices allow an administrator to remotely see the display and control the keyboard and mouse of a computer over the network, as shown in Figure 1.4.

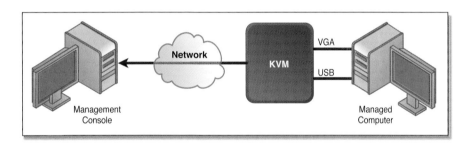

Figure 1.4   An IP/KVM Device Connected to a Managed Computer

Since this device stands on the side of the computer, it can be trusted and can't easily be compromised through the network. Such devices can't generally monitor or control the power state of a computer and are relatively expensive because they must take the video out of the computer and encode it in such a way as to be sent over the network. For mission critical computers this is an excellent option, but it is not an option that can be deployed widely. It is also impractical for large scale deployments.

For years now, large servers have had baseboard management control-lers (BMC), which are small embedded controllers that monitor the larger server. Since these controllers are effectively separate from the main computer and have many connected sensors, they can be trusted and perform accurate diagnostic and monitoring of a large server, as shown in Figure 1.5.

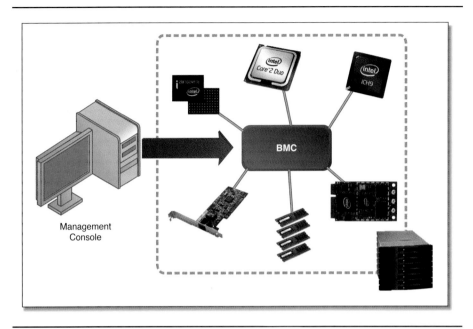

Figure 1.5 Baseboard Management Controller (BMC)

Many new BMCs also combine an IP/KVM feature making them very powerful. Administrators can turn a computer on and off remotely, take control of it and monitor system temperatures, fan controls, and much more. BMCs can be very useful, but they also add significantly to the cost of the platform and so are reserved for high end servers.

In effect, today's solutions are ether software-only or an effective but costly combination of software and hardware.

In-Band versus Out-of-Band

When looking at various management solutions, we have to look at how the management solution communicates with the management console. This is important because how a management console communicates with a managed computer affects the robustness and cost of the communication link.

In-band management solutions run within the operating system and use the operating system resources and network communication, as illustrated in Figure 1.6. For example, a corporate agent might monitor the computer and report back to a main server about the health of the computer.

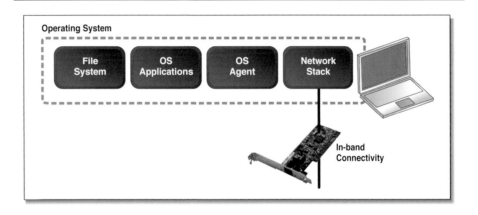

Figure 1.6 In-Band Connectivity: This Is the Usual Flow of Network Traffic from the Operating System to the Network.

Out-of-band management solutions run alongside the main operating system and use an alternate communication path that does not depend on the operating system running properly. A good example would be an IP/KVM device that runs alongside the main computer and uses a separate connection to the network. Another example involves sharing some of the hardware used by the operating system but using a separate network stack.

Out-of-band management solutions can be built within the computer itself, but they are considered out-of-band when they don't depend on the operating system. Sometimes, they can use a different communication path like a separate serial port or the same path as the operating system (such as sharing an Ethernet port), as shown in Figure 1.7.

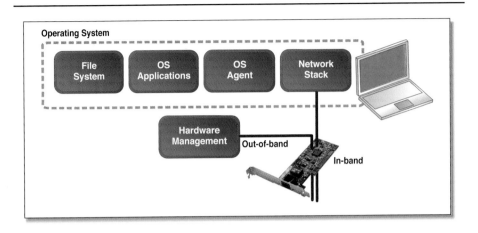

Figure 1.7   Out-of-Band Management: Both the Operating System and Hardware Management Traffic Can Use the Same Network Hardware.

Out-of-band communication is typically more reliable since it's more often available than the in-band channel. The Wake-on-LAN (WOL) feature that has been available on most computers for many years is a good example of a primitive out-of-band channel. When the computer is sleeping and the operating system is not running, the Ethernet controller on the computer is still on, waiting for a packet that will instruct the wakeup of the computer.

Wake-on-LAN is a good example of what we mean by out-of-band. It's built right into the motherboard or network card of many computers and uses the same Ethernet connection and components as the in-band channel. Yet, because it does not depend on the operating system, it is considered to be out-of-band.

The difference between in-band and out-of-band is important because as we look at how to solve today's management problems, we quickly come to the conclusion that out-of-band management has many interesting benefits: it's dependable, it can be trusted, and more interestingly, it's available more often than in-band solutions.

Management Agents

One of the staples of network management has been the management agent. In the context of computer manageability an agent refers to software running on each managed computer on the network that facilitates the task of the remote administrator. Agents come in many forms and generally run as a background task within the operating system. Agents can do many things like performing system checks, reporting when the computer is present on the network, allowing the administrator to remotely control the computer, and so on. Almost all management software vendors have agents as part of their solutions. Agents have access to many of the computer's resources and can perform many tasks, but they have key drawbacks.

Trust and reliability are two of the main problems facing agents running in the operating system. Rogue software can replace, stop, or completely remove a running agent, making it impossible to manage the computer. Even without the presence of rogue software, agents are often disabled by the users or applications that attempt to clean up the operating system startup sequence. As a result, even the best agent is limited in how reliable and trusted it can be when running on a computer.

Connectivity is another problem facing agents. Even when running properly, the user may enable a firewall or other software that will block agent network connectivity. This often happens when the user changes firewall policies or installs new network filtering software. In this case, the running agent may try to solve the problem by resetting the firewall settings, but this is not always possible.

Since agents are an undeniable part of network manageability solutions, network administrators have been seeking solutions to solve the trust, reliability, and connectivity problems. One of the best solutions is to run the agent completely outside the operating system, such as, for example, on a completely separate computer or baseboard management controller (BMC), as shown in Figure 1.8. These solutions are expensive, but the general idea is a good one.

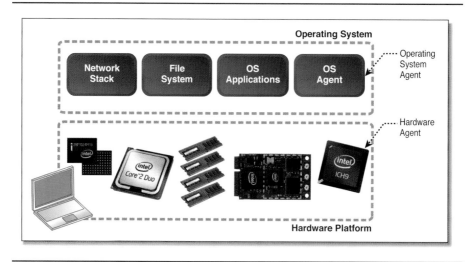

Figure 1.8 Agent within Operating System versus Agent in Hardware

If sufficient portions of the network management functionality run outside the main operating system in a separate and trusted environment, it could makes agents completely optional. Some computers would therefore run without management agents in an "agent-less" configuration.

Out-of-Band and Agent-less

Out-of-band communications and running agent features outside the operating system should be viewed as separate. However, both are logically related. It is possible for an agent running in the operating system to use an alternate means of communication such as a serial port, and it is possible for management features outside the operating system to use in-band communications.

While separate, using management features that run outside the operating system along with a connectivity path that is also outside the operating system's control provides trust, reliability, and connectivity that is desired in an ideal managed computer.

Management in Low Power States

Another management feature that is on the top of the manageability solution wish list involves being able to manage computers regardless of their power state. This is especially important in an era of rising energy costs and heightens sensitively to waste of power. Manageability solutions based on software agents require the computer to be on for any manageability feature to be available. Software agents can work along with the Wake-on-LAN feature to allow the computer to turn off and be woken up when manageability operations need be performed. Software agent along with Wake-on-LAN is not an ideal solution. When the computer is in low power, Wake-on-LAN cannot be queried to determine if the computer is still connected unless the computer is woken up first. Also, Wake-on-LAN may work on desktop PCs, but on mobile platforms that move from network to network, it's generally impossible to manage.

An ideal solution would offer some management features even when the computer is in low power states, making it easy to query and wake up the computer when appropriate.

Summary

In this chapter we reviewed various solutions and technologies from a historical perspective. We also defined the basic components that make a computer a manageable one. Connectivity, trust, and relativity are all factors that differentiate manageability solutions.

As we will see later in this book, running agent-like management functionality outside the main operating system along with trusted and reliable execution along with out-of-band connectivity is the basic idea behind Intel Active Management Technology (Intel AMT), a major component of Intel vPro technology platforms.

In the next chapter we look at the history of manageability.

Chapter **2**

History of Manageability

Civilizations in decline are consistently characterized by a tendency towards standardization and uniformity

— Arnold Toynbee (1889–1975)

Manageability, as a unique discipline, has historically evolved from the growing need to configure and maintain the computer systems, applications, and networks. As more and more of these entities provided capabilities that could be adapted, changed, and optimized for a particular use or preference, the need for manageability grew. With a low number of systems, it was possible to have system administrators individually log into the system locally and manage each system independently. However, as these systems grew in number and became more and more complex, administrators needed to manage a large number of resources from a central management site. The use of remote management tools became important. This led to development of several protocols for remote management. In the beginning, most of these were proprietary in nature, which meant that a system from one manufacturer could only be managed with a management console from the same manufacturer. This led the industry to work on interoperable standards that allow the systems from multiple manufactures to be managed with common tools.

Protocol and Data Model

Remote management interfaces can be logically viewed as a combination of a communication protocol and the payload that is exchanged via that communication protocol.

Historically, this separation has not always been very clear or emphasized, and some standards have treated them with a very tight binding. However, making this logical separation has clear advantages as illustrated in Figure 2.1.

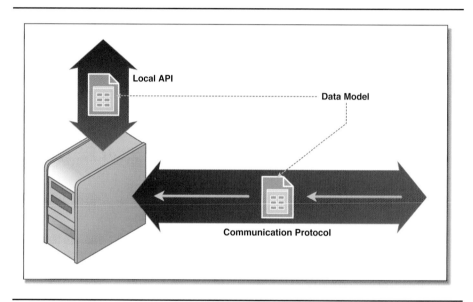

Figure 2.1 Separation of Communication Protocol and Data Model

The communication protocol defines how the messages from one system are to be encoded and sent to another system. It does not depend on the contents of the messages. In much the same way that TCP/IP as a protocol allows a reliable transmission of the packets from one network node to another and does not concern itself with the content of the packets, a good management protocol is agnostic of the management payload or the data model.

The data model defines the actual content that allows the request for specific changes to be made to the managed entity and communicated via the communication protocol to the managed system.

The separation of the two also allows the designer of the system to provide different access mechanisms while keeping the same management data model. For example, a local application programming interface (API) can provide an alternate mechanism for management while keeping the same semantics for the data model.

Simple Network Management Protocol

Simple Network Management Protocol (SNMP) is a management standard that came into existence in late 1980s and achieved widespread acceptance over the next decade. A majority of network devices, routers, switches, and gateways have been using SNMP as the standard management protocol.

The name SNMP suggests that it is only a network protocol. However, this standard defines more than a protocol. SNMP is based on the manager/agent model, consisting of the manager, agent, a database of information, managed objects, and the network protocol.

The manager and the agent communicate use a Management Information Base (MIB) and a set of well defined commands to exchange the information. MIBs are organized in a tree structure with each MIB given its unique place in the tree. Within an MIB, eventually the actual management information is defined through MIB variables. Each individual MIB variable is identified via a unique identifier, called an Object Identifier (OID).

The OIDs are assigned based on where the MIB appears in the MIB tree, and how the variables are defined within the MIB. For example, a standard MIB called mib-2 is defined by `iso(1).org(3).dod(6).internet(1).mgmt(2).mib-2(1)`. Based on this structure, all variables in mib-2 will have a prefix of 1.3.6.1.2.1. Within this mib-2, the complete OID of the variable `sysDescr` (as shown in the following excerpt of mib-2) is 1.3.6.1.2.1.1.3.

```
mib-2       OBJECT IDENTIFIER ::= { mgmt 1 }
system      OBJECT IDENTIFIER ::= { mib-2 1 }
sysDescr OBJECT-TYPE
    SYNTAX  DisplayString (SIZE (0..255))
    ACCESS  read-only
    STATUS  mandatory
    DESCRIPTION
            "A textual description of the entity.  This value
            should include the full name and version
            identification of the system's hardware type,
            software operating-system, and networking
            software.  It is mandatory that this only contain
            printable ASCII characters."
    ::= { system 1 }
```

SNMP uses five basic messages (GET, GET-NEXT, GET-RESPONSE, SET and TRAP) to communicate between the manager and the agent, as illustrated in Figure 2.2. GET and GET-NEXT messages allow the manager to request information for a specific variable. The agent receiving these messages then uses a GET-RESPONSE message to provide the information requested, or an error indication if the request cannot be processed. A SET message allows the manager to change the value of the variable, and thus change configuration data or control a particular object, such as disabling a network interface. The agent uses the GET-RESPONSE message to indicate the changed value or the error condition. There is no specific SET-RESPONSE message, since the content of the messages is exactly same as in case of GET. The TRAP message allows the agent to spontaneously inform the manager of a critical event.

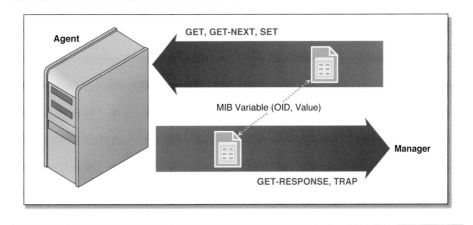

Figure 2.2 SNMP Protocol Messages

The SNMP protocol is built on top of UDP/IP, and uses a simple connectionless mechanism. The protocol is a basic query/response protocol. TRAPs are the only packets that are sent by the agent without a request from the manager. There is no acknowledgement defined for the TRAP messages, so TRAPs are not necessarily guaranteed to be received by the manager. Managers often periodically poll the agent to receive information, in case the TRAP message is missed.

The small number of commands, simplicity, and therefore ease of use led to the widespread usage of the protocol. However, the same simplicity is holding back further progress of SNMP into the Internet and Web era. The first version of SNMP had next to no security (a simple plain text community string as a password). SNMPv2 and SNMPv3 enhanced the security but lost the simplicity, and hence were not readily adopted. Even with what is available in these versions, it is no match for the security and reliability demands of today.

Newer web-based standards, as described later in this chapter, are slowly replacing SNMP deployments. No new standards work is going on for enhancement of SNMP.

Desktop Management Interface

SNMP was widely adopted in the networking segment. However, as people started to look into managing computer systems, components within a system, operating system components, and applications parameters, it became clear that SNMP was not designed to do this. A local API standard was needed. A network-based protocol was not ideal for local management by application, and the OID structure defined by SNMP was very rigid and cumbersome to manage thousands of variables in the system. In 1994, several system vendors including Intel, Dell, HP, IBM, and Compaq formed a standards consortium under the name of Desktop Management Task Force (which was later renamed to Distributed Management Task Force) to embark on the task of defining such a standard. The Desktop Management Interface (DMI) was a result of that effort.

DMI defines the data model in a much simpler format using Management Information Format (MIF). The MIF uses a more text-based definition that can be parsed by a machine as well as easily read by humans. The information is organized into groups of attributes (equivalent to SNMP variables). The groups are uniquely identified based on their Group ID (a string). Any number of groups can be combined together and organized in a MIF file. The flexibility of DMI makes it very easy to organize MIF groups in any arbitrary collection based on a specific implementation. So, if an implementation only needs one group, no other groups need be implemented. Group attributes have a name, description, type, read/write properties, and other information that gives enough guidance to a management application to interpret the attribute value.

A sample MIF segment containing a single group is shown here.

```
Start Group
     Name = "ComponentID"
     Class = "DMTF|ComponentID|001"
     ID = 1
     Description = "This group defines the attributes "
       "common to all components.  This group is required."
     Pragma = "SNMP:1.3.6.1.4.1.412.2.1.1 ;"

     Start Attribute
          Name = "Serial Number"
          ID = 4
          Description = "Serial number for this system."
          Access = Read-Only
          Storage = Specific
          Type = DisplayString(64)
          Value = ""
     End Attribute
     // Additional Attributes Deleted from illustration //
End Group
```

DMI operations are modeled along the same lines as SNMP. However, instead of defining a protocol and on-the-wire messages, DMI defines an API-style interface, which is much simpler and readily usable by software programs.

The DMI API defines calls to enumerate (list) DMI Components, Groups, Attributes, and Class names. This provides a discovery mechanism to find out what exists. Once the management application has discovered that a specific group is instrumented, then it can call DmiGetAttribute or DmiSetAttribute to operate on the values of the attributes in the group. Some groups can have multiple instances, like rows in a table. For such groups, the API provides add and delete row operations to allow manipulations of the group instances. A mechanism to register for a callback in case of an event is also specified.

In addition to the management API, DMI also defines a pluggable manager and provider architecture. As shown in Figure 2.3, this centers around a DMI Service Provider (SP) as the manager of the information, a Component Interface (CI) for registering one or more components (also called instrumentation) providing information, and a Management Interface (MI) for management applications. This provides a very modular architecture, where multiple vendors can plug in their instrumentation and multiple management applications can use that information.

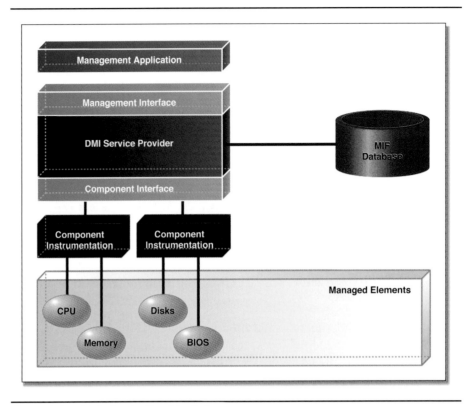

Figure 2.3 DMI Service Provider Infrastructure

This structured format came as a benefit to system vendors, who could take components and instrumentations from their component suppliers and integrate all of it into a cohesive solution. Several hardware and computer system vendors developed instrumentations and built solutions based on DMI infrastructure.

However, DMI's strong definition of infrastructure and interfaces was not warmly welcomed by Microsoft, as it was not aligned with the rest of the Windows management infrastructure. Microsoft started working on an alternate architecture, Windows Management Instrumentation (WMI), which then started the foundation of next generation of DMTF standard, as described later in this chapter.

Wired for Management

As DMTF was defining the DMI standards on standardizing the management information format and the infrastructure to allow consistent management of multiple components in the platform, Intel started working with the system vendors and component vendors to define a baseline of management information that a system must present. Wired for Management (WFM) defined such a baseline. The baseline was defined in terms of the DMI groups and attributes that must be instrumented to meet WFM compliance.

In addition, mechanisms and structures were also defined (with the effort led by BIOS vendors) for the BIOS to collect the information from the system and put it in BIOS structures. This was defined by the SMBIOS (System Management BIOS) specification, later standardized by DMTF. SMBIOS structures also follow the data defined by DMI groups and attributes definitions. However, since BIOS is under a space constraint, the structure uses lower level bits and bytes definitions.

Another technology that came out of the WFM effort was the Preboot eXecution Environment (PXE) specifications. The PXE environment allowed the remote boot of a computer system from a network image. This is often used today in a variety of enterprise environments to do a "bare-metal" provisioning. Bare metal here refers to a system that is fresh out of the box and has not yet been provisioned with an operating system. PXE allows the system to be booted from a remote image, which can then in turn install the operating system. PXE can also be used for diskless systems to always boot from a network image.

PXE is being used today in enterprise environments, but is not scalable and lacks security. So, it is unlikely that PXE usages will grow much unless the scalability and security issues are resolved. Later in the book, we discuss some alternate mechanisms that address these issues.

Intelligent Platform Management Interface

As standards were being developed by DMTF and others to define mechanisms for management applications to manage systems (that is, external view), the server system vendors were facing another challenge. This was to look inside the system and define efficient ways of combining hardware components from multiple vendors and provide a way of collecting the management information from these hardware components inside the platform (system) via some standard management bus. Intel, Dell, HP, and NEC led the creation of the Intelligent Platform Management Interface (IPMI) to address this need. IPMI defines standardized, abstracted interfaces to the platform management subsystem. IPMI includes the definition of interfaces for extending platform management between boards within the main chassis, and between multiple chassis.

The term *platform management* is used to refer to the monitoring and control functions that are built in to the platform hardware and primarily used for the purpose of monitoring the health of the system's hardware. This typically includes monitoring elements such as system temperatures, voltages, fans, power supplies, bus errors, system physical security, and so on. It includes automatic and manual recovery capabilities such as local or remote system resets and power on/off operations. It includes the logging of abnormal or out-of-range conditions for later examination and alerting where the platform issues the alert without aid of runtime software. It also includes inventory information that can help identify a failed hardware unit.

IPMI defines an Intelligent Platform Management Bus (IPMB), which is an I²C-based bus that provides a standardized interconnection between different boards within a chassis. The IPMB can also serve as a standardized interface for auxiliary or emergency management add-in cards.

IPMI also specifies an Intelligent Chassis Management Bus (ICMB), which provides a standardized interface for platform management information and control between chassis.

IPMI was developed as a complementary technology to provide low-level management information to broader frameworks based on SNMP, DMI, and CIM (discussed later in this chapter). However, since it provided information about hardware, and the information needed to be made available to remote management consoles in OS-absent scenarios, it did define a simple UDP based Remote Management Control Protocol (RMCP) to send IPMI messages to a remote system. It also based its Platform Event Trap Format definition on SNMP traps, which provided a mechanism to send asynchronous alerts to management consoles.

Alert Standard Format

While Server vendors were busy solving the platform management problem and building a modular and scalable framework with IPMI, client vendors, led by Intel and IBM, had been working on Alert on LAN (AOL) technology, which initially focused on providing OS-independent alerting mechanisms, for events like OS failures, from the LAN devices directly to the management consoles. This technology was later standardized as Alert Standard Format (ASF), and submitted to DMTF in due course. IPMI (for servers) and ASF (for clients) continued to evolve together, sometimes sharing technologies, and at other times developing parallel technologies. ASF adopted Platform Event Trap Format defined by IPMI, and IPMI adopted Remote Management and Control Protocol (RMCP) defined by ASF. However, the actual messages under the covers of these common protocols (RMCP and PET) are quite different between ASF and IPMI.

For inside the platform interfaces, ASF also defined System Management Bus (SMBus) for connecting a small number of sensors. It is also an I²C-based bus, but is not as extensible as IPMB. In fact, IPMB comprehends connecting to SMBus based sensors, and is thus a superset.

Common Information Model

SNMP was focused on managing the network devices. DMI was created to manage components in a platform from host OS-based applications. IPMI and ASF were more focused on inside the platform as well as out-of-band and OS-absent management. Software, applications, and services didn't really have any widespread standard for management. All this, coupled with the need to have an end-to-end management of all infrastructure, led to the concepts of a Common Information Model (CIM), unifying all the previous management models.

The need for end-to-end management, across multiple components, in a distributed environment is a reality and is now a requirement. It is no longer sufficient to manage personal computers, servers, subnets, the network core, storage, and software in isolation. These components all interoperate to provide connectivity and services. Information passes between these boundaries. Management must pass across these boundaries as well.

These are the problems addressed by the Common Information Model. The goals of CIM are to address both FCAPS management (fault, configuration, accounting, performance, and security management) and to support the abstraction and decomposition of services and functionality. The information model defines and organizes common and consistent semantics for computing and networking equipment and services. The model's organization is based on an object-oriented paradigm, promoting the use of inheritance, relationships, abstraction, and encapsulation to improve the quality and consistency of management data.

The value of CIM stems from its object orientation. Object-oriented design provides support for the following capabilities that other "flat" data formats do not allow.

Abstraction and Classification

To reduce the complexity of the problem domain, high level and fundamental concepts (the "objects" of the management domain) are defined. These objects are then grouped into types ("classes") by identifying common characteristics and features ("properties"), relationships ("associations") and behavior ("methods").

Object Inheritance

By creating subclasses from the high level and fundamental objects, additional detail can be provided. When created, a subclass "inherits" all the information (properties, methods, and associations) defined for its higher level objects. Subclasses are created to put the right level of detail and complexity at the appropriate level in the model. This can be visualized as a triangle, where the top of the triangle is a "fundamental" object, and more detail and more classes are defined as you move closer to the base.

Ability to Depict Dependencies, Component and Connection Associations

Relationships between objects are extremely powerful concepts. Before CIM, management standards captured relationships in multidimensional arrays or cross-referenced data tables. The object paradigm offers a more elegant approach in that the relationships and associations are directly modeled. In addition, the way that relationships are named and defined describes the semantics of the object associations. Further semantics and information can be provided in properties (specifying common characteristics and features) of the associations.

Standard, Inheritable Methods

The ability to define standard object behavior (methods) is another form of abstraction. Bundling standard methods with an object's data is called *encapsulation*. Imagine the flexibility and possibilities of a standard able to invoke a Reset method against a hung device, regardless of the hardware, operating system, or device.

Summary

In this chapter we reviewed various manageability standards and technologies from a historical perspective. The next chapter provides details on the current state-of-the-art management technologies, such as CIM and Web Services–based management, which are gaining widespread acceptance.

Chapter 3

Manageability
Standards

The nice thing about standards is that there are so many of them to choose from.

—Andrew S. Tanenbaum

Fortunately, bringing some relief to IT managers and system administrators, the industry is starting to converge on a common set of standards for management of applications, systems, and platforms. Common Information Model (CIM) for representation of various manageable entities and Web-based access to this model is fast becoming a prevalent standard. This chapter discusses these current and upcoming standards.

Common Information Model (CIM)

Common Information Model is a standard that started in DMTF in 1997. During the past 10 years, the CIM standards have grown to cover a wide variety of manageable entities, including systems, network, storage, applications, and services.

CIM is an abstraction and representation of the entities in a managed environment, their properties, attributes, operations, and the way that they relate to each other. It is independent of any specific repository, software usage, protocol, or platform.

Chapter 2 provided a high level overview of CIM. In this chapter we explore in more detail how classes are represented and defined in CIM.

UML Diagram

Figure 3.1 shows an example of CIM classes. The classes are represented in a UML (Unified Modeling Language) diagram.

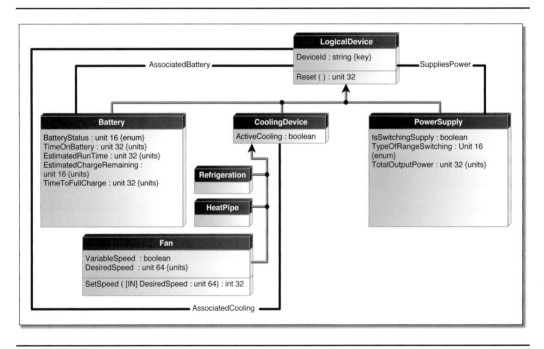

Figure 3.1   Example of CIM Classes

The example shows a LogicalDevice, which is an abstract class that represents a wide variety of devices that may be present in a platform. Battery, CoolingDevice, and PowerSuply are further specialization of the LogicalDevice. These devices are inherited (derived) from LogicalDevice as shown by the blue arrows. Additional specific properties are added to these classes. When these classes are instantiated as objects, they represent the respective specialized devices. At the same time, they inherit the properties of the parent class, and hence are LogicalDevice objects as well. All of the

LogicalDevice behavior is common across all these objects. For example, all the logical devices can be reset by invoking the Reset() method of the corresponding object representation.

The red lines in the diagram represent Association objects. These Associations connect two unrelated object together with certain behavior. In the example shown, the AssociatedCooling association helps us figure out which cooling device is cooling a particular LogicalDevice. This can be used to differentiate a system fan from a processor fan. If one of these fans fails, a management console can quickly isolate the component impacted because of this failure.

Managed Object Format (MOF)

Although UML diagrams are nice to get an overview of the overall class hierarchy and associations, it is not a formal machine-readable representation as defined by DMTF.

Common Information Model (CIM) Infrastructure Specification defines a formal language to describe the CIM classes and objects. This is called Managed Object Format (MOF). Complete MOF syntax and grammar rules are defined in the CIM specification.

The following example shows an excerpt from the definition of a CIM class (CIM_Sensor) in MOF syntax.

```
//=================================================
// Sensor
//=================================================
    [Abstract, Version ( "2.6.0" ), Description (
        "A Sensor is a hardware device capable of measuring the "
        "characteristics of some physical property - for example, "
        "the temperature or voltage characteristics of a "
        "Computer System.")]
class CIM_Sensor : CIM_LogicalDevice {
        [Description (
            "The Type of the Sensor, e.g. Voltage Sensor. "
            "description of the different Sensor types is as follows:  "
            "..........................deleted   text… "."),
        ValueMap { "0", "1", "2", "3", "4", "5", "6", "7", "8", "9",
            "10", "11", "12" },
        Values { "Unknown", "Other", "Temperature", "Voltage",
            "Current", "Tachometer", "Counter", "Switch", "Lock",
            "Humidity", "Smoke Detection", "Presence", "Air Flow" },
        ModelCorrespondence { "CIM_Sensor.OtherSensorTypeDescription" }]
```

```
      uint16 SensorType;

   [Description (
       "PossibleStates enumerates the outputs of the Sensor. "
       "For example, a \"Switch\" Sensor may output the states "
       "\"On\", or \"Off\". Another implementation of the Switch "
       "may output the states \"Open\", and \"Close\". Another "
       "example is a NumericSensor supporting thresholds. This "
       "Sensor can report the states like \"Normal\", \"Upper "
       "Fatal\", \"Non-Critical\", etc. A NumericSensor that "
       "does not publish readings and thresholds, but stores this "
       "data internally, can still report its states."),
     MaxLen ( 128 )]
  string PossibleStates[];

   [Description (
       "The current state indicated by the Sensor. This is always "
       "one of the \"PossibleStates\"."),
     MaxLen ( 128 )]
  string CurrentState;

};
```

Let us discuss a few key components of this definition. CIM_Sensor is the main *class* defined in this example. This class inherits from a parent class called CIM_LogicalDevice. Class level *qualifiers* provide more information about the class. For example, the qualifier Abstract defines that the class cannot be directly instantiated into an object, but an implementation must further derive a Concrete class to instantiate an object. The CIM_sensor class shown in the example MOF segment lists the properties SensorType, PossibleStates[] and CurrentState. The actual class definition has more properties, but these are omitted from this illustration. SensorType is an unsigned integer, PossibleStates[] is an array of strings, and CurrentState is of the type string. Property level *qualifiers* provide additional information about the properties. For example, *ValueMap* and *Values* arrays provide enumeration values to the SensorType property. This allows applications to understand that if, for example, SensorType = 3, then the sensor is a "Voltage" sensor. Another property level qualifier *MaxLen(128)* restricts the length of the string property CurrentState to 128 bytes.

CIM Object Manager (CIMOM)

Let's delve a little bit into an implementation of the CIM infrastructure. Figure 3.2 shows a conceptual architectural diagram of a CIM-based infrastructure.

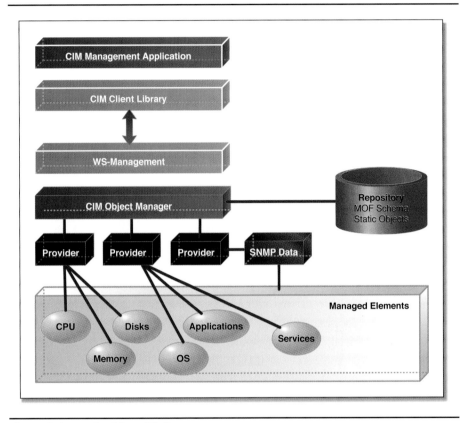

Figure 3.2   A CIM-based Infrastructure

In a typical implementation of CIM infrastructure, a CIM Object Manager (CIMOM) provides the most of the object management functions. The CIMOM provides capability to compile the MOF or XML Schema files and store them into a database. It allows providers to register to provide object instantiations of the CIM classes. The providers are typically controlling a managed resource, such as a disk drive, a networking stack, an application, or a service. These providers register with CIMOM to provide a CIM representation of the managed resource. When an application wants to read specific information, such as "Disk Capacity," the CIMOM routes the call to the appropriate Disk provider. The Provider translates this call to a resource specific interface, and in this case, sends the requests to the disk driver.

Requests to change an object property are handled in the same way. The infrastructure also allows for a resource to send asynchronous event to the provider, which in turn allows the CIMOM to send it to the applications that are interested in receiving this event.

The CIMOM implementations typically provide a network protocol interface for the management applications to communicate with the CIMOM. Web Based Enterprise Management (WBEM) defines this layer of communication. We will discuss this in more detail later in this chapter.

CIM Server

Not all the designs require a full CIMOM implementation. An external management console communicates to a CIMOM via the network protocol interface. The management console does not know (or care) if the object manager it is talking to provides underlying pluggable architecture with provider interfaces. In fact, a simpler CIM server may be able to satisfy the requests from the management consoles just as well as a full CIMOM. There is no complete definition of a CIM server, and it can be as highly optimized as the need dictates. The only requirement is that it must support a network protocol and retrieval of CIM object instances. Internally, an implementation could just store all data in a few variables, and return values when queried. A CIM server may not be able to parse MOF files, implement object inheritance, or support elaborate queries. Most of the embedded implementations just implement a CIM server, and not a full CIM object manager.

Management Profiles

DMTF has spent a considerable amount of time in providing comprehensive definitions of almost every aspect of platform management. There are CIM definitions for hardware components, disk, network, operating systems, applications, services, and security to name a few. Each of these areas has a number of CIM classes defined. At present, over 2000 CIM classes are defined. Implementations can chose to instrument the classes and properties that are important for the resources they need to manage. Since CIM classes do not mandate that a particular class or a property be implemented, it becomes hard for a management application to manage resources in a consistent way across the network. Furthermore, CIM as a data model does not specify the behavior of the system as a whole when a property value is changed or a method is called. This has led DMTF to further create *profiles* that define this behavior.

A *profile* is a specification that defines the CIM model and associated behavior for a management domain. The management domain is a set of related management tasks. For example, a server system may have a set of redundant power supplies that work together to provide power to the system. These power supplies are organized in a power domain, and a management console can query if the power domain is healthy and all the power supplies are active, and it can register for an event if one of the power supplies fails and the redundancy is lost. Such a behavior is specified in a power supply profile. Similarly, a mobile laptop system may have an instrumented battery. The management console can query all the instrumented laptops for their expected battery life. Such a behavior is documented in a system battery profile.

A *profile* contains the definition of a set of mandatory, as well as recommended classes, properties, methods and events. A *profile* also specifies the behavior of the system when some of these parameters are changed.

DMTF has two initiatives, System Management Architecture for Server Hardware (*SMASH*) and Desktop/Mobile Architecture for System Hardware (*DASH*), that have defined a number of profiles that are applicable for systems hardware management, which is the focus of this book.

DASH and SMASH have many profiles in common, while a few profiles are specific to each domain. Following are some of the examples of the profiles that are defined by DASH and SMASH.

- Power supply profile
- OS status profile
- Media redirection profile
- Platform watchdog profile
- Sensor profile
- PCI device profile
- LED profile
- KVM redirection profile
- BIOS management profile
- Alarm device profile
- Battery profile

More details on these profiles can be obtained from the DMTF Web site.

Web-Based Enterprise Management (WBEM)

Web-Based Enterprise Management (WBEM) provides the ability to exchange CIM information in an interoperable and efficient manner. WBEM includes protocols, query languages, discovery mechanisms, mappings, and anything else needed to exchange CIM information.

Today, WBEM defines three protocols for the communication between a management console and the CIM infrastructure.

CIM-XML over HTTP was the very first protocol defined by DMTF as a way to transport CIM objects over the network. Some implementations, particularly in storage industry, use this protocol heavily.

Windows Management Instrumentation (WMI), Microsoft's CIM implementation, had used a DCOM based remote network interface to communicate with the network console. Although not defined by DMTF, this has been commonly used.

DMTF has now published the new WS-Management protocol, which is composed using the latest Web services–based standards. We feel this protocol is likely to become the dominant standard for the network communications with a CIM infrastructure.

In addition to the above programmatic web-based protocols, DMTF also has defined an interactive Command Line Protocol (SMASH-CLP). This allows the network operators to use a simple text based interface to communicate with a backend CIM infrastructure.

WS-Management

The WS-Management architecture is based on a suite of specifications that define rich functions from which designs may be composed to meet varied service requirements. It is based on general SOAP-based Web services protocols, as illustrated in Figure 3.3.

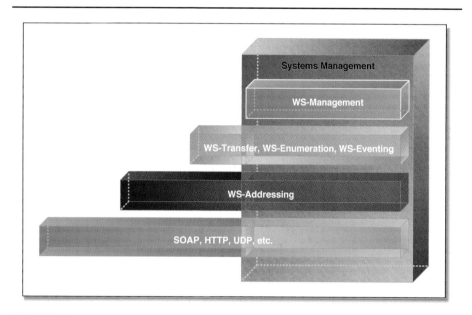

Figure 3.3 Systems Management with the WS-Management Protocol

To promote interoperability between management applications and managed resources, this specification identifies a core set of web service specifications and usage requirements to expose a common set of operations that are central to all systems management. This comprises the abilities to

- Discover the presence of management resources and navigate between them.

- Get, Put, Create, and Delete individual management resources, such as settings and dynamic values.

- Enumerate the contents of containers and collections, such as large tables and logs.

- Subscribe to events emitted by managed resources.

- Execute specific management methods with strongly typed input and output parameters.

In each of these areas of scope, the WS-Management specification defines minimal implementation requirements for conformant web service implementations. An implementation is free to extend beyond this set of operations, and may also choose not to support one or more areas of functionality listed above if that functionality is not appropriate to the target device or system.

As shown in Figure 3.3, the WS-Management specification uses underlying Web Services specifications, namely WS-Transfer, WS-Enumeration, and WS-Eventing. These are also sometimes referred to as TEEN (Transfer, Eventing, and Enumeration) specifications. These specifications are originally defined by World Wide Web Consortium (W3C, www.w3.org), and are evolving. On the other hand, the WS-Management specification is owned by DMTF, and is under a different release cycle. To minimize ever-changing dependencies, DMTF picked a version and included it in the WS-Management specification. Console vendors must be careful if using the W3C version of the TEEN specifications. Some of the changes in W3C TEEN specifications are not backward compatible with WS-Management.

The following example illustrates the WS-Management messages in a more detail. In this example scenario, the management console starts with querying the WS-Management server and enumerating all of the management objects it supports. Once it enumerates the objects, it makes further query to get the object and see the property values.

Figure 3.4 will help in understanding the protocol flow.

Figure 3.4 WS-Management Protocol Flow

Let's examine these messages in more detail.

Step 1: Management console sends the Enumerate request to the managed system. The managed system is hosting the WS-Management service. The message directed to a specific ResourceURI (`http:......./PhysicalElements`) as shown in the `<To>` tag of Figure 3.5. The `<Action>` specifies that this is an Enumerate request.

```
<Envelope>
  <Header>
    <To>
      http://192.168.0.100/agent?ResourceURI=
        http://schemas.dmtf.org/wbem/wscim/1/
        cim-schema/2/CIM_PhysicalElement
    </To>
    <Action>
      http://schemas.xmlsoap.org/ws/2004/09/
        enumeration/Enumerate
    </Action>
    <MessageId>
      uuid:1778973d-10e9-477D-ae07-34e424e6577a
    </MessageId>
    <ReplyTo>
      http://schemas.xmlsoap.org/ws/2004/08/
        addressing/role/anonymous
    </ReplyTo>
  </Header>
  <Body>
    <Enumerate>
      <Expires>expiry time</Expires>
    </Enumerate>
  </Body>
</Envelope>
```

Figure 3.5   WS-Management Enumerate Request

Step 2: The response from the WS-Management service to the above Enumerate request is shown in Figure 3.6. This response starts the enumeration of all PhysicalElement objects provided by the WS-Management service for this targeted URI. This response primarily contains an Enumeration-Context, which then can be used to walk through the elements in the list. Think of this as a file handle that is used in remaining calls to read the contents of the file.

```
<Envelope>
  <Header>
    <To>
      http://schemas.xmlsoap.org/ws/2004/08/
        addressing/role/anonymous
    </To>
    <Action>
      http://schemas.xmlsoap.org/ws/2004/09/
        enumeration/EnumerateResponse
    </Action>
    <RelatesTo>
      uuid:1778973d-10e9-477D-ae07-34e424e6577a
    </RelatesTo>
    <MessageID>
      uuid:dc0eeb8f-d025-4A45-a859-2b4ca640a1ff
    </MessageID>
  </Header>
  <Body>
    <EnumerateResponse>
      <EmumerationContext>█</EmumerationContext>
    </EnumerateResponse>
  </Body>
</Envelope>
```

Figure 3.6   WS-Management Enumerate Response

Step 3: Now that the EnumerationContext is known, the management console can issue the request to start the walkthrough of the list as shown in Figure 3.7. It starts by sending the request Enumeration/Pull with the EnuerationContext provided in the previous response. Management console can further specify how many maximum elements it wants to receive in the reply.

```
<Envelope>
  <Header>
    <To>
      http://134.134.201.169/agent?ResourceURI=
        http://schemas.dmtf.org/wbem/wscim/1/
          cim-schema/2+/CIM_PhysicalElement
    </To>
    <Action>
      http://schemas.xmlsoap.org/ws/2004/09/
        enumeration/Pull
    </Action>
    <MessageId>
      uuid:9180bb55-9f9d-4808-93ca-72a6e922105a
    </MessageId>
    <ReplyTo>
      http://schemas.xmlsoap.org/ws/2004/08/
        addressing/role/anonymous
    </ReplyTo>
  </Header>
  <Body>
    <Pull>
      <EmumerationContext>█</EmumerationContext>
      <MaxElements>█</MaxElements>
    </Pull>
  </Body>
</Envelope>
```

Figure 3.7   WS-Management Enumeration Pull

Step 4: The response to the Pull request is shown in Figure 3.8. Note that the response returned the two elements Data1 and Data2. The EnumerationContext is also changed, so that the subsequent requests can be made to return the rest of the elements following the ones that are already returned.

```
<Envelope>
  <Header>
    <To>http://schemas.xmlsoap.org/ws/2004/08/
      addressing/role/anonymous</To>
    <Action>
      http://schemas.xmlsoap.org/ws/2004/09/
        enumeration/PullResponse
    </Action>
    <RelatesTo>
      uuid:9180bb55-9f9d-4808-93ca-72a6e922105a
    </RelatesTo>
    <MessageID>
      uuid:6500bf62-72e6-4468-8c2d-cd969ed0bd56
    </MessageID>
  </Header>
  <Body>
    <PullResponse>
      <EmumerationContext>
        ▉
      </EmumerationContext>
      <Items>
        <CIM_PhysicalElement>
          ▉DATA▉
        </CIM_PhysicalElement>
        <CIM_PhysicalElement>
          ▉DATA▉
        </CIM_PhysicalElement>
      </Items>
    </PullResponse>
  </Body>
</Envelope>
```

Figure 3.8   The Response to the enumerationPull Request

The two data items returned are the XML representations of the CIM objects, as shown in Figures 3.9 and 3.10.

```
<CIM_PhysicalElement>
  <Tag> 406ACME-08K8198</Tag>
  <Description>
    Physical media (SATA disk)
  </Description>
  <ElementName>SATA Disk</ElementName>
  <Manufacturer>ACME Inc.</Manufacturer>
  <Model>SATA Disk, The Big Cahuna 2005</Model>
  <SKU>AABB8900</SKU>
  <SerialNumber>78999999999999</SerialNumber>
  <Version>1.0</Version>
  <PoweredOn>True</PoweredOn>
  <ManufacturerDate>Jan 30, 2005</ManufacturerDate>
  <VendorEquipmentType>
    SATA Cahuna
  </VendorEquipmentType>
  <CanBeFRUed>True</CanBeFRUed>
</CIM_PhysicalElement>
```

Figure 3.9   XML Representation of the Data Object (Item 1)

```
<CIM_PhysicalElement>
  <Tag> 406BigBlobMem-08K8198</Tag>
  <Description>
    Physical Memory (DDR memory)
  </Description>
  <ElementName>DDR memory</ElementName>
  <Manufacturer>BigBlobMem Inc.</Manufacturer>
  <Model>DDR memory, The Big Blob</Model>
  <SKU>99000ababab</SKU>
  <SerialNumber>756568432</SerialNumber>
  <Version>1.0</Version>
  <PoweredOn>True</PoweredOn>
  <ManufacturerDate>Jan 30, 2005</ManufacturerDate>
  <VendorEquipmentType>
    DDR, Blob
  </VendorEquipmentType>
  <CanBeFRUed>True</CanBeFRUed>
</CIM_PhysicalELement>
```

Figure 3.10   XML Representation of Data Object (Item 2)

Step 5: If the management console has knowledge (as a result of prior enumeration) that a target object exists on the managed system, then it can make a direct GetRequest call, as shown in Figure 3.11. In this example, a specific call to get the Processor object is shown. The Selector of CPU0 selects the specific instance of the Processor object. The transfer/Get specifies the action, indicating that this is a Get operation as per WS-transfer protocol semantics.

```
<Envelope>
  <Header>
    <To>
      http://192.168.0.100/
        wsman?ResourceURI= http://schemas.dmtf.org/
          wbem/wscim/1/cim-schema/2+/CIM_PhysicalElement
    </To>
    <Action>http://schemas.xmlsoap.org/ws/
      2004/09/transfer/Get
    </Action>
    <SelectorSet>
      <Selector="DeviceID">████</Selector>
    </SelectorSet>
    <ReplyTo>
      http://schemas.xmlsoap.org/ws/2004/08/
        addressing/role/anonymous
    </ReplyTo>
    <MessageID>
      uuid:da649f50-3368-4646-bc90-9b294ea058fb
    </MessageID>
  </Header>
  <Body/>
</Envelope>
```

Figure 3.11   WS-Management Get Request

Step 6: The response to the Get request comes in the form of GetResponse, shown in Figure 3.12.

```
<Envelope>
  <Header>
    <To>
      http ://schemas.xmlsoap.org/ws/2004/08/
        addressing/role/anonymous
    </To>
    <Action>
      http://schemas.xmlsoap.org/ws/2004/09/
        transfer/GetResponse
    </Action>
    <RelatesTo>
      uuid:da649f50-3368-4646-bc90-9b294ea058fb
    </RelatesTo>
  </Header>
  <Body>  DATA  </Body>
</Envelope>
```

Figure 3.12   WS-Management Get Response

The Data element in the message shown in Figure 3.12 is expanded in Figure 3.13. Again, this is an XML representation of the CIM_Processor object.

```
<CIM_Processor>
  <Family>165</Family>
  <DeviceID>CPU0</DeviceID>
  <OtherFamilyDescription>
    "Intel (R) Xeon (TM)"
  </OtherFamilyDescription>
  <MaxClockSpeed>3000</MaxClockSpeed>
  <CurrentClockSpeed>3000</CurrentClockSpeed>
  <DataWidth>32</DataWidth>
  <AddressWidth>32</AddressWidth>
  <LoadPercentage>2</LoadPercentage>
  <Stepping>5</Stepping>
</CIM_Processor>
```

Figure 3.13   XML Representation of Data Object Embedded in Get Response

Other operations supported by WS-Management are WS-Transfer:Put and WS-Transfer:Delete. WS-Management also supports events, which is based on WS-Eventing specification. WS-Eventing allows a management console to create, delete, and renew event subscriptions. Once subscribed to events, a management console receives the events in a similar way as most of the responses discussed above.

Putting It All Together

Having looked at the different components of the standards-based management infrastructure, let's look at how these pieces fit together. Figure 3.14 provides a bird's eye view of the different technologies discussed in this chapter.

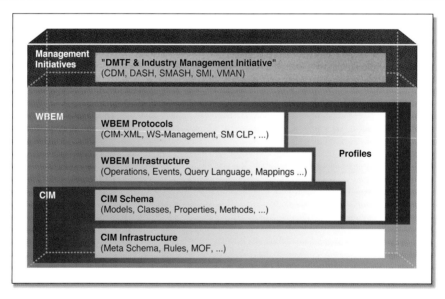

Courtesy of dmtf.org

Figure 3.14 Manageability Standards and Initiatives

CIM Infrastructure defines the language, MOF, UML, and the rules that provide a foundation of Common Information Model.

CIM Schema comprises the over 2000 CIM classes that define various objects, their properties, and methods.

WBEM defines the infrastructure and protocols that specify how management applications interact with the Common Information Model.

Profiles define the system behavior and implementation requirements for classes and properties. This allows for interoperability among different implementations.

To provide an overall interoperability guarantee of how these components play together, initiatives such as SMASH and DASH put the processes in place such as interoperability events and compliance requirements.

Summary

In Chapter 1, we discussed the general concepts of systems and platform management. We then, in Chapter 2, looked at the manageability from a historical perspective. In this chapter, we reviewed the prevalent management standards. These standards are used by Intel® Active Management Technology (Intel AMT), which is a major feature of Intel® vProTM technology. In the next chapter, we start looking at the capability of Intel vPro platforms, and then dive into a discussion of Intel AMT for a majority of the book. In Chapter 19, we will circle back and discuss the standard profiles supported by Intel AMT.

Chapter 4

Overview of Intel® vPro™ Technology

Computers are useless. They can only give you answers.
—Pablo Picasso (1881–1973)

Intel® vPro™ technology is a collection of high performance, energy efficient, and robust out-of-band management capabilities that enable IT professionals to monitor, manage, and repair computers remotely, regardless of operating system health or computer power state. The same techniques that have been used to lower the cost of ownership and power use, and to increase the reliability and security of large servers, are built into platforms with the Intel vPro technology.

Intel vPro technology is more than Intel Active Management Technology (Intel AMT). While Intel AMT is the main focus of this book, computers marked with the Intel vPro technology brand include a dual core 64-bit processor or better, gigabit Ethernet, RAID controller for storage speed and reliability, Wake-on-LAN, and power saving features such an Ethernet adapter capable of dropping to lower speeds when the computer is sleeping. All these features allow IT professionals to identify platforms that meet the manageability and security requirements of today's business computing.

Intel® vPro™ Technology Value Vectors

Manageability, security, and energy-efficient performance are three key value vectors of Intel vPro technology.

The manageability capabilities embedded in the platform with Intel vPro technology allow the IT system administrator to carry out manageability operations like collecting system inventory and asset information, detecting the act of disabling of critical system software like virus scanners by malware or the users, remotely diagnosing and repairing issues with software or firmware on the platform. Having this capability embedded in the hardware allows the IT system administrator to perform these actions remotely, irrespective of the state of operating system or the system power state, and thereby considerably reducing the number of desk side visits.

For home users, Intel vPro technology means that they can press a Help button (or a key sequence) when they need support, rather than making a phone call. PCs can "phone home" for help or for regular maintenance even if located outside the firewall.

The security benefits for platforms with Intel vPro technology lie in the capabilities to detect and isolate infected systems from the network to prevent the infection from spreading. Once isolated, the infected systems can be placed on a quarantine network allowing the IT system operator to remotely repair and update the critical security agents. Platforms with Intel vPro technology can automatically run heuristics to determine if the system is infected, take policy-based actions to automatically isolate them from the network and notify the IT system administrator.

System hardware can take part in network authentication even prior to start of the operating system, allowing administrators to be sure that their network access protections are in place before allowing systems on the network.

Intel vPro technology provides hardware-based data encryption capabilities providing the end users protection from theft.

While providing the manageability and security benefits, Intel vPro technology provides energy efficiency in core silicon and other hardware components, leading to reduced power consumption and longer battery life. Additional remote power control operations allow systems to stay longer on standby power while maintaining emergency contact with the remote system administrator. In certain areas of the world (such as Japan) and specific installations (such as schools) people like to turn the systems off in the evening and turn them on in the morning. Providing a way to do this in an automated fashion helps in saving power.

Intel® vPro™ Technology Ingredients

In this chapter, we look at the overall capabilities of platforms equipped with Intel vPro technology and how these capabilities are exposed through standards-based interfaces, which allows a wide variety of management applications to use them. This open architecture allows greater interoperability and provides flexibility to IT systems administrators to deploy manageability and security solutions.

Intel® Core™2 Processor with Intel vPro™ Technology

The Intel Core™2 Quad processor or Intel Core2 Duo processor (or later versions as the products evolve) are essential parts of the Intel vPro technology ingredients. These are built on Enhanced Intel Core microarchitecture. The 45-nm technology used in these processors brings higher performance and lower power usage than the previous generations with up to a 12 MB L2 cache and a 1333 MHz Front Side Bus. These processors include several technologies that are essential to deliver many of the capabilities of Intel vPro technology.

Enhanced Intel SpeedStep® technology brings a unique combination of power-optimized performance. This technology allows automatic switchover from high performance mode to power-optimized mode by adjusting the processor speed and voltage as the system is switched from AC power to battery power. The smooth transitions make it completely transparent to the operating system and the user. Furthermore, the power adjustments are done on a per-core basis to further enhance efficiency.

Processor features support Intel Virtualization Technology (Intel VT) and Intel Trusted Execution Technology (Intel TXT) to bring unique benefits for creating secure virtual partitions. We describe these features in more detail later in this chapter.

New Intel Streaming SIMD Extensions 4 (Intel SSE4) instructions bring improved performance for multimedia and graphics and enhanced video encode and decode capabilities. Intel SSE4 brings over 50 new instructions to the IA instruction set. The general concept behind these instructions is to combine certain common operations into one smooth operation: rather than a series of *multiple* instructions required for, say, discovering the dot product of two vectors, Intel SSE4 provides one dedicated instruction. Intel SSE4 reduces complex operations into native instructions, and this can greatly improve the efficiency of the processor in certain applications. Most of the new instructions are related to vector operations, which are the core of graphics and multimedia processing. Also included are primitives that increase the speed of streaming and improves access to device memory.

Chipsets

The Intel Q45 Express Chipset and Intel Q43 Express Chipset (and later versions as the products evolve) work in conjunction with Intel Core 2 processors to provide key parts of the ingredients in Intel vPro technology. Intel AMT is the heart of these capabilities delivered by these chipsets and is the main focus of this book.

Intel Anti-Theft Technology allows encryption of user data and makes sure that the data cannot be retrieved if the system is stolen. Statistics indicate that thieves are usually after the data rather than the system itself, and the thief is less likely to steal a system if he knows that the data is locked.

Intel Matrix Storage Technology provides the reliability and performance for building RAID solutions.

Integrated DVI and display port as well as dual independent digital displays provide enhanced graphics performance and usability and productivity.

Gigabit Ethernet

In addition to the obvious speed and performance benefits of Gigabit Ethernet, an additional capability that the Intel Gigabit Ethernet controller brings is the packet filtering. There are two types of filters. One type, Out-of-Band filter, allows delivering the manageability traffic received from the network to the manageability engine. This capability allows Intel AMT to be connected over the network to the IT system administrator at all times irrespective of the state of the host operating system. The other type of filter allows Intel AMT to create policies to detect certain anomalous network patterns, thereby detecting a condition such as outbreak of a network worm. In such conditions an Ethernet controller can be instructed to stop all or some of the traffic going to or from the host. These packet filters in the Integrated Gigabit Ethernet controller are key elements of the network security capabilities provided by the Intel AMT technology. This capability is discussed more in detail in later chapters.

Wireless Networking

Faster wireless networking with 802.11n in Intel Centrino® platforms provides high throughput connectivity options for multiple environments. It provides flexibility to connect to wireless home network and public wireless LAN hotspots located in airports, hotels, restaurants, and coffee shops around the world. Intel AMT capabilities are accessible via wireless networks in the same way as through the wired LAN. TCO filters in the wireless controller work the same way as described above.

Platform BIOS

Platform BIOS is an important ingredient that enables the features in the processors and chipsets. The BIOS has been used traditionally on desktop and mobile client platforms to configure and enable key platform features for use by the operating system. On some platforms, a management controller can directly configure certain features and provide an interface to the user to set a configuration parameter.

In platforms with Intel vPro technology, the BIOS must be able to enable and configure the following capabilities such that they can be used by the operating system and applications:

■ Intel® Virtualization Technology

■ Intel® Trusted Execution Technology and the Intel® Trusted Platform Module

■ Intel® Active Management Technology

Software Applications

Software applications which use Intel AMT are another important part of managing platforms with Intel vPro technology. The capabilities of Intel vPro technology are exposed using standards-based interfaces allowing easy interoperability and integration with wide variety of manageability and security solutions. Intel has done significant work in collaborating with independent software vendors (ISVs) to create the ISV manageability ecosystem.

Key Intel® vPro™ Technologies

Three key set of ingredient technologies are fundamental to Intel vPro technology: Intel Active Management Technology (Intel AMT), Intel Virtualization Technology (Intel VT) and Intel Trusted Execution Technology (Intel TXT).

Out of these three, Intel AMT is the most user-visible and it is described further in the remainder of the book. The following sections provide an overview of Intel VT and Intel TXT.

Intel® Virtualization Technology

Intel Virtualization Technology provides hardware support that simplifies processor virtualization, enabling reductions in virtual machine monitor (VMM) software size and complexity. Resulting VMMs can support a wider range of legacy and future operating systems on the same physical platform while maintaining high performance.

To understand the concepts of Intel VT, let's first briefly understand the challenges associated with virtualizing the processor. In order to virtualize the processor, the VMM needs to:

- Protect itself from the guest operating system and applications
- Isolate guest operating systems from each other
- Present a virtual platform to the guest operating system

To achieve this, the VMM must be able to control and virtualize the CPU, memory, and devices on the platform. This requires the VMM to be executing as the most-privileged software on the processor. Intel processors provide protection based on the concept of a privilege level, using 0 for most-privileged software and 3 for least-privileged. The privilege level determines whether privileged instructions, which control basic CPU functionality, can execute without fault. It also controls address-space accessibility based on the configuration of the processor's page tables and segment registers.

For an OS to control the CPU, some of its components must run with privilege level 0. Because a VMM cannot allow a guest OS such control, a guest OS cannot execute at privilege level 0. Thus, VMMs must use ring de-privileging, a technique that runs all guest software at a privilege level less than 0 (numerically greater).

However, since the guest OS is not written to run at this privilege level, it introduces inefficiencies and security problems. A number of Intel Architecture (IA) instructions like LAR, LSL, SIDT, and CPUID when executed at lower-privilege rings (rather than ring 0 as intended) do not fault. Hence the VMM, even though running at ring 0, cannot intercept and virtualize them. In order to effectively switch the context between multiple guest operating systems, the VMM needs mechanisms to save and restore the processor state. Some of the IA processor state, like the hidden segment states, cannot be easily saved and restored. Additionally, executing operating systems in higher privilege levels can lead to excessive and un-necessary faulting leading to inefficient execution. Numerous problems, such as interrupt virtualization, inefficient transitions back and forth from VMM to guest OS, and so on, make this software approach problematic.

To address the virtualization challenges VMM designers developed creative techniques for modifying guest software (source or binary). The source-level modifications technique is called paravirtualization. Developers of these VMMs modify the source code of a guest OS to create an interface that is easier to virtualize. Paravirtualization offers high performance and does not require changes to guest applications. A disadvantage of paravirtualization is that it limits the range of supported operating systems. VMMs that rely on paravirtualization cannot support an OS whose source code the VMM's developers have not modified.

A VMM can support unmodified operating systems by transforming guest-OS binaries on-the-fly to handle virtualization-sensitive operations. Such VMMs support a broader range of operating systems than VMMs that use paravirtualization.

Intel VT eliminates the need for CPU paravirtualization and binary translation techniques, simplifying the implementation of robust VMMs that can support a broad range of unmodified guest operating systems while maintaining high levels of performance.

Intel VT consists of two main components. Intel VT for IA-32 Intel Architecture (Intel VT-x) provides processor extensions for CPU virtualization, and Intel VT for Directed I/O (Intel VT-d) provides processor extensions for device virtualization.

Intel VT-x augments IA-32 with two new modes of CPU operation: VMX root mode intended for use by a VMM and VMX non-root mode intended for guests' virtual machines. Both modes of operation support all four privilege levels, allowing guest software to run at its intended privilege level, and providing a VMM with the flexibility to use multiple privilege levels.

Intel VT-x defines two new transitions: a transition from VMX root operation to VMX non-root operation is called a VM entry, and a transition from VMX non-root operation to VMX root operation is called a VM exit. VM entries and VM exits are managed by a new data structure called the virtual-machine control structure (VMCS). The VMCS includes a guest-state area and a host-state area, each of which contains fields corresponding to different components of processor state. VM entries load processor state from the guest-state area. VM exits save processor state to the guest-state area and then load processor state from the host-state area.

Processor operation is changed substantially in VMX non-root operation. An important change is that many instructions and events cause VM exits. Some instructions, such as INVD, cause VM exits unconditionally when executed in VMX non-root operation. Other instructions, such as INVLPG, can be configured to cause VM exits conditionally using VM-execution control fields in the VMCS.

VM entry and VM exit provide an efficient way of switching the context from a VMM to a guest and back. The result is better performance without sacrificing the security while running unmodified guest OS.

Intel VT-d extends Intel VT to include support for I/O device virtualization. It is important to have protected access to I/O resources from a given virtual machine (VM), such that it cannot interfere with the operation of another VM on the same platform. This isolation between VMs is essential for achieving availability, reliability, and trust. The second major requirement is the ability to share I/O resources among multiple VMs. In many cases, it is not practical or cost-effective to replicate I/O resources (such as storage or network controllers) for each VM on a given platform.

In the case of the enterprise client, virtualization can be used to create a self-contained operating environment, or *virtual appliance*, that is dedicated to capabilities such as manageability or security. These capabilities generally need protected and secure access to a network device to communicate with down-the-wire management agents and to monitor network traffic for security threats. For example, a security agent within a VM requires protected access to the actual network controller hardware. This agent can then intelligently examine network traffic for malicious payloads or suspected intrusion attempts before the network packets are passed to the guest OS, where user applications might be affected.

The virtualization of I/O resources is an important evolution of usage models in the data center, the enterprise, and the home. VT-d support on Intel platforms provides the capability to ensure improved isolation of I/O resources for greater reliability, security, and availability.

To help with this, Intel VT-d supports the remapping of I/O DMA transfers and device-generated interrupts. The architecture of Intel VT-d provides the flexibility to support multiple usage models that may run unmodified, special-purpose, or virtualization-aware guest operating systems. The Intel VT-d hardware capabilities for I/O virtualization complement the existing Intel VT capability to virtualize processor and memory resources. Together, this offers a complete solution to provide full hardware support for the virtualization of Intel platforms.

Readers who need more information on Intel VT will be interested in the book *Applied Virtualization Technology* By Sean Campbell and Michael Jeronimo (Intel Press 2006)

Intel® Trusted Execution Technology

Intel Trusted Execution Technology (Intel TXT) is a hardware extension that is intended to provide users and enterprises with a higher level of trusted platform while accessing, modifying, or creating sensitive data and code. It is useful as a way to defend against software-based attacks aimed at stealing sensitive information.

Intel TXT consists of a series of hardware enhancements that allow for the creation of multiple separated execution environments, or partitions. One critical component is the Intel® Trusted Platform Module (Intel® TPM), which allows for secure key generation and storage, and authenticated access to data encrypted by this key. The private key stored in the Intel TPM is not available to the owner of the machine, and never leaves the chip. Intel TXT comprises of the following capabilities.

The processor allows creation of a segregated private environment for applications, so that the hardware resources (such as memory pools) are locked to the calling applications and cannot be accessed by any other process running on the platform.

User input paths (keyboard, mouse) are protected, allowing users to interact with trusted platform applications without the risk of their inputs being observed or modified by other software. Secure display interface enables trusted platform applications to send display data securely on output devices without the risk of their output being observed or modified by other software.

The Intel TPM allows the system administrator to configure a launch control policy and in conjunction with the Intel TXT allows the performance of a measured and verified launch of the system software. The Intel TPM also provides secure storage and sealing for keying material and other secrets such that the secrets are made available to only trusted applications. The Intel TXT and Intel TPM can be used to securely record various system measurements and provide trusted attestation of the system status.

Thus Intel TXT capability helps reduce IT support costs with improved services, enables decentralized or remote computing, and verifies platform configuration with a higher level of assurance.

Intel TXT allows local or remote verification of the platform state. Local verification uses the measurement capability of Intel TXT to allow the local user to have confidence that the platform is executing in a known state. The confidence comes from the hardware ability of Intel TXT to properly measure the launched configuration and store the measurement in the Intel TPM. Remote verification takes the measurements obtained by Intel TXT and stored in the Intel TPM, and uses the Intel TPM to inform remote entities (those not executing on the platform) about the current platform configuration. The essence of this use model is that the remote entity can rely on the protective properties of Intel TXT.

Readers who need more information on Intel TXT will be interested in the book *Dynamics of a Trusted Platform: A building block approach* by David Grawrock (Intel Press 2009).

Summary

Intel vPro technology provides manageability, security, and energy efficient computing capabilities using technologies like Intel AMT, Intel VT and Intel TXT. A number of ingredients in the platforms, such as CPU, chipset, LAN, and BIOS work together to provide the capabilities of Intel vPro technology. The rest of the book focuses on Intel AMT and the ingredients that are specifically used in delivering these capabilities.

Chapter 5

Intel® Active Management Technology Overview

Management is doing things right; leadership is doing the right things.
—Peter Drucker (1909–2005)

As we discussed in the last chapter, Intel® Active Management Technology (Intel AMT) is a major component of the Intel vPro™ platform that differentiates this platform from other platforms. Let's look more closely at the details of the capabilities that Intel AMT provides. In this chapter we look at different end-user solutions that are built using the Intel AMT capabilities.

Key Characteristics

Before we examine the functional capabilities of Intel AMT, let's briefly look at the key characteristics that make it different from traditional management based on OS agents.

Out of Band Access

Intel AMT is powered by a separate hardware engine: the Manageability Engine in Intel chipsets. This hardware engine has its own processor, its own portion of the memory, its own portion of Flash, its own sideband access to the networking controllers, and so on. It therefore provides the out of band access benefits that we looked at in Chapter 1. We will go into details of these Intel AMT components in Chapter 7. At this point, it is enough to say that Intel AMT can operate independent of the main CPU and independent of the operating system state. Intel AMT is always available and always accessible.

Low Power Operation

The Manageability Engine from which Intel AMT operates can function in lower power states. The system can be in the low-power standby or hibernate mode or even turned off, and Intel AMT will continue to function.

Operation in Various System States

Advanced Configuration and Power Interface (ACPI) is an industry specification that defines the system sleep states (S-states). S0 is the state when system is fully powered on. S3 state is called system standby state, where the OS image is intact in the system memory. System memory contents are maintained in self-refresh mode. The processor, disk and all the peripherals are turned off. S4 state is when the memory contents are transferred to disk, and memory is powered off. This is also called hibernate. S5 is system off state. Intel AMT is available in all these system S-States.

When the system is in S0 (fully powered) state, the system may still be in various states of OS or BIOS operations. These states are not defined by ACPI, but we make this further distinction based on accessibility to the platform from a remote management console.

When the OS is fully operational and networking access is functional, agent-based methods can usually be used to manage the system. Intel AMT works in this state and coexists with these mechanisms.

When the OS is not functioning normally, an agent or a device driver has crashed, the networking software is running slow, some rogue application is hogging the CPU, or the OS is hung or has crashed, OS-based agents are not accessible by management consoles. Intel AMT is functional in these states and can be used to bring the system back to its normal functioning state.

In the pre-OS environment, when the OS has not yet started or the system does not yet even have an OS installed, or in certain cases when the BIOS encounters failures, Intel AMT continues to work and provides critical remediation services to allow the system to be fixed.

OS-Independent Agent-less Solution

Intel AMT does not require any agent in the OS for its core operations; this makes it OS independent. Intel AMT capabilities are available whether the system has Windows, Linux, or any other operating system installed, or for that matter even if no operating system is installed.

Tamper-Resistant Solution

Intel AMT components execute in an isolated environment and are not accessible by any software from either the main system operating system or applications. Malware cannot change or modify any code module in Intel AMT. Intel AMT is protected at the hardware level. The only access to Intel AMT is through a well defined API, which requires authenticated credentials to access. No mechanisms are provided to download a software component into Intel AMT, which prevents any malware from getting into the Intel AMT execution environment.

Discover, Heal, and Protect

Having looked at the key characteristics of Intel AMT, let's look further into its various capabilities.

Key Intel AMT usage models are centered around the three pillars of Discover, Heal and Protect.

A management console can *discover* all Intel AMT systems on the network and collect hardware and software inventory information from those systems. Intel AMT is able to do all this regardless of system power or health state, and regardless of OS state.

A management console can get alerts from the Intel AMT system when things are failing or about to fail. Once these alerts are received the system administrator can remotely diagnose and *heal* the system with tools such as remote login, remote boot, text console redirection and remote media redirection.

Intel AMT provides hardware-based capabilities to watch the operation of the critical security agents and can alert the system administrators when these events are accidentally or purposely stopped by malware. Some versions of Intel AMT also provide a mechanism to watch outgoing network traffic and detect anomalous patterns that are indicative of a spreading worm. Thus, Intel AMT provides capabilities to *protect* the systems and the network from malware.

Key Capabilities

In this section, we walk through the key capabilities of Intel AMT. In the next chapter, we look at how we can build various solutions using these capabilities.

Hardware Inventory

Intel AMT keeps all the hardware inventory data in a nonvolatile RAM (NVRAM). In some cases, the manageability engine is directly connected to various components on the platforms, and Intel AMT collects that information directly. In other cases the BIOS scans the hardware, collects the asset information and relays it to Intel AMT to store in the NVRAM. The information includes the make, model number, asset tag, and so on. This information is made available through a management console.

Software Inventory

Intel AMT has the capability to keep software asset information in NVRAM as well. OS services, drivers, and applications can relay this information to Intel AMT, which stores it in Third Party Data Store (described later in this chapter). This information is then made available to management consoles even when the OS is unavailable. This is particularly useful when the OS and applications fail and the system administrator needs to know the system configuration to be able to fix it.

Hardware Health and Platform Sensors

Intel AMT monitors various hardware components such as processor, memory, chipset, networking controller, and disk controllers on the platform and proactively reports any failures or impending failures to the management console. Several sensors on the platforms collect readings from various physical places on the platform and contribute to determining the overall health status. These sensors include CPU presence and error sensors, temperature sensors, voltage sensors, chassis integrity sensors, and fan sensors.

Remote Power Control

Intel AMT allows a remote system administrator to reset or power off a system even when the normal access methods to reach the operating system may not work. For example, the OS is hung or crashed, or an OS is not installed. Furthermore, a system administrator can even reach a system that is powered off and send it a command to turn it on.

Boot Control

This capability allows a system administrator to control how the system is booted. A specific boot device can be selected. For example, the system can be instructed to boot from a hard disk, a CD-ROM, a network controller (PXE boot) or a remote IDE device (explained below). Additionally, options can be provided to change the display of BIOS messages on the local console, or redirect the messages to the remote console.

Text Console Redirection

This feature is also often known as serial redirection or serial over LAN (SOL). Intel AMT hardware emulates a serial COM port for the system. This allows all text output to this COM port, to be packaged by Intel AMT into network messages and sent to remote console over the network. Conversely, the keyboard input is captured at the remote console and sent through the network packets to the Intel AMT system. Intel AMT takes that keyboard sequence and sends it to the COM port as if it were the local keyboard input.

This capability allows all the pre-boot BIOS text output and input to be controlled by a remote management console. Pressing a function key to change BIOS settings can be achieved using this functionality.

Disk Redirection

This feature is also known as IDE Redirection (IDE-R). This allows a remote system administrator to mount a storage media, which can be a local disk on system administrator's console, a disk volume, a CD-ROM, and ISO image, a USB flash drive, or any other storage device to be accessed by the Intel AMT system as if it is a local IDE drive.

Intel AMT hardware emulates a local IDE disk drive interface for the system. All the writes are captured by Intel AMT and packaged into network packets and send to the console. Console software takes those packets and writes it to the mounted media. Similarly any read requests from an Intel AMT system go through the remote console and content is returned via network packets. To the local system, this all appears as if it is communicating with a local IDE drive, except for the somewhat slower performance compared to local access.

Persistent NVRAM Log

Intel AMT maintains a log of all critical platform events in NVRAM. This log is a persistent historical record of the events that happened on the platform. It is embedded in the platform and is more reliable than the traditional disk-based logs that are prone to be lost if the disk fails or is replaced. Like the rest of the Intel AMT capabilities, this log is accessible in all platform states, thereby providing an important diagnostic tool.

Alerts

Intel AMT can be configured to send directed alerts to one or more configured IP addresses. These alerts can be for configured critical or informational events. The alerts can go out as SNMP traps, or can be delivered using a more sophisticated WS-Management event registration and delivery mechanisms.

Third Party Data Store (3PDS)

Intel AMT provides the capability for a third party to have a programmatic and secure access to a fixed size reserved block in the NVRAM. This allows a software application to keep a critical portion of the data in this persistent storage and not get affected by disk wipes or by malware access. Another reason to keep the data in NVRAM is that it is accessible all the time independent of the system state. One example of this is a virus definition file for the virus scanner software. A system administrator can update all the systems on the network with the version number of the latest virus definition files without worrying about the fact that some systems may not be up and running. When the systems are booted or brought up from sleep, the virus scanner software agent can check if it needs to pull the latest virus definition files from the server.

Agent Presence

Intel AMT provides a watchdog capability that allows a local application on Intel AMT system to be configured to periodically send a heartbeat message to the Intel AMT hardware. If the application fails to send the heartbeat within a pre-defined time interval, the Intel AMT hardware can generate an alert and notify the remote console, as well as send a local notification to display on the console. This allows critical software agents to be watched for presence. This is very useful to watch critical security agents on the platform.

System Defense

The system defense feature allows a remote system management console to define and enforce network security policies. A system defense policy contains a set of filters that are applied to incoming or outgoing packets, along with a set of actions to perform when the filter is matched, or not-matched. Once these policies are loaded into Intel AMT and activated, Intel AMT constantly monitors the incoming and outgoing network packets and takes specified actions. The actions can include sending an alert to the system management console, logging an event in event log, taking autonomous action to throttle incoming or outgoing traffic, or even completely stopping the network traffic. While the network traffic to host is stopped, Intel AMT is still accessible over the network for remediation actions.

Endpoint Access Control

Intel AMT helps secure network endpoints by validating their compliance with network policies. The Endpoint Access Control (EAC) feature allows the system administrators to implement differentiated policy enforcement and configuration based on the security state of the endpoint. At every connection, or on demand, a client system's profile is securely surveyed in a trusted manner. The system posture (including credentials, configuration, and system data) along with Intel AMT configuration parameters (Firmware Version, TLS enabled, SOL enabled, and so on) is compared to current requirements. For systems not meeting the minimum standards, network access is restricted, and a user notification is displayed to convey to the end user that normal network operation will be delayed until remediation is complete.

Full authentication and posture checking before allowing network access can greatly reduce the potential for malware to propagate onto the network, and this allows the IT administrator to maintain all systems in compliance with current policies and limits rogue or visitor systems from gaining network access. Intel AMT enables the acquisition of accurate endpoint state and attributes information for network admission control, via "always-available" communication, regardless of the PC's power state, the state of the OS, or the absence of management agents. Accurate identification of machines in a pre-boot environment results in improved automation and enforcement of secure network policies.

Interfaces and Protocols

Intel AMT capabilities are accessed in a secure manner from a management console or from an application running locally on the Intel AMT platform. Several mechanisms for Intel AMT access exist and are listed below.

Network Access

All communications with Intel AMT system from a remote management console happen over the standard networking protocols. This communication is supported over wired (Ethernet) or wireless (Wi-Fi†) connections.

Intel AMT can have its own IP address, or can share the IP address with the host. Shared IP address is the most commonly used configuration. When the IP address is shared, only certain packets destined to Intel AMT ports are filtered and sent by the networking controller to Intel AMT. This communication happens without any OS assistance via a sideband connection between the networking controller and the Intel AMT manageability engine hardware.

Intel AMT supports communication over fully encrypted secure channel provided by TLS (HTTPS). With the secure communication channels, all network traffic is protected against.

All Intel AMT communications require authentication of the user credentials. Intel AMT manages the access controls based on the permissions set for the user. Intel AMT uses passwords and can also integrate with Kerberos and Active Directory security mechanisms.

External Operations Interface

Intel AMT has traditionally supported a SOAP-based network interface called External Operations Interface (EOI). EOI has been the interface since the first release of Intel AMT. EOI works over HTTP and HTTPS transport protocols.

WS-Management Interface

Intel AMT today supports the standard WS-Management interface. This is the preferred interface for the future generations of Intel AMT. Intel AMT supports WS-Management over HTTP and HTTPS as well.

Platform Event Traps

Intel AMT alerts can be sent via Platform Event Traps (PET), which are defined using SNMP packet format, and are delivered using SNMP protocol. The PET format is a standard defined by DMTF.

In addition to PET alerts, Intel AMT can also send events using WS-Management event formats.

Local Access

Intel AMT allows local applications to access some of the Intel AMT functionality through a device driver and higher-level software layers.

Intel® Management Engine Interface

Intel Management Engine Interface (Intel MEI) is a hardware interface that is used to communicate to the Intel AMT subsystem. Intel MEI is essentially a PCI device interface. Intel MEI is bidirectional, as either the host OS or Intel AMT firmware can initiate transactions.

Communication between the local host OS and Intel AMT is accomplished by means of the Intel MEI driver.

The BIOS typically sends messages directly through the Intel MEI interface. Most OS-based applications go through another layer of software that sits on top of Intel MEI and provides the higher level of abstraction.

Network-Compatible Interface

Local Manageability Service (LMS) is a service that runs locally in the user space of the host OS. LMS exposes Intel AMT functionality through standard network-compatible interfaces (EOI and WS-Management as described above). LMS listens for the request directed to the Intel AMT local host and when an application sends a SOAP/HTTP message addressed to the local host, LMS intercepts the request and routes the request to Intel AMT via the Intel MEI driver.

Intel® AMT SDK

Intel AMT SDK provides the documentation for interfacing with Intel AMT along with necessary libraries and also provides sample source code.

For example, if you want to read/write data to the third party data store (3PDS) then your application uses the storage library API to accomplish the task. The storage library talks to the LMS interface and that in turn talks to the Intel MEI driver to access the 3PDS. As far as the client application is concerned, it simply talks to the LMS or Storage Library (Intel AMT SDK) and the message gets routed to the Intel Management Engine via the Intel MEI driver.

Intel® AMT and Enterprise Infrastructure

Intel AMT needs to work with existing enterprise infrastructure, as most of the Intel vPro platforms are deployed within a standard IT environment. In order to facilitate this integration, Intel AMT provides a number of capabilities to make the deployment in enterprise environments straightforward. Most of these components are not required in smaller environments.

Active Directory Integration

For the IT environments that deploy Active Directory for authentication, authorization, and access control, Intel AMT can be configured to use Active Directory. Intel AMT is also capable of using Kerberos Authentication and Active Directory–based authorization and access controls.

Setup and Configuration Server

In order to make large-scale Intel AMT deployments easier, a setup and configuration service can be deployed. This service can be integrated into management consoles. The Setup and Configuration service discovers the new Intel AMT systems on the network and can send them the configurations parameters in a secure manner.

Management Consoles

Management consoles are a key part of providing overall manageability solutions for Intel vPro platforms. Management consoles can use the standard WS-Management interfaces or legacy EOI interfaces to communicate with Intel AMT platforms. The Intel AMT SDK provides another higher level of API abstraction to make this integration even simpler.

If the enterprise is not setup with Active Directory integration, then the management console has to setup the passwords on the system with for password/digest authentication, deploy Intel AMT access control realms on the system with Intel AMT, and manage that over time.

Management consoles also have the responsibility to maintain the up-to-date time in the Intel AMT subsystem. The periodic time synchronization is part of the management console responsibility.

Certificate Server

If the enterprise needs to support TLS and HTTPS, then it needs to provide services from a Certificate Server to generate certificates for Intel AMT. These certificates are deployed in systems with Intel AMT.

BIOS

Although the BIOS is technically a component on the platform itself, we include it in this list because changes are required for Intel AMT to work properly. On Intel AMT systems, the BIOS must contain an Intel Manageability Engine BIOS Extensions (Intel MEBX) module to be able to enable and configure Intel AMT. This has to be considered when performing BIOS upgrades. Typically, the vendor that supplies Intel MEBX–enabled BIOS with the platform will include it in the updates, so this generally should not be a problem.

Intel AMT also provides the capability to check the firmware and measure its different components as they are initialized. This measurement can be matched against a pre-stored value. The BIOS typically does this and makes a policy-based decision if the measurements do not match.

Routers, Access Points, and Servers

As described earlier regarding Endpoint Access Control capability, Intel AMT needs to operate in an 802.1x network to provide the posture information to the access points or backend network. The policies have to be configured for Intel AMT to get access to the network if the posture information is as expected.

DHCP and DNS

Intel AMT integrates with DHCP to obtain an IP address. Then it uses DHCP options to provide its discovery information and update DNS servers, which is later used to discover the Intel AMT systems on the network.

Wi-Fi Access Points

Intel AMT can be accessed over a Wi-Fi network. Intel AMT can work with access points that do not support encryption. It also supports WAP and WPA keys. Profiles with these keys need to be provisioned in systems with Intel AMT. Intel AMT can also synchronize the profiles with the OS.

Security Compliance Suites

Several security compliance suites need to audit the activities on a platform. Intel AMT provides a well secured audit log that records all actions that are performed with Intel AMT. Compliance suites can retrieved this audit log and analyze it as part of the overall platform audit log.

Summary

Intel AMT provides a number of capabilities that allow discovery, healing, and protection of the platform and resources. These capabilities can be accessed using local or network interfaces in a secure manner. In the next chapter, we see how these capabilities are used to solve real world problems.

Chapter 6

Solving End User Problems with Intel® vPro™ Manageability

The ideal engineer is a composite ... He is not a scientist, he is not a mathematician, he is not a sociologist or a writer; but he may use the knowledge and techniques of any or all of these disciplines in solving engineering problems.

—N. W. Dougherty, 1955

None of the features of Intel® Active Management Technology (Intel AMT) would be of any use if they could not be combined to solve real world problems. In this chapter we will review a set of real world scenarios and how Intel AMT features can be used to solve them. It's also important to note that in most or all of these scenarios, software-only solutions would either not work at all or not solve the problem as effectively or as securely.

Protect from a Worm Outbreak

Virus outbreaks have cost organizations much time and money. As employees come in early in the morning, companies would post announcements telling them not to use their computers until further notice. In these situations each hour a network is down is a huge burden and a fix must be deployed quickly.

When Intel AMT is present and set up on a computer; IT can quickly deploy hardware network filters that stop specific traffic types. If it is determined that a virus attempts to scan a given port on all computers, IT can deploy one or more hardware filters that block inbound and outbound packets that match a given traffic type. Hardware counters can also be used to count how many packets of this type where dropped, making it easy to determine if a computer is infected.

Here is a typical scenario: An employee uses a USB flash stick to transfer files onto a work computer. One of the files is infected with a new and unknown network worm. The worm then proceeds to scan the network for vulnerable computers. The worm spreads quickly throughout the company slowing down the network and making computers unusable. IT determines that the worm is scanning the network for a custom application that is specific to this organization. This application listens to a specific UDP port and determines that the worm must be exploiting vulnerability in the software. Having a fleet of Intel vPro computers, IT pushes a network filter blocking inbound and outbound packets to this port. It also assigns a hardware network packet counter to these filters, as shown in Figure 6.1.

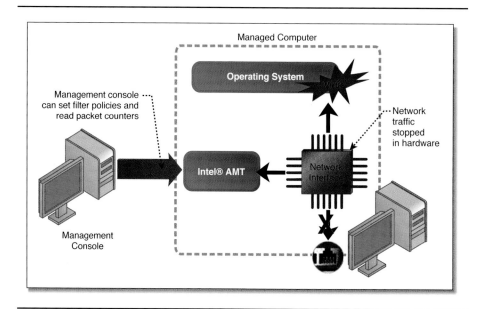

Figure 6.1 With the Infected Computer's Network Traffic Cut Off, the Administrator Can Still Communicate with Intel® AMT

IT is now in a position to monitor each computer and see which ones are infected with the worm. It can do so without requiring any software to be installed or running on each computer, or without worry that the worm itself would tamper or disable monitoring software running on each computer.

In an extreme case, IT could also disable all network traffic going in and out of a computer, or disable all traffic except for a give type. In our example, the worm attacks some of the computers in the company and these are now isolated and can't attack any other computer. In order to fix computers remotely, IT places a policy that allows traffic to and from the management console to be permitted through. This allows the administrator to contact services running within the operating system and attempt to fix the problem, as shown in Figure 6.2.

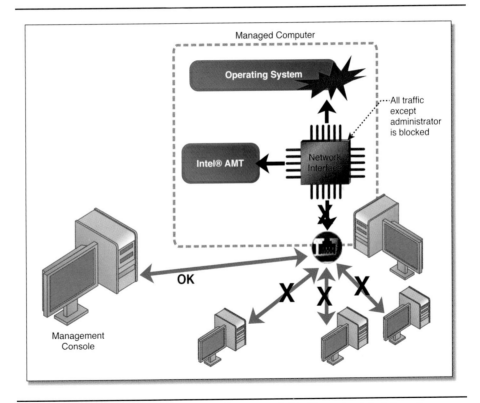

Figure 6.2   All Traffic Cut Off Except for Network Traffic to the Administrative Console. This Allows for Safe Remote Repair.

With Intel AMT 3.0, an additional feature may be useful in this scenario. Heuristic filters can be setup in advance to automatically detect and stop computers that attempt to scan the network. In our scenario, all computers with Intel AMT 3.0 would automatically detect and stop the worm from attempting to find other vulnerable computers.

Tracking Hardware Assets

Hardware theft is a big problem. Universities and corporations operating in poor countries are known to be especially at risk, but no one is immune to hardware theft. Thieves may steal a computer, but can also replace parts. They can replace the computer's CPU with a lower value one or remove some of the RAM, remove one of the PCI cards, and so on.

Let's suppose a scenario where a university campus is the target of occasional RAM theft. Computers still run, but a portion of the RAM is removed.

Using Intel AMT, the university IT department gets the hardware inventory of all of the computers on campus every day. It gets a very accurate picture of the inner components of each computer. Each time the hardware inventory is gathered; it is compared against the previously known inventory for this computer and stored into a database, as illustrated in Figure 6.3.

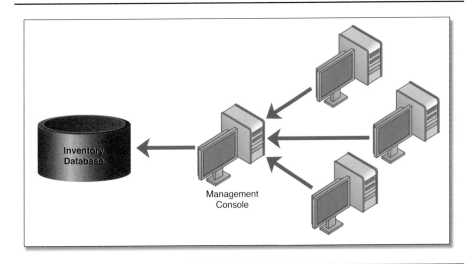

Figure 6.3 Hardware Asset Information Gathered into a Searchable Database

IT has a full inventory of all hardware assets within the university and can print a report showing, among other things, the total amount of RAM for all of the computers in the entire university. When a computer's RAM is decreased, a warning is automatically displayed on the administrator's management console.

In this scenario, administrators can find the computer with the missing memory and start to investigate. So far, the hardware asset inventory of all computers in the university is only taken every 24 hours and so it may take some time before the stolen RAM is detected. Intel AMT also supports the case intrusion switch and can send an alert to the administrator each time a computer case is open. Even if the computer is not connected at the time of the theft, the next time power and network is connected back, the computer will send the case intrusion alert to the administrator console. The university console can then turn the computer on remotely and automatically verify that the entire hardware inventory is still the same as before. Using the case intrusion switch allows the console to perform asset inventory check more frequently and exactly when needed. The administrator can also detect cases where lower quality RAM is replaced into a computer since Intel AMT reports the speed and serial number of each RAM stick.

Another similar and much more serious scenario has to do with hard disk theft. Intel AMT also reports each hard disk installed on a computer and for each disk, the size and serial number of disk. Administrators can quickly identify and react to a hard disk replacement or theft since Intel AMT does not depend on software or an operating system running on the PC. When a thief steals a hard disk from a computer, the case intrusion switch is triggered and the alert is sent, the administrator can take action.

Lastly, to protect mission critical data and computer assets the university management console can connect to any Intel AMT computer even if it is sleeping. This is useful because the software console can get up to the second report on the connectivity of all university computers. A thief attempting to steal a computer will have to disconnect it from the network causing the console to stop receiving network responses from that computer and the university security can automatically be advised of the problem.

In the past, this type of live monitoring would require the computer to stay on all the time, consuming and wasting energy increasing overall cost of operation. With Intel AMT, computers can be monitored around the clock while staying in full sleep or hibernation mode.

Fixing a "Blue Screen"

One of the most difficult problems to fix remotely is a complete crash of a computer. Luckily the well known "blue screen of death" occurs much less frequently now than it did only a few years ago as operating systems have gotten more reliable. Still, there are cases where such a crash can be costly to repair.

In this scenario, a company operates cash registers for a chain of stores. If one of the cash registers crashes, it may be costly to send someone to go fix it. The preferred solution is to fully diagnose and possibly fix the problem completely remotely. Older crashed cash registers would no longer be reachable through the network, but in our scenario the cash registers are running Intel boards that support Intel AMT. Even when the cash register has crashed, it is still possible to connect to Intel AMT and attempt to diagnose the problem.

Using the IDE redirect (IDE-R) feature, an administrator can remotely boot a recovery operating system (ROS). The administrator uses a CD-ROM disk image (.iso file) containing the recovery operating system and uses the management console software to boot the disk image on the cash register, as shown in Figure 6.4. Once completed, a set of diagnostic tools can be run and actions can be taken to fix the problem.

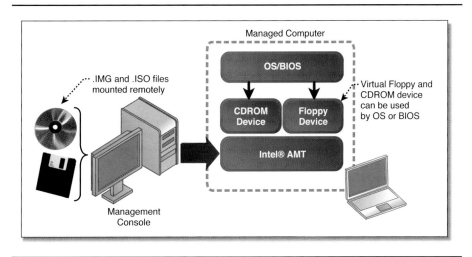

Figure 6.4 A Console Can Redirect a Floppy and CD-ROM Drive to a Managed Computer and Use Them for Remote Repair

In our case, the administrator realizes that files were accidently corrupted in the operating system and decides to reformat the hard disk with the original factory software. All of the software and tools needed to perform these operations are located on the ROS image file. If the administrator does not have the right tools, a different ROS can be used. The administrator changes the ROS disk image and causes another remote reboot using the new disk image.

This scenario equally applies to remote kiosks, corporate computers, ATM machines, and much more. IDE redirect is a powerful tool for fixing many types of problems remotely.

Compliance Network Alert

A healthy network starts with healthy computers that run up to date anti-virus, firewall, and repair agent software. A computer is said to be compliant with IT policies if it is running all of the correct IT software. Keeping track of computers that are not in compliance can be a problem.

Thanks to the agent presence feature of Intel AMT, it's possible to monitor what applications are running within the operating system. To do this, applications must periodically send a heartbeat to announce their presence to Intel AMT. Serving as a trusted entity on behalf of the network administrator, Intel AMT can report back on any changes in the running state of an application, as shown in Figure 6.5. In this way, many applications can be tracked and compliance maintained.

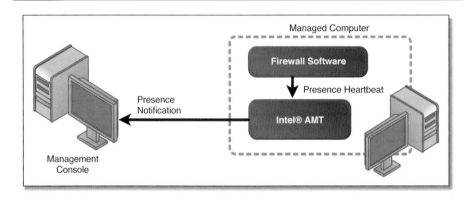

Figure 6.5   Intel® AMT Agent Presence Feature Monitors the Running of Firewall Software and Can Notify the Console of the Running State

When an application starts or stops reporting its presence, Intel AMT can send a network alert to the management console and/or log this as an event on the platform's event log. Since the event log is kept on the motherboard flash memory, it can be retrieved later, as shown in Figure 6.6. Keeping presence information in the event log can be very useful.

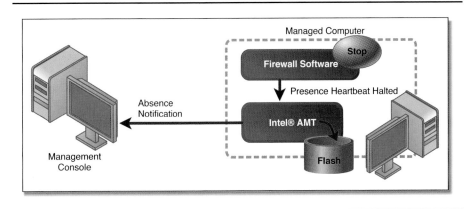

Figure 6.6 If the Firewall Software Is Stopped, the Console Can Be Notified with a Network Alert and an Event Can Be Stored in the Intel® AMT Event Log

For mobile platforms, the administrator can monitor compliance even when the computer is not connected to the managed network. When connected again, the event log can be examined to see if compliance was maintained.

Tracking Power Usage

For the first time, with Intel vPro technology, a network administrator can query over the network the power state of a computer without waking it up. This means that administrators can tell the difference between a computer that is powered on, a sleeping computer, and one that is disconnected from the network altogether. This feature in Intel AMT makes it easier to know if operating system configured power saving policies are working correctly. It also makes it possible for administrators to see in near real time how many computers are in which power state and which ones are currently disconnected from the network, as shown in Figure 6.7.

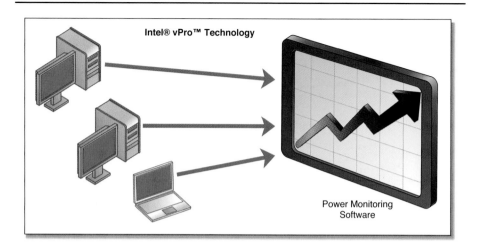

Figure 6.7   Power Monitoring Software Can Collect Power State for Many Computers and Show an Overview Graph of the Organization's Power Use

For Experts

There are a few tricks for using Intel AMT for power monitoring. On its own, Intel AMT will not send a network alert to a monitoring application when a computer changes power state. Events generally occur when a computer first boots up, but this will not help the monitoring software know when a computer goes to sleep and back, sometimes many times within a day.

The usual way to gather this data is to poll all computers with Intel AMT for their power state every few minutes. This works well, but may not be optimal. One clever trick is to use the Intel AMT agent presence feature and setup a new dummy watchdog that no application will ever use. Within Intel AMT, an agent presence watchdog will change to the "Suspended" state when the computer is in any sleep state, and back to "Expired" when it wakes up again. By causing this watchdog to send alerts, the monitoring software can be notified when a computer changes power state. When going to sleep, the monitoring software can then query the computer for its exact power state: S1 to S5.

This trick can help monitoring software get more accurate power data without continually polling all of the computers for their power state. Still, continual polling does have one important benefit. There is no way a computer can send a network alert notifying the monitoring software that it has been disconnected from the network. This information may be important and so, routinely performing a PING on each computer in addition to getting power notifications can insure both good power data in addition to knowing if the computer is still connected on the network.

Changing BIOS Settings Remotely

Probably one of the easiest and most immediately compelling demonstrations of Intel AMT is remote BIOS changes. Suppose a BIOS setting is incorrect such as the booting order of disk drives is not set correctly. The administrator can use Intel vPro–enabled administrative console software to remotely reboot the computer into BIOS and redirect the text mode display to the Intel AMT virtual serial port. The administrator can then send keystrokes back to the BIOS that will be acted upon just as if the user was typing that key, as shown in Figure 6.8.

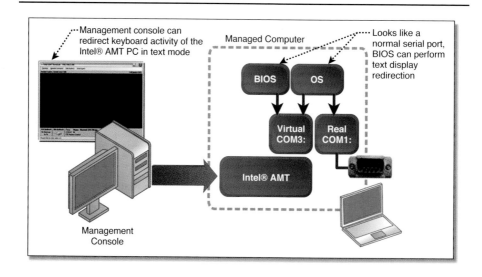

Figure 6.8   A Virtual Serial Port Is Redirected to the Management Console Allowing Remote Control When the Managed Computer Is in Text Mode Display

The administration console gets a complete remote view of the BIOS and, on some platforms, can even block local keyboard input from the local user. This is a very powerful feature but it can be augmented even further with terminal scripting on the administrator console. Because the terminal is text mode, it can easily be scripted, and manual changes in the BIOS can thus be automated.

Terminal scripting is especially valuable when a single BIOS change must be done on many computers, or when BIOS settings on many computers have to be audited. A script can read existing settings or perform the correct operations to make changes. Of course, because BIOS takes different forms the script may have to adapt to the specific BIOS that is present on the target computer.

Once the BIOS changes are completed, it's then possible to save the changes and reboot the computer normally. This is usually done in the same way that it's done when sitting in front of the managed computer. If needed, Intel AMT can be used to power cycle the computer.

Remote Platform Diagnostics

The Intel AMT event log records events from various sources and can be helpful in remotely diagnosing platform level problems. If an application fails, the operating system logs are a good source of information on what caused the problem. If the platform fails to boot, the Intel AMT event log plays the same role at the platform level, as shown in Figure 6.9.

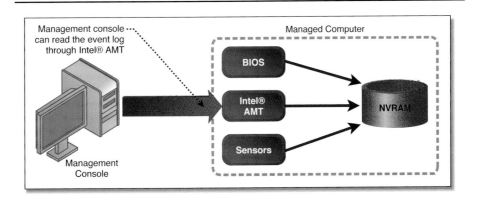

Figure 6.9　The Management Console Can Access Events Sent by Various Sources through Intel® AMT's Event Log Stores in Platform Flash Memory

The event log is stored in the platform's flash memory and so, is kept regardless of the health of disk storage. It gets events from three main sources: BIOS, platform sensors, and Intel AMT itself. BIOS events generally include boot up events and system failures. Platform sensors include the case intrusion switch, processor, add-in cards, and sometimes temperature warning sensors. Lastly, Intel AMT will record many events such as system defense and agent presence state changes, and so on.

The combination of all these events recorded into flash makes the Intel AMT event log an interesting place to start when trying to remotely diagnose platform level issues.

The event log can be accessed using most Intel vPro–enabled console software as shown in Figure 6.10 and also using the built-in Intel AMT Web server shown in Figure 6.11.

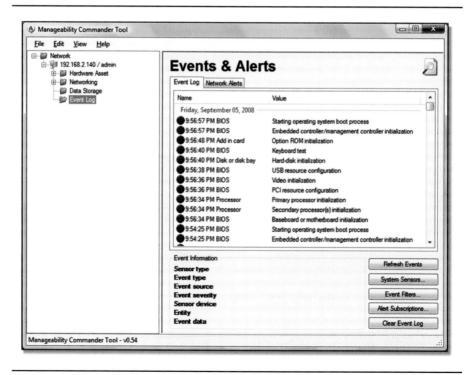

Figure 6.10 Event Log as Displayed within Intel Manageability Commander

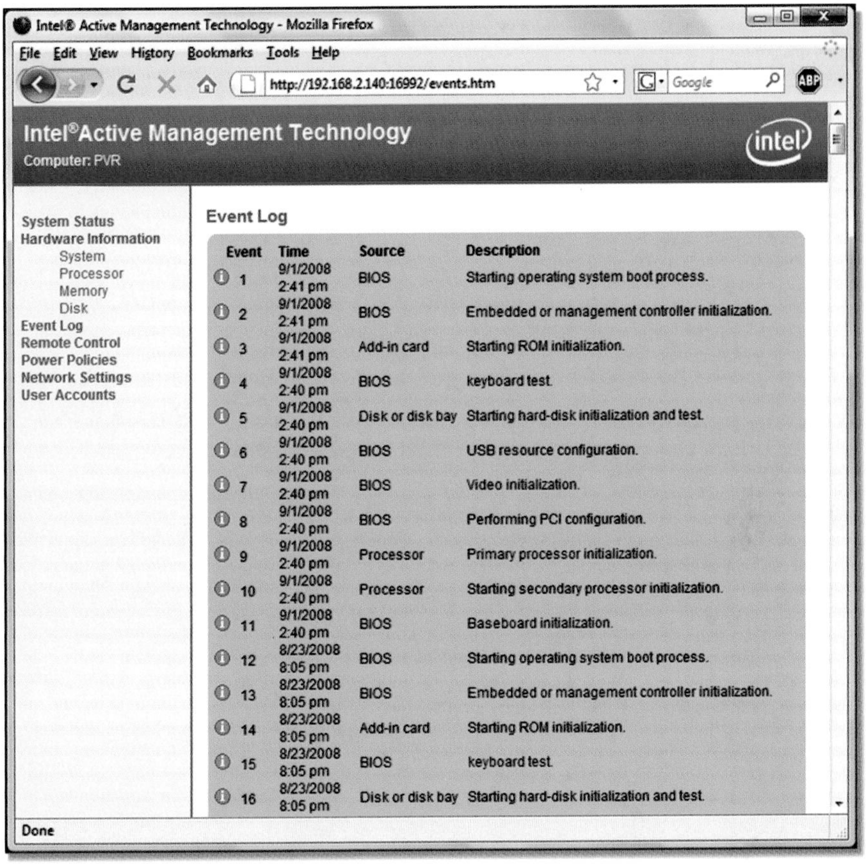

Figure 6.11 Event Log as Displayed in the Intel® AMT Web Page

Lockup Detection and Power Control

Another powerful feature of Intel AMT allows the administrator to remotely control the power state of the computer: power up, power down, power cycle, and detect an operating system hang. As an example, a remote tourist kiosk is locked up and has become unusable. In the past, the kiosk would no longer be reachable through the network and any remote operation was impossible. Such a kiosk would stay locked up for hours or days until someone manually performed a power cycle.

With Intel vPro, the Intel Manageability Engine Interface (Intel MEI) driver (called the HECI driver in the past) periodically notifies Intel AMT that it is running correctly. Since it's a driver and runs at a higher privilege level, a stop in these notifications indicates that something quite serious has happened to the operating system. A management console can read the operating system lock-up flag when reading the power state of the computer; it's the same call that reports both.

In our example, a tourist kiosk can lock up and the administrative console can notice this using the agent presence feature indicating the tourist application is no longer running and/or reading the lock-up flag. Once the determination is made of an operating system lockup, the administrator can power cycle the system remotely, as shown in Figure 6.12.

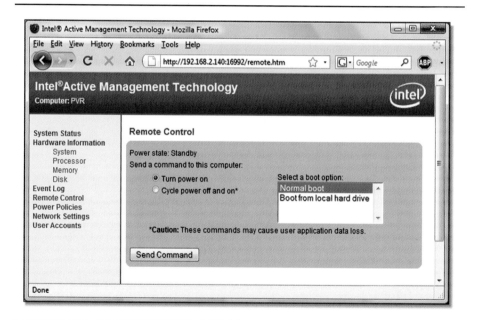

Figure 6.12 Remote Control Feature in the Intel® AMT Web Page

Obtaining the current power state and performing remote power operations is also available within the Intel AMT built-in Web page. For our tourist kiosk example, one of the tourist guides with minimal knowledge of Intel AMT can log into the Web page of the locked-up computer and reset it. No additional software is needed.

Summary

We have reviewed some of the most typical discover, heal, and secure scenarios that can be solved using Intel AMT. In the next few chapters we will take a look at the details of these scenarios and how a developer can add these and other Intel AMT features into their own management software. A good understanding of the features available with Intel AMT means that developers and users can make the most of them.

Chapter **7**

The Components of Intel® Active Management Technology

What we need to do is learn to work in the system, by which I mean that everybody, every team, every platform, every division, every component is there not for individual competitive profit or recognition, but for contribution to the system as a whole on a win-win basis.

—W. Edwards Deming (1900–1993)

In the previous chapters we described Intel® Active Management Technology (Intel AMT) platforms from a functional standpoint, that is, the kind of problems Intel AMT solves and the collection of features that help solve those problems. This chapter presents an overview of the architecture of Intel AMT. This includes the architecture of the hardware, firmware, and software, all of which need to come together to make Intel AMT work. At a very high level, Figure 7.1 shows how these pieces stack up.

The hardware for Intel AMT is comprised of the Intel chipset (which includes the wired Ethernet network controller), wireless communication chip, nonvolatile flash memory for code and data storage, and the communication links and buses. The firmware comprises the runtime environment, kernel, drivers, services, and firmware applications. The software is made up of OS drivers, OS/ISV agents, and console applications. Console software could reside on the same computer's OS (in the form of host-based services), or on a different computer located somewhere else on the network (network-based console). Several vendors (such as Microsoft, Symantec, and LANDesk) provide console applications and suites that utilize Intel AMT capabilities for platform management. An up-to-date and complete list of ISV software suites that work with Intel AMT is available on Intel's Web site.

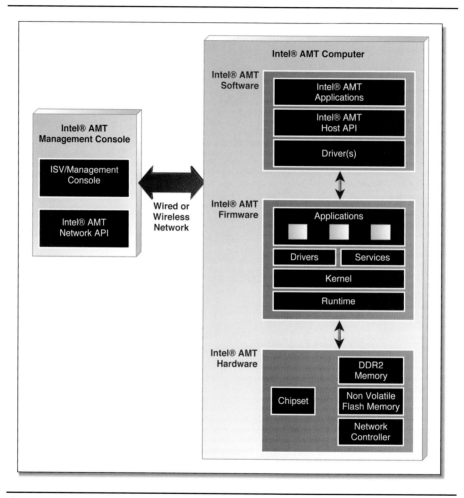

Figure 7.1   High Level View of Intel® AMT components

The next few sections go deeper into the architecture and design of the hardware, firmware, and software components that constitute Intel AMT.

One point to note here is that the architecture described in this chapter is based on the currently shipping Intel platform architecture, which includes the CPU and the two-chip chipset—Northbridge and Southbridge (see Figure 7.2). In the new architecture, a majority of Northbridge functionality is being integrated into the CPU Core and Uncore, and the rest of the functionality is being combined with the Southbridge (see Figure 7.3). This Southbridge chip is internally called as the PCH (Platform Controller Hub) within Intel. This is a very significant change to the platform architecture, but from the standpoint of Intel AMT, the architecture of all of the components described below remains largely unchanged.

Hardware Architecture

The primary hardware pieces of Intel AMT reside in the Intel chipset (Northbridge and Southbridge). The Northbridge, also called the Graphics and Memory Controller Hub (GMCH), contains a micro controller called the Intel Manageability Engine (Intel ME), which is the heart of Intel AMT. It is the engine that runs the Intel AMT firmware services and applications. The GMCH also contains the memory controller that provides access to the system memory. A small portion of the system memory is used by the Intel ME for its runtime memory needs. This memory is separated from the memory accessed by the OS using special hardware mechanisms. The architectural mechanism that creates the separation is called Unified Memory Architecture (UMA). The Southbridge, also called the I/O Controller Hub (ICH), contains the Ethernet network controller, network filters, and non-volatile flash memory controller, among other things. The wireless LAN (Wi-Fi†) network controller is connected to the ICH over a PCI Express† bus. The network controllers, wired LAN (Ethernet) and wireless LAN (Wi-Fi), and the network filters provide out-of-band (OOB) communication access to the Intel ME. OOB communication allows the Intel ME to communicate over the network without having any dependence on the OS or the drivers that reside therein. OOB communication is capable of working even when the computer is in some states where the OS is not working or is sleeping, such as when the OS has crashed, or is in standby state or hibernate state. The flash controller in the ICH provides access to the flash memory, also called the nonvolatile memory (NVM), on the computer's motherboard. This NVM houses the BIOS code, Intel ME code, and data, among other things. The GMCH and ICH communicate with each other using the DMI[1] bus and Controller Link (C-Link) bus. The C-Link bus is a proprietary interface that can be used even when the computer is in sleep or hibernated states, in addition to being used when the OS is operational. Figure 7.2 shows the hardware architecture of the Intel CPU and chipset based computer. We won't go into details of each and every component shown in the picture, but we will cover a good amount of detail on the components that make up Intel AMT, in the next few sections.

---

1   Direct Media Interface (DMI) is the chip-to-chip interconnect between the ICH and the (G)MCH. This high-speed interface ensures that the I/O subsystem (PCI Express, Intel High Definition Audio, SATA, USB, and so on) receives the bandwidth necessary for peak performance.

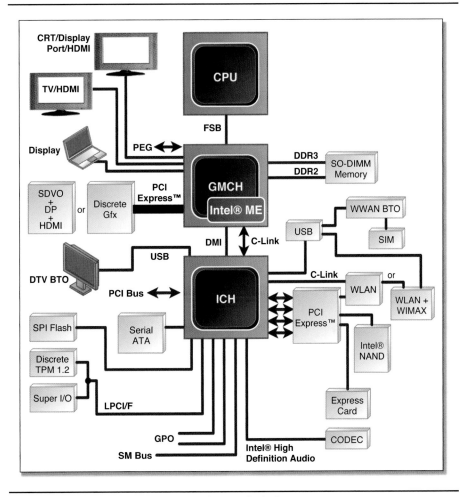

Figure 7.2 Hardware Architecture of an Intel Platform

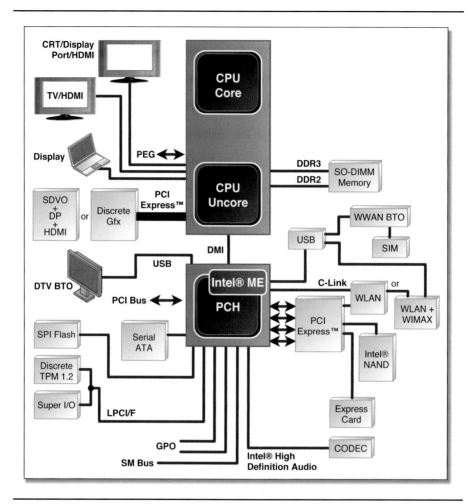

Figure 7.3   Hardware Architecture of Future Intel Platforms

Intel® Manageability Engine (Intel ME)

The Intel Manageability Engine is the core hardware component of Intel AMT. A high level picture of the Intel ME is shown in Figure 7.4.

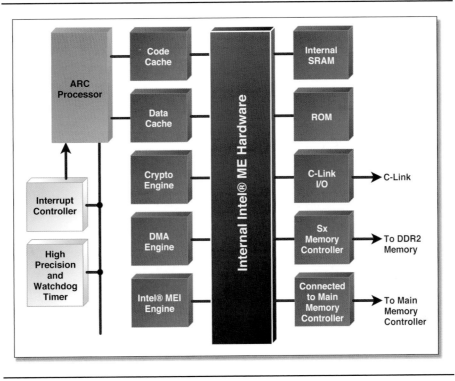

Figure 7.4   Hardware Architecture of the Intel® Manageability Engine

The Intel ME is made up of several components such as an ARC processor, code and data caches, a DMA engine, a crypto engine, ROM, C-Link interface, Intel MEI, memory controller interface, interrupt controller, and high precision and watchdog timers. These are connected together over an internal hardware bus.

The code and data caches help to accelerate Intel ME functionality by reducing the memory accesses to system memory. The DMA engine helps to move data to and from the OS memory and Intel ME UMA memory. However this DMA engine is only accessible by the Intel ME, not the OS. Also, it does not provide any generic interfaces to the OS to access this DMA engine. The crypto engine provides hardware offloads to accelerate the cryptographic operations done inside the Intel ME for secure communication protocols like wireless security, HTTP security via TLS, and so on. The initial boot code for the Intel ME is located and executed from the ROM. The C-Link interface is used for communication between the GMCH and ICH in low power states such as sleep or hibernate. Some Intel ME–specific devices in the ICH communicate with the Intel ME exclusively over C-Link, while some devices can communicate over DMI as well as C-Link (for example, the network controller).

Memory for the Intel® ME

A small portion of the main system memory is used by the Intel ME for its runtime memory needs. This separation is done using the UMA mechanism. The Intel integrated graphics controller in the GMCH also uses the same mechanism to use a portion of the main system memory for its needs. The size of this memory is 16 MB, which is less than 1 percent of the total system RAM in a computer having 2 to 3 GB of DRAM. From the perspective of the OS the Graphics UMA memory portion will appear to be a little larger than on computers that do not have the Intel ME.

Nonvolatile Storage for the Intel® ME

The Intel ME uses a NOR flash nonvolatile memory (NVM) present on the motherboard, for persistent storage of the code, configuration data, user data, and so on. This NVM is also used to store the BIOS code and other OEM specific data. It is used for other purposes by the network controllers, which we won't discuss here. The NVM is divided into specific regions, one each for the Intel ME, the BIOS, and the network controller. The NVM contains an access control descriptor at the very beginning of the NVM (at address 0) which specifies the permissions for accessing the various regions of the NVM. The ICH hardware ensures that these permissions are enforced. The controller that the ICH uses for accessing the NVM is the based on Serial Peripheral Interface (SPI). The Intel ME region of the NVM is further divided into regions for code, recovery code, internal configuration data and variable storage, event logs, and user/ISV relevant 3PDS data. Figure 7.5 shows a high level map of the NVM showing the various regions. Chapter 14 explains more details about the protection mechanisms applied to the NVM.

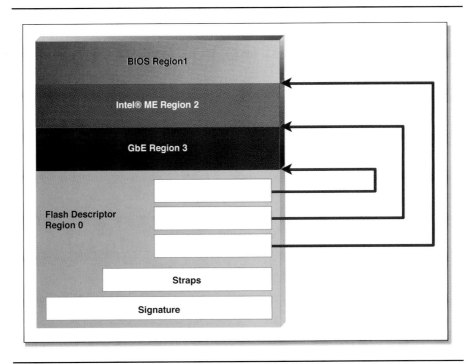

Figure 7.5   High Level Map of the Nonvolatile Memory

Network Access to Intel® ME

On desktop platforms, only the Ethernet network adapter is connected to the Intel ME. On mobile platforms, the Intel ME has access to both Ethernet and Wi-Fi network controllers and this, both when the OS is functional or not (crashed, sleeping, and so on). The Intel network controllers (Ethernet and Wi-Fi) communicate with the Intel ME using the C-Link interface. Intel ME accesses traffic from the Gigabit Ethernet controller differently from how it accesses traffic from the Wi-Fi controller. It always sends and receives traffic over the Ethernet controller directly without going via the OS. However, in the case of Wi-Fi, some design limitations require that the network controller has a single master. Therefore, when the OS is operational, the Wi-Fi traffic is routed via the Wi-Fi driver in the OS to the Intel ME. However when the OS crashes or goes to sleep, the Intel ME assumes ownership of the Wi-Fi network controller and does the communication directly.

Intel AMT provides for remote communication with computers from a management console (using the HTTP and WS-Management protocols) over these interfaces. This mechanism allows the Intel ME firmware to share a common LAN MAC, hostname, and IP address with the OS, helping to minimize the IT infrastructure cost to support functionality based on Intel AMT. The details are explained in Chapter 11.

Figure 7.6 shows the filters supported by the Ethernet network controller.

The out-of-band communications architecture supports the following filters:

- ARP: Forwards ARP packets containing a specific IP address to the host and/or the Intel ME

- DHCP: Forwards DHCP Offer and ACK packets to the host and/or the Intel ME

- IP Port Filters (HTTP and Redirection): Redirects incoming IP packets on a specific port to the Intel ME

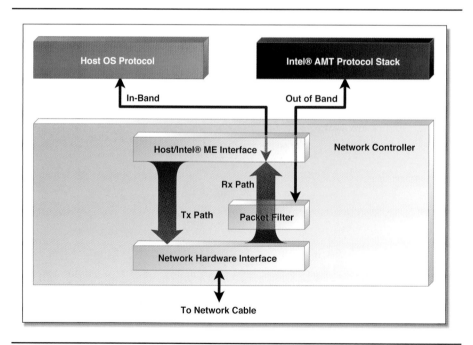

Figure 7.6 Network OOB Filters for Gigabit Ethernet

Protected Clock

The Intel ME has access to a special purpose clock on the chipset called Protected Real Time Clock (PRTC). This clock is not accessible by the OS, but only by the Intel ME. The clock is used for its time related verifications (such as certificate validations, Kerberos time stamp checks, and so on), instead of relying on the system Real Time Clock (RTC). The RTC can be changed (back-dated or moved forward) by the user or a malware in the OS, hence the Intel ME does not rely on the RTC. This PRTC is powered by the same coin battery that powers the RTC. So the PRTC maintains the time even when the computer is completely powered off.

> **For Experts**
>
> When Intel AMT is provisioned in Small Business mode, the protected clock is synchronized with the BIOS clock at boot time and both generally represent local time. When provisioned in Enterprise mode, the clocks are separate and it is recommended that the protected clock be set to GMT time

True Random Number Generator

The Intel ME also has access to a True Random Number Generator (TRNG), which is based on thermal noise variants. This TRNG is very helpful for assisting in cryptographic transactions such as generating random session keys, tokens, nonces, and so on. The TRNG outputs 32-bit random numbers at a time. Chapter 15 covers the TRNG in detail.

Chipset Key

The chipset has a 128-bit key for use by firmware in symmetric encryption and integrity protection operations. This key is generated during manufacturing of the chipset at the Intel manufacturing plants, by randomly blowing fuses dedicated for this purpose. The Intel ME is the only component that can access this keying material, and it provides the root of trust for several operations. No one outside the Intel ME knows the value of this key.

Firmware Architecture

This section describes the firmware architecture of the various components that constitute Intel AMT. This includes the Intel ME ROM, the kernel running on the Intel ME, common services modules (such as networking services, security services, and configuration services), and the applications in the firmware (such as 3PDS, remote control, asset inventory). A high level block diagram of the firmware is shown in Figure 7.7.

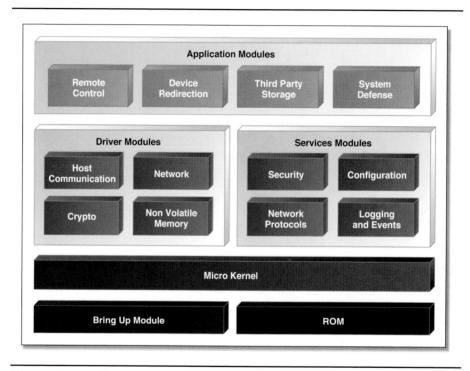

Figure 7.7   Intel® Management Engine Firmware Block Diagram

Intel® ME ROM

The Intel ME ROM is masked into the silicon of the GMCH chip. The ROM contains the reset vector (the very first set of instructions to execute after the Intel ME is reset). The ROM is only accessible by the Intel ME and not by the host or OS. Because ROM code is masked in the chip during manufacturing, it can never be changed and hence is secure by nature. Therefore no integrity check is performed on the ROM. The size of the ROM is on the order of a few kilobytes. The main operations of the ROM include configuring the Intel ME memory areas, initializing certain critical hardware pieces, checking the integrity and signature on the firmware image on the NVM, and transferring control to the firmware image. The ROM is the root of trust of the Intel ME firmware.

Intel® ME Kernel

The Intel ME Kernel module is composed of services and drivers that provide the base functionality of the Intel ME environment. The kernel provides the basic set of services that are expected for any general purpose execution environment. These services include:

- Bootstrap and initialization
- Task and thread management
- Memory management
- Interrupt management
- Timers
- Messaging and events
- Security and cryptographic functions
- Drivers for local and network interfaces, storage, and so on
- Power management
- Interface discovery
- Firmware update

Since the Intel ME houses some very security-sensitive technologies apart from Intel AMT, such as the Intel® Trusted Platform Module (Intel TPM)[2], there is a need to provide a high degree of separation and isolation right from the kernel level between the highly security-sensitive applications and others. For this reason the kernel is partitioned into privileged and non-privileged portions. The privileged portion includes the ROM, the initialization modules (such as a loader and bring-up modules), a portion of the kernel called the

---

2   Intel Trusted Platform Module is only available on some Intel® vPro™ technology platforms.

privileged kernel, and the Intel TPM firmware. The non-privileged portion includes the remaining portion of the kernel called the non-privileged kernel, support modules, common services modules, and other firmware applications. Firmware that executes in privileged mode has access to privileged hardware resources, such as certain memory ranges and certain hardware registers. Non-privileged firmware that attempts to access privileged resources will cause an exception or interrupt to occur. A register in the Intel ME contains the address of the code for entering and exiting out of the privileged mode. Using these addresses, the firmware code transitions between privileged mode and non-privileged mode. Figure 7.8 shows the privileged and non-privileged partitioning of the Intel ME kernel.

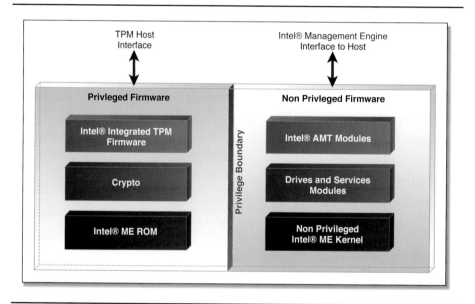

Figure 7.8   Intel® ME Kernel: Privileged and Non-Privileged Partitions

Intel® ME Common Services

The Intel ME Common Services are a set of services provided by the Intel ME firmware for different Intel ME applications such as Intel AMT applications. These services include network services, security services, and configuration services. These services are implemented on top of the Intel ME Kernel. Figure

7.9 shows the various service modules available inside the Intel ME Common Services component of the firmware.

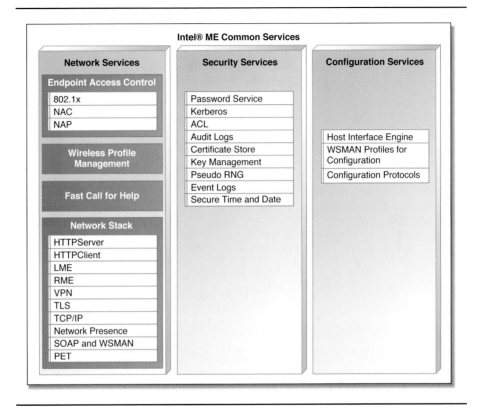

Figure 7.9 Intel® ME Common Services

Tables 7.1 through 7.3 describe briefly the role of each of the modules within the Common Services components.

Networking Services

The networking services component provides the access to various networking stacks and protocols that firmware applications use for communication, as described in Table 7.1.

Table 7.1 Networking Services

Module	Description
Network Presence	The module that establishes presence of Intel® AMT on the network by initiating DNS and DHCP transactions. DHCP helps the Intel AMT subsystem to obtain an IP address if the OS is not up, or Intel AMT and the OS are not sharing IP addresses.
TCP/IP	The TCP/IP protocol stack in firmware
TLS	The TLS protocol stack in firmware providing session encryption and integrity to keep eavesdroppers away
LME	Local Manageability Engine – this is the module that implements the firmware end of the local manageability interface with the host OS. The local manageability interface allows for communication between the local host OS and Intel AMT via a TCP/IP network connection, albeit with some constraints. We will go into this in detail in Chapter 11.
RME	Remote Manageability Engine – this is the module that implements the firmware end of the remote manageability interface. The remote manageability interface allows for communication with Intel AMT over the network from management consoles.
VPN	The VPN firmware module that allows for manageability communication through the host VPN mechanism.
Fast Call for Help (FCFH)	The FCFH firmware module that implements the FCFH capability. More details are available in Chapter 12.
HTTP Server	The HTTP server implemented in firmware to host most of the manageability applications
HTTP Client	An HTTP client module implemented in firmware for certain scenarios where Intel AMT needs to operate as a HTTP client and communicate with HTTP servers on the network.
Wireless LAN profile management	Firmware module that manages WLAN profiles and settings in Intel AMT. This allows Intel AMT to communicate using the specified wireless profiles and policies over the wireless connection.
802.1x supplicant	The 802.1x supplicant in firmware that communicates with the 802.1x enabled network infrastructure to allow Intel AMT to obtain authenticated network access.
802.1x profile management	Firmware module that manages 802.1x profiles and settings in Intel AMT.

Table 7.1 Networking Services (Continued)

Module	Description
NAC/NAP	Firmware module in firmware that communicates with the NAC/NAP enabled network infrastructure to allow Intel AMT to obtain authenticated network access. This module provides a signed posture of Intel AMT to the NAC/NAP backend infrastructure, which is evaluated for compliance with the network policies before Intel AMT can access the network.
SOAP and WSMAN	The SOAP and WSMAN protocol layer modules in firmware
PET	The PET (Platform Event Trap) alert generation module to send out PET alerts to the management console as configured by the IT administrator

Security and Utilities Services

Table 7.2 describes the security and utilities services provided that are required by most firmware applications such as authentication, access control, session encryption, auditing, and so on. It also provides some utility services such as event logs, date, and time. Most of these topics are covered in detail in Chapters 14, 15, and 16.

Table 7.2   Security and Utilities Services

Module	Description
Password Service	A password service in Intel® AMT that ensures that access to Intel AMT BIOS interfaces is allowed only after proper password authentication from the BIOS.
Kerberos	A module in the firmware that hosts a Kerberos-based service making authentication to Intel AMT integrated with the enterprise's Active Directory infrastructure in a Single Sign On manner. Using the services of this module, Intel AMT grants seamless access to privileged administrators of Intel AMT without requiring additional authentication specifically for Intel AMT.
Access Control Lists	A module that manages the permissions of authenticated administrators of the Intel AMT subsystem. Not all authenticated administrators have equal privileges in Intel AMT. This module allows for managing the permissions and enforces those permissions at the time of administrator logon and subsequent access to Intel AMT.
Security Audit Logs	A module that keeps a secure and undeniable log of the actions taken by an authenticated administrator in the Intel AMT subsystem. This module is like the video camera inside the firmware. With awareness of this capability, administrators are deterred from misusing their privileges in Intel AMT.
Certificate Store	A secure store for certificates. Certificates are used for configuration, TLS, Audit Logs, and so on. Secure storage for certificates is a necessity wherever they need to be used.
Key Management	A module that manages the various keys inside the firmware. There are various types of keys inside the Intel AMT subsystem such as TLS private key and Kerberos key.
Pseudo RNG	A pseudo–Random Number Generator module in the firmware. This takes in a true random number from the hardware based TRNG, and from there on generates pseudo-random numbers on demand. Random numbers are used by several Intel AMT and common service modules.
Event Logs	A simple logging mechanism for system events. This keeps track of various happenings in the firmware. It can be used to troubleshoot problems in the deployment or functionality of Intel AMT or for other similar purposes. This is not a secure log, and is not the same as the Security Audit Log.
Secure Time and Date	A module that manages the hardware PRTC and provides write access to the PRTC after proper authentication and authorization. It also provides read access to the PRTC to Intel AMT and common service modules.

Configuration Services

Table 7.3 describes the configuration services provided for initial configuration of Intel AMT and other firmware applications, WS-Management services, and so on.

Table 7.3 Configuration Services

Module	Description
Provisioning and Configuration	A module that manages the configuration process of Intel® AMT. This is covered in detail in Chapter 17.
WSMAN Configuration Profiles	The WSMAN (WS-Management) configuration profiles used by the WSMAN module for configuration of Intel AMT.

In this section, we have been able to cover the Intel ME common services briefly, with the intent of familiarizing the reader with the extent and breadth of the services available to firmware applications in Intel AMT. Several of these services and protocols and the mechanisms to communicate with them are explained in much greater detail in the rest of this book.

Intel® AMT Firmware Applications

The Intel AMT applications implemented in the firmware are the heart of Intel AMT. These applications implement the actual logic of the various Intel AMT features that we discussed in Chapter 5.

Software Architecture

Intel AMT software can be divided into a BIOS component, local components and remote components. The BIOS component performs certain configuration and bootstrap operations for Intel AMT. Local components consist of software drivers, services, and applications that run on the host OS of the computer that has Intel AMT. Examples are the Intel MEI driver, LMS module, UNS, and Tray Icon, as explained below. Remote components are the components that help services and applications that run on the systems that manage the Intel AMT computer over the network using management consoles. Examples are the Intel AMT SDK, Intel AMT Storage Library, and Intel AMT Redirection Library.

Intel® AMT BIOS Component

Intel AMT computers have a BIOS component integrated into the BIOS. This component is called the Intel ME BIOS Extension (Intel MEBX). It is a BIOS binary that is very similar to the other extension ROMs (also known as OPROM) commonly present in BIOS. This component provides the IT administrator the ability to configure and change the Intel ME subsystem's policies. We will come across this component at several places in this book. Some of the operations performed by the Intel MEBX component are as follows:

- Authenticate (via a password) the user before allowing any configuration changes.

- Collect the system hardware inventory information from the main BIOS and feed it into the Intel AMT subsystem so that it can be monitored by the IT administrator at a remote console. The Intel MEBX passes this information to the Intel AMT subsystem over the Intel MEI. Therefore the Intel MEBX also needs to implement an Intel MEI driver.

- Display the configuration options on the Intel MEBX screen that allows the user to view/change various Intel ME policies settings. The Intel MEBX screen is usually reached by pressing the Ctrl-P key combination at the time of system startup.

Local Software Components

Figure 7.10 shows a block diagram of the local software components of Intel AMT. The blue components depict the Intel provided components. The orange component is the host application developed by the ISV.

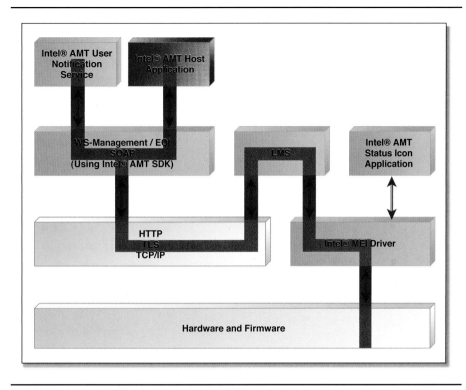

Figure 7.10 Local Software Components of Intel® AMT

The Intel Management Engine Interface (MEI) driver is the device driver for the Intel MEI that is the main communication channel between the Intel AMT firmware and the local host. In Windows, it is a WDM driver that supports Windows XP and Vista. In Linux, this is a character device driver that supports the main kernel based distributions.

The purpose of the Local Manageability Service (LMS) component is to enable Intel AMT to expose a similar interface for both local and remote applications. Basically LMS allows local applications to open a virtual "network" connection to Intel AMT firmware. From the local application point of view, it opens a network connection and uses EOI or WS-Management over SOAP. LMS redirects the network traffic over Intel MEI to the Intel AMT firmware.

Intel AMT computers have a system tray icon application that will inform the user about the existence and the enabled/disabled status of Intel AMT.

The application also points to the Intel AMT Web site so that users will be able to get detailed information about the technology and its capabilities. This is covered in more detail in Chapter 16.

User notification service (UNS) module in the Intel AMT firmware enables Intel AMT firmware to send events to the local user. The role of this software component it to listen to such events and record them in the operating system event log.

The yellow highlighted line in Figure 7.10 shows the path of communication from the Intel AMT host application to the Intel AMT subsystem in the firmware/hardware. The same path is also taken by the Intel AMT User Notification Service to communicate with the Intel AMT subsystem in the firmware/hardware.

Remote Software Components

Figure 7.11 shows a block diagram of the remote software components of Intel AMT. The blue components depict the Intel provided components. The orange component is the Management Console application developed by the ISV.

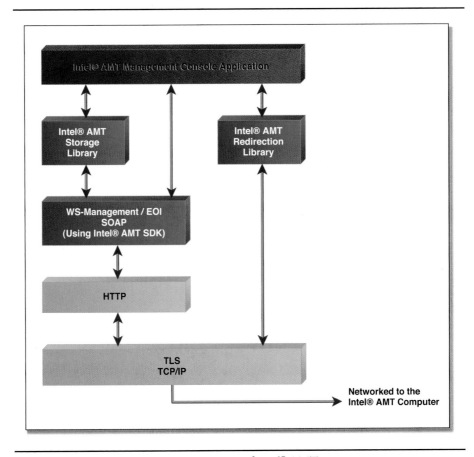

Figure 7.11   Remote Software Components of Intel® AMT

The purpose of Intel AMT SDK is to enable software developers to easily develop applications that communicate with Intel AMT and bundle Intel AMT features into their existing management consoles and other applications.

The SDK is comprised of the documentation, WSDL files for EOI/SOAP interface, and MOF files for WS-Management interface, and code samples for a majority of Intel AMT features (both EOI and WS-Management). The SDK is designed for both Windows and Linux environments, and primarily for C++ and C#, but any language that supports SOAP/WS-Management can be used (such as Java, for which a sample is included with the SDK).

The purpose of the Intel AMT Storage Library is to provide a clean programmatic interface to applications that use the third party data store feature and hide the underlying details of EOI/SOAP commands. There are Windows and Linux versions of the library. The interface to applications is in the form of a static C/C++ library.

The purpose of Intel AMT Redirection Library is to provide a clean programmatic interface to applications that use Serial over LAN or IDE Redirection features and hide the underlying details of the redirection protocols. There are Windows and Linux versions of the library. As with the Intel AMT Storage Library, the interface to applications is in the form of a static C/C++ library.

Power Management States of Intel® AMT

The Intel AMT subsystem has the capability to operate in all states when the main operating system is running and when it is sleeping (S3 state), hibernating (S4 state), or shut down (S5 state). These states were described in Chapter 5, but here is the recap. The S0 state is when the computer is working, that is, the operating system and applications are running. The S1 and S2 states are not commonly implemented on modern systems, so we will skip them. S3 is the standby state. In this state, most of the computer is powered off. Only the main memory (RAM) is powered on and in self-refresh mode, to retain its data. The resume time from S3 to S0 is therefore fairly quick, since the memory already contains the state of the operating system and applications, and execution begins in a matter of a few seconds. S4 is the hibernate state. All the components in the computer are powered off, and the operating system and application state is stored on the hard disk. Resume from S4 to S0 is relatively much longer since the state has to be restored from the disk to RAM. S5 is the state when the computer is fully powered off and the operating system has shut down, maintaining no state.

Intel AMT provides configuration options to the user (usually via the MEBx configuration screens) to let the user choose the power management policies for Intel AMT. For example, the user may choose not to keep Intel AMT operational when the computer is in S3, S4, or S5. Figure 7.12 shows a sample Intel MEBX screen where various power management options are displayed.

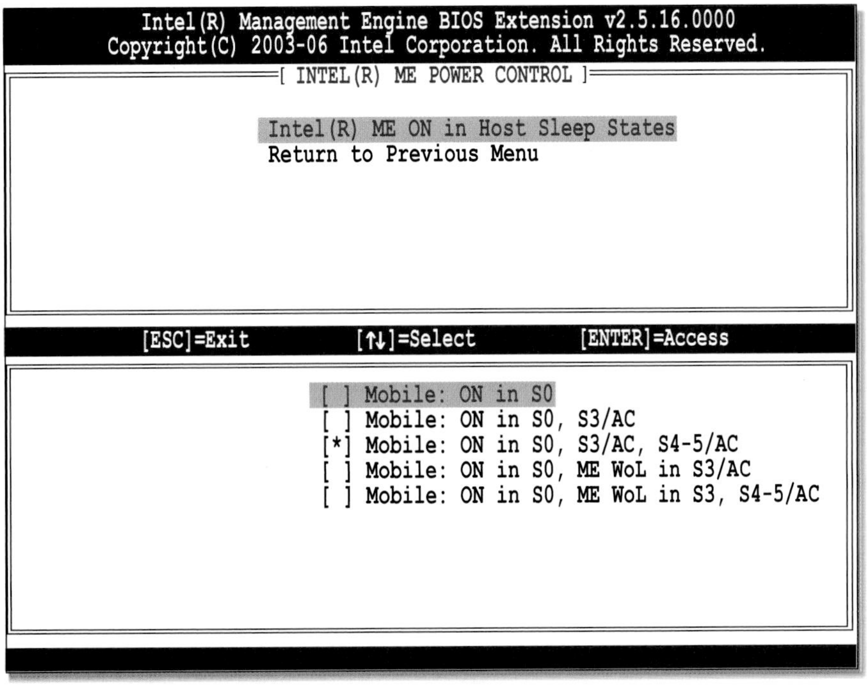

```
          Intel(R) Management Engine BIOS Extension v2.5.16.0000
          Copyright(C) 2003-06 Intel Corporation. All Rights Reserved.
        =[ INTEL(R) ME POWER CONTROL ]=

                   Intel(R) ME ON in Host Sleep States
                   Return to Previous Menu




     [ESC]=Exit         [↑↓]=Select          [ENTER]=Access

                    [ ] Mobile: ON in S0
                    [ ] Mobile: ON in S0, S3/AC
                    [*] Mobile: ON in S0, S3/AC, S4-5/AC
                    [ ] Mobile: ON in S0, ME WoL in S3/AC
                    [ ] Mobile: ON in S0, ME WoL in S3, S4-5/AC
```

Figure 7.12   Intel® AMT Power Management Options in the Intel® MEBX

The Intel AMT subsystem defines its own power states, called *M-States*. These states are M0, M1, and M-Off. The Intel AMT subsystem is in the M0 state when the overall system is in S0. All the components of Intel AMT are powered on and operational. Figure 7.13 shows the computer in M0 state. The Intel AMT subsystem can be either in M1 or M-Off when the overall system is in S3/S4/S5, depending upon the policy configured in Intel MEBX. Intel AMT functionality is available in S3/S4/S5 states only when Intel AMT is in the M1 state, not M-Off. In the M1 state, all the components that take part in making Intel AMT work are powered on (for example, the Intel ME, some portion of RAM, NVM, networking components, and so on). The rest of the computer is off. Figure 7.14 shows the computer in M1 state. In the M-Off state, all the components are powered off. Figure 7.15 shows the computer in M-Off state.

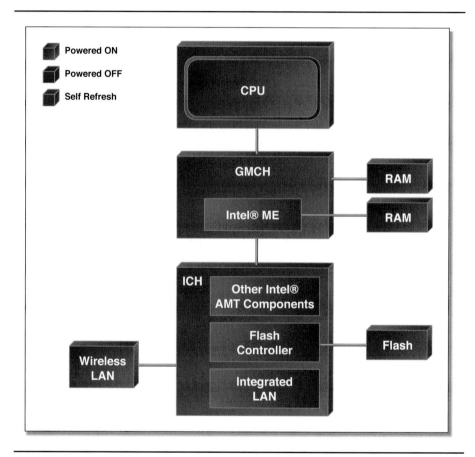

Figure 7.13 An Intel® AMT Computer in S0 and M0 State

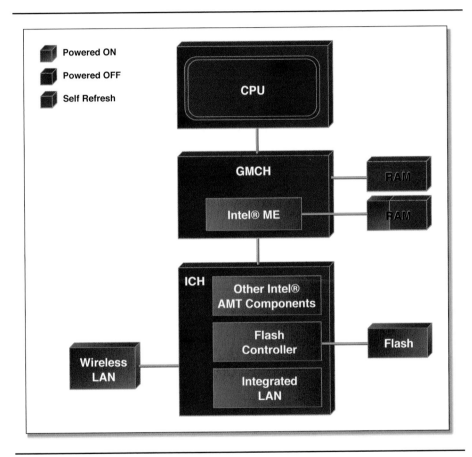

Figure 7.14 An Intel® AMT Computer in S3 and M1 State

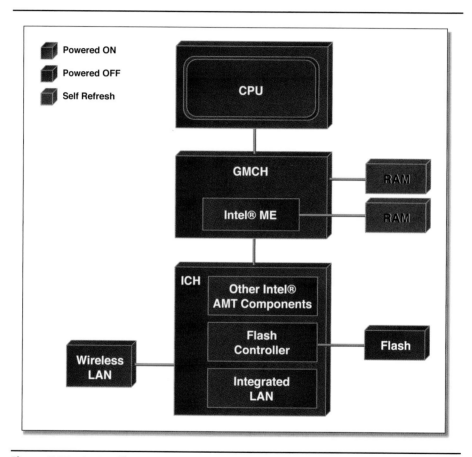

Figure 7.15 An Intel® AMT Computer in S3 and M-Off State

Summary

In this chapter we briefly covered all the important components that make up Intel AMT. This included the hardware components such as the Intel ME inside the chipset, the nonvolatile storage, memory, network controller, and so on. Then we described the firmware components such as the Intel ME kernel, common services, and firmware applications. We also discussed some details of the software components that reside on the host OS of the computer that has Intel AMT, as well as components that reside on management consoles on computers remotely located over the network. Finally we discussed the power management operations within Intel AMT and what enables Intel AMT to be operational even when the computer is in a sleep, hibernated or off state. In the next few chapters we go into more depth on the various aspects and features of Intel AMT.

Chapter 8

Discovery of Platforms and Information

Discovery consists of seeing what everybody has seen and thinking what nobody has thought.

—Albert Szent-Gyorgyi (1893–1986)

The act of doing discovery in the context of Intel® Active Management Technology (Intel AMT) means locating, connecting, and acquiring real time information about the remote computer regardless of its power state. Discovery is important because it's generally the necessary starting point for further use of Intel AMT features.

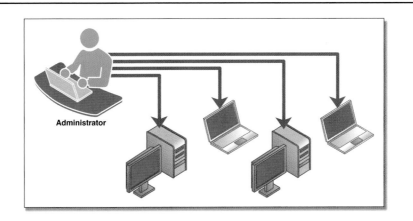

Figure 8.1 Administrators Must First Discover the Computers on the Network before Managing Them

Performing Intel AMT discovery can be summed up in three phases: The first phase involves scanning a network for computers with Intel AMT support. The second phase involves obtaining the list of supported Intel AMT features for this specific computer. The third phase is obtaining available management information from a given computer.

When using modern management software, the first step of this process will rarely have to occur. Most management consoles will have a database of all managed computers that support Intel AMT. This database will grow each time a new computer is provisioned or when a computer is added manually by the network administrator.

The second step is crucial since many different versions of Intel AMT are on the market and with more to come, being able to discover what version of Intel AMT a computer supports becomes increasingly important. Lastly, available management information about a computer is retrieved.

Network Scanning for Intel® AMT

It is sometimes useful to scan a range of IP addresses to find computers that support Intel AMT. Different approaches can be used with varying degrees of efficiency. The basic technique is to attempt a TCP connection to both ports 16992 and 16993, hoping that one of these ports successfully connects.

In the case where port 16992 successfully connects, one can send a basic HTTP get request on this connection and obtain the Intel AMT server in the response's SERVER field. Figure 8.2 shows a typical HTTP HEAD requests and responses given back by the Intel AMT HTTP server.

HTTP Request to port 16992

```
HEAD / HTTP/1.1
   Host: hostname.domain.com
```

HTTP response from Intel AMT 2.0 computer

```
HTTP/1.1 303 See Other
   Location: http://hostname.domain.com/logon.htm
   Content-Length: 0
   Server: Intel(R) Active Management Technology 2.1.2
```

HTTP response from Intel AMT 3.0 computer

```
HTTP/1.1 303 See Other
   Location: http://hostname.domain.com/logon.htm
   Content-Length: 0
   Server: Intel(R) Active Management Technology 3.0.1
```

Figure 8.2   Discovery Requests and Responses

Note that with Intel AMT 1.0, the version is simply omitted and must be assumed to be 1.0 by the management console.

If port 16992 fails to connect, a connection attempt to port 16993 can be attempted. This time a TLS session could also be attempted. A successful TCP connection to port 16993 could indicate that Intel AMT is unprovisioned and awaiting setup, or that Intel AMT is already set up with TLS security. If a TLS session successfully connects, the same HTTP request performed above can also be accomplished through TLS to determine the computer's Intel AMT information.

Attempting a TCP connection sweep of many IP addresses on a network can take a very long time, especially with the connection limitations included in Microsoft[†] Windows XP SP2 and Microsoft Vista[1]. The network sweep

---

1   The TCP/IP stack now limits the number of simultaneous incomplete outbound TCP connection attempts. After the limit has been reached, subsequent connection attempts are put in a queue and will be resolved at a fixed rate. Under normal operation, when applications are connecting to available hosts at valid IP addresses, no connection rate-limiting will occur.—Microsoft TechNet.

can be significantly speeded up by using a combination of ARP and PING. In Figure 8.3 we have a possible state machine for network discovery of Intel AMT computers.

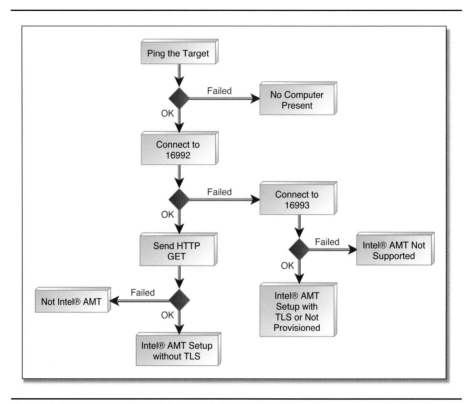

Figure 8.3   Basic Intel® AMT Network Scanning State Diagram

Basic discovery can be performed without having an authorized user-name and password. Note that this state machine assumes that Intel AMT is set to respond to PING requests, a feature that may be turned off by the administrator. Also, if a computer accepts TCP connections on port 16993, we can't conclude that the computer is provisioned and ready to go. Computers that are not provisioned will expect connections on port 16993 for a provisioning server. Once we know that computer with Intel AMT is present on the network at a given IP address, authentication is required to complete the second part of the discovery process.

Obtaining Intel® AMT Features

Once a management console has determined the presence of Intel AMT it must use appropriate credentials (username and password or Kerberos) to authenticate itself. This done, the second phase of the discovery involves obtaining information necessary to talk to Intel AMT itself. Two critical pieces of information are needed by a management console to talk to Intel AMT. First the management console needs to determine the Intel AMT version and second whether it communicates using the older EOI (SOAP based External Operations Interface) messages or the newer WS-Management based WSDL. Intel AMT 1.x and 2.x support only the older EOI while Intel AMT 3.x to 6.x support both EOI and WS-Management, with EOI having a progressively more limited set of features as WS-Management becomes the standard.

As illustrated in Figure 8.4, the first call a management console should make is the GetCoreVersion method in the SecurityAdmin SOAP service. By analyzing the response to this call, software can determine a lot of information. It should first be noted that the same GetCoreVersion method is also present in the GeneralInfo service, but that service was not present in Intel AMT 1.x, so we will use the one in SecurityAdmin. It is possible for a computer to be in WS-Management-only mode; in this case none of the EOI actions are available and Intel AMT will respond with a 404 "HTTP Not Found" error. Consoles receiving this error should try to switch over to using WS-Management on Intel AMT 3.0 or higher.

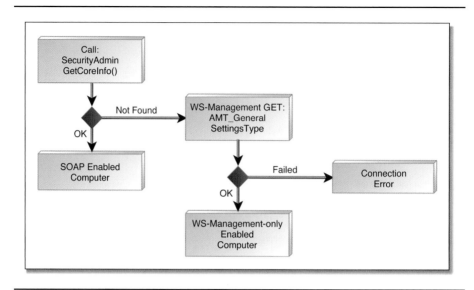

Figure 8.4   Basic Intel® AMT Connection State Diagram

The authentication used by the console could have limited access to Intel AMT features. In other words, the username and password that were used might not have had all security realms associated with it. A console could optionally then try to check if it is logged as administrator by calling GetAdminAclEntry. This method returns the name of the administrator account, generally "admin". If the console is not logged as administrator, the list of realms can be obtained using GetUserAclEntries method.

If at any time a call returns a forbidden error (HTTP 403) it is a good chance that the attempted call is not allowed because the account does not have the correct associated permission realm. The following diagram shows a possible algorithm a console could use to determine available features. For advanced developers, there is also a way to detect that a console is talking to Intel AMT locally, through the LMS service. This is useful in cases when the administrator is performing discovery on his own computer locally. A telltale sign that this is happening is that the call to GetCoreVersion will return an HTTP 401 unauthorized. In that case, other calls can be attempted to determine if a local LMS connection is indeed occurring.

Information about the computer's name, unique identifier, version, protocol, and permissions can be stored in a database for future use. When communicating again with the same computer, this information could be used to skip the first two phases of discovery with an important caveat: Since the Intel AMT settings of a computer could change without notice; it's probably good practice to perform the feature check upon each connection. After all, software developers should not assume that their own software is the only software being used to configure or manage Intel AMT.

Obtaining Management Information

Finally, now that we know more about this Intel AMT computer we are communicating with, we are in a position to start gathering useful management information about this computer itself. Here are four basic categories of management information that could be of use:

- Asset inventory
- Event log
- Power, battery, and lockup state
- Third party data storage

Other management information such as network filter counters, heuristic filter state, and agent presence state will be covered in Chapter 10.

Asset Inventory

One of the most basic features of Intel AMT allows the console to read hardware information about the computer that was gathered by the BIOS upon the last boot up. Hardware assets are often the first features developers write code for when first starting with Intel AMT since it's one of the simplest. These include:

- Computer system
- Base board
- BIOS
- Memory modules
- Hardware modules (such as PCI cards)

- Media devices (such as disk drives)
- Processors
- Batteries (mobiles only)

Developers must be aware that it is possible for all of this information to be completely missing in the rare case that Intel AMT was just provisioned and no host reboot has occurred since then. In this case, software should behave appropriately and indicate to the administrator that this information is not currently available.

When using EOI, this information is gathered using the Hardware Asset service. With WS-Management, similar information is obtained through many CIM objects. Examples of how to obtain asset information with both EOI and WS-Management are available in the Intel AMT SDK.

Hardware asset information can change when, for example, memory is changed, a PCI card is added, or the BIOS is updated. Most of these changes require a reboot of the computer, and the updated information will be reflected within Intel AMT once the reboot occurs. When a change to a hardware asset occurs, there are no events logged or notification given. It is therefore the management console's responsibility to occasionally get the hardware asset inventory of each computer and compare with the previously obtained one to see if anything has changed. Determining if such a change has occurred can be very useful to track inventory and detect theft.

Developers often ask if USB or 1394 devices are part of the hardware inventory and no, they are not. Listing these devices and other information can be done using the third party data storage (3PDS) and the assistance of OS software covered later in this chapter.

Figure 8.5 shows one of the Intel AMT Web pages for system inventory. This information is also available to management consoles using a programmatic interface- EOI or WS-Management interface.

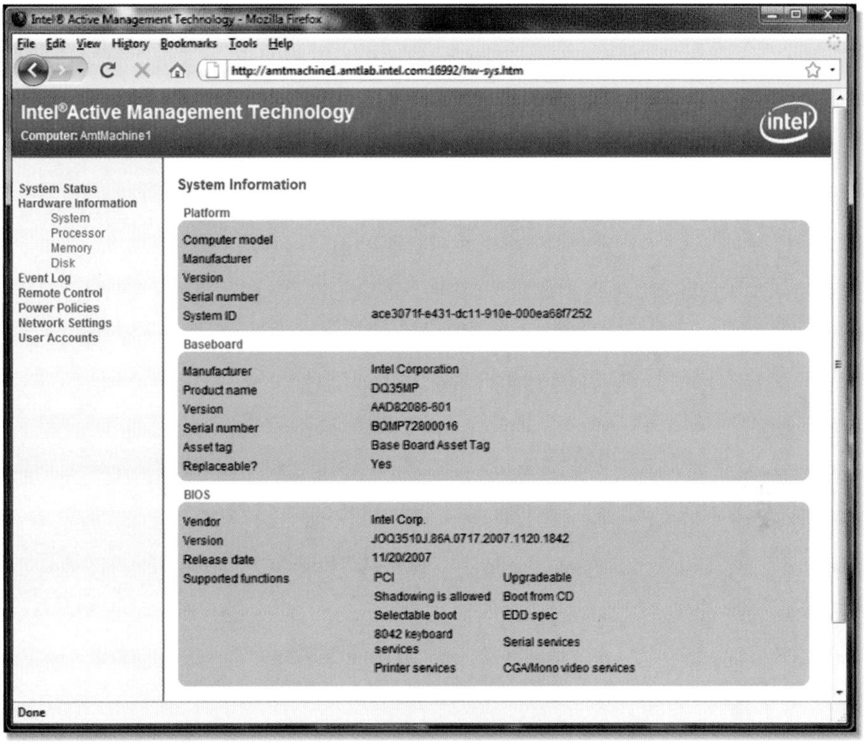

Figure 8.5 Intel® AMT Web Page for System Inventory

Intel® AMT Event Log

This log provides basic historical information about the computer: reboots, errors, case intrusion, and much more.

The event log can serve as a computer's "black box" and can sometimes be helpful in determining problems that occurred in the past. On most platforms, the event log keeps 390 events and once full, the older events are automatically deleted to make way for new events. For mobile computers the event log allows network administers to get historical data about the computer even if in the past it has not been connected to the office network.

The event log is cleared when Intel AMT is first provisioned and gathers event information from three main sources: Intel AMT, the BIOS, and system sensors. For most computers with Intel AMT on the market today, the case intrusion sensor, if connected, is the only sensor that will cause a logged event, but this can change depending on the board vendor.

It is important to note that events coming from the BIOS vary greatly from one BIOS vendor to another, and so management software should not make assumptions about events coming from the BIOS without first checking the computer's BIOS vendor. There is no formal list of what vendor supports what events. Figures 8.6 and 8.7 show the difference in the events logged between two different BIOS vendors.

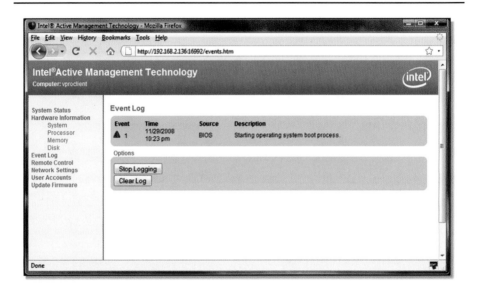

Figure 8.6 Single Reboot on a Third Party Motherboard

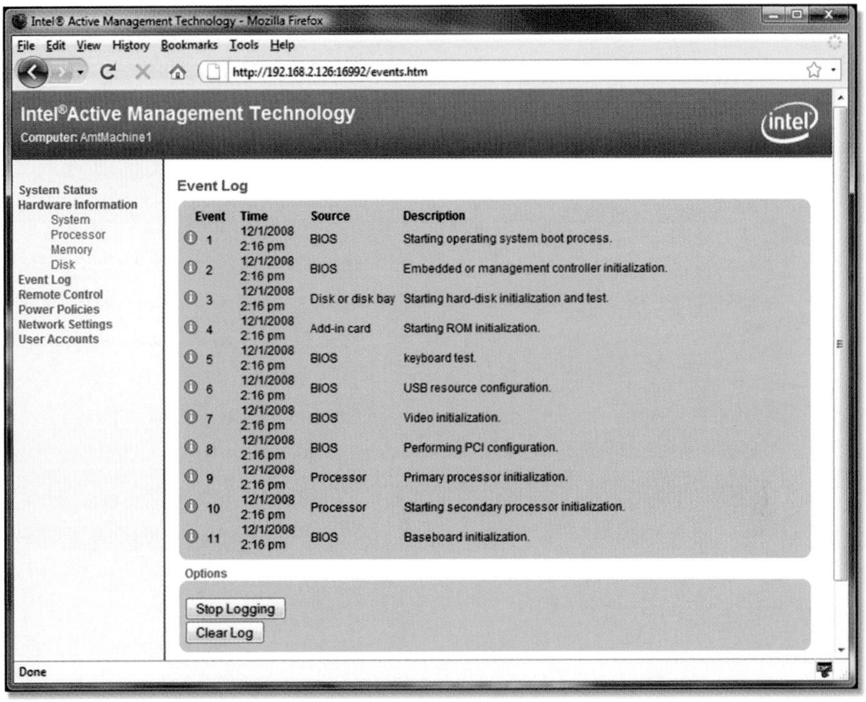

Figure 8.7 Single Reboot on an Intel Motherboard

Like the hardware asset inventory feature, the Intel AMT SDK has samples for retrieving all events using both EOI and WS-Management. Developers will notice that when retrieving events using EOI, the events are ordered sequentially with the most recent event being retrieved first. This is not the case when retrieving using WS-Management and as a result, developers using WS-Management must sort the list of events using the event's time stamp before displaying the events to the administrator. The time stamp used to mark each event is based on the Intel AMT clock and so management consoles should take care to set the Intel AMT clock correctly. If the computer is provisioned in enterprise mode, Intel AMT makes use of UTC time and the console may need to perform appropriate time zone conversion.

A few administrative operations are allowed on the event log. First, an administrator with the proper rights can clear the event log. Since the event log can grow to be very long and take a long time to retrieve, network administrators may opt to clear the event log from time to time, especially if the log is stored in a central database. The other management operation allowed on the event log is a freeze. In this case, the log no longer records events. This could be useful if the network administrator is about to perform a long series of operations on a computer and does not need this information to be logged into the Intel AMT event log.

One question that is often asked regarding the event log is how does an event entry, which is a short set of numbers, convert to a string readable by humans? A prime example of this is the Intel AMT Web UI, which has a human readable event log.

When reading events using WS-Management, the same human-readable string that is visible in the Web UI is provided. This string is only in English and so does not help with internationalization and contributes to making the event log in WS-Management very slow to retrieve.

With EOI, the event log can be retrieved much faster but no human-readable string is provided. When building the Manageability DTK and Manageability Commander, each new EOI event was manually compared to the Web UI and appropriate code was added to perform the conversion. This also has the benefit of being available in many different languages.

Because of a known bug in some versions of Intel AMT, it's not always possible to retrieve the event log using WS-Management and perform the same value-to-text conversion that is possible when using EOI. As a result, avid international users of Intel AMT Commander will notice that the event log will be displayed in, for instance, Japanese when using EOI, but only in English when using WS-Management.

Intel® AMT Network Alerts

Since we just covered the Intel AMT event log in some detail, it is a good place to talk about the Intel AMT support for network alerts. A console could opt to regularly read the event log and take note of new events, but this would be very inefficient. Intel AMT supports network alerts. A management console can subscribe to network alerts by placing the console's IP address in the Intel AMT alert subscription list along with an event filter. Once this is done, every new event that matches the filter will cause a network alert to be sent to the console.

There are two ways Intel AMT can send a network alert: SNMP traps and WS-Eventing.

SNMP Traps

All versions of Intel AMT support sending alerts using SNMP traps. They are UDP packets sent to port 162 of the console. The packet contains all the basic information about the alert. Since it is UDP and not reliable, the packet is sent three times at a few second intervals with an identical sequence number. The management console must then remember what packets it got from each IP address and what sequence number it already received to remove any duplicates. Because SNMP trap packets are un-authenticated, are sent in the clear, and can be spoofed, they are not considered secure. One solution is to go back to the computer with Intel AMT that sent the alert and read the event log to confirm that the alert truly came from this computer. In any case, SNMP trap alerts should not be used if the administrator does not wish anyone on the network to see these events in plain text. Lastly, it's often assumed that because Intel AMT supports SNMP traps, that it also supports SNMP. This is not the case: Intel AMT does not have any support for SNMP.

In Figure 8.8, we show the SNMP trap viewer built into the Manageability Commander tool. This screen gives a good idea of what information is encoded in the SNMP trap packet. In Manageability Commander, this screen is accessible through the Alert Viewer on the File menu.

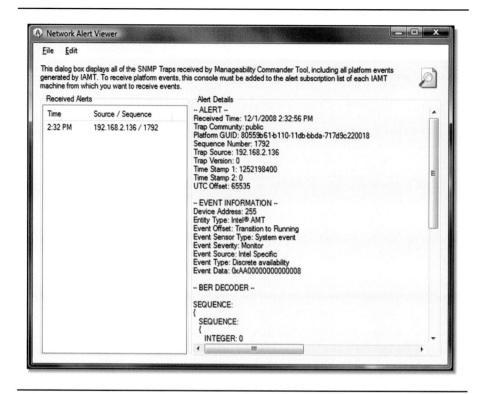

Figure 8.8 Manageability Commander SNMP Alert Viewer

WS-Eventing

Starting with Intel AMT 3.0, a management console using WS-Management to talk to Intel AMT can subscribe to alerts using the much more secure WS-Eventing standard. Unlike SNMP traps, which are rather simple, WS-Eventing assumes that a Web server is located on the console and ready to receive events in the form of a full HTTP or HTTPs connection. Such alerts are much more involved since they require opening a TCP connection and possibly performing TLS negotiation before the alert it sent to the console. This said, the alert is much more reliable and securely sent to the console.

Event Log and Alert Filters

The event log and network alerts are only as useful as the information they store or carry. In order to prevent excessive events from being logged or alerts to be sent to a management console, Intel AMT supports the concept of an event filter. Up to 16 of these can usually be present and by default, most or all of these 16 slots are populated with default filters.

Event filters can be added, removed, and changed at will by an authorized administrator. They can be used to filter the types of events to be stored in the event log or sent as network alerts. In general, it's best to stick to the default filters if possible. Since, if many consoles and monitoring applications access the same Intel AMT computer, they may conflict in how they want to use alerts and the event log.

In EOI, the event log, event filters, and network alerts are all controlled by the EventManager service. This service and its features are fairly straight-forward.

Computer's Power, Battery, and Lockup State

During the discovery phase, it's often useful to obtain the computer's current power state. As we will see in this section, this little piece of information can be very powerful.

Using EOI, the Remote Control service offers a method called `GetSystemPowerState`. In WS-Management the same information is obtained using the Power State property of the CIM_AssociatedPowerMan-agementService object. In both cases, the management console can retrieve the current power state of a computer. The Intel AMT SDK has a table of possible return values, but in practice, only a few are really used:

- S0 – Fully on
- S1 – Sleeping with power on, devices off
- S3 – Sleeping, suspend to memory
- S4 – Hibernating, suspend to disk, auxiliary power only
- S5 – Off, auxiliary power only

Retrieving the current power state can be important during discovery because other Intel AMT operations do not makes sense when the computer is off.

This information can also be used to track how effective power savings are or make sure that a critical server has not been turned off.

In the Manageability DTK, a sample tool called Intel AMT Monitor can be used to poll the power state of many computers every few minutes. The tool draws a colored graph showing the power state of each computer over time making it easy to determine which computers are staying on all night and which are saving the most power. Intel AMT can't tell the administrator exactly how much power is being used by a given computer; the exact power use of a computer changes depending on many factors including disk usages and CPU work load. Still, if we give each power state a relative power efficiency score, we can build a tool that computes the overall energy savings of an entire network of computers with Intel AMT. All of this is thanks to Intel AMT allowing us to query the computer's power state over the network without waking the computer up.

Querying for the power state also gives us two other pieces of interesting information. Two bits in the `GetSystemPowerState` method allow us to determine if a laptop is running on battery power and if a computer is locked up. The battery power bit is not always implemented by vendors, but when on, it should give the administrator a little warning not to perform operations on this computer that may excessively drain the battery. The lockup bit is actually implemented in cooperation with the Intel MEI driver running in the OS. If for any reason the Intel MEI driver fails to shutdown correctly, Intel AMT will turn on this bit, indicating a possible incorrect shutdown of the computer.

Third Party Data Storage (3PDS)

So Intel AMT does not provide all of this information you want when the computer is powered off? No problem. Third Party Data Storage allows developers to extend what information is available by allowing software to store data into the computer's onboard flash for later retrieval by a trusted administrator.

Imagine a small OS agent that starts each time the computers boots into the operating system and stores such things as:

■ List of connected USB devices

■ Installed software

■ Summary of last blue screen kernel dump

■ Currently logged user

■ OS boot up and shutdown times

■ OS errors

■ Location of the latest backup

Such information would be stored periodically in the computer's flash memory and an administrator could retrieve this set of OS level historical information and use it to diagnose current problems. If a computer has a critical error, information contained in the flash could indicate what was going on before the error occurred. It could also be used for USB hardware and general software asset inventory. Being able to read from the platform's flash where to get the latest backup in the case of a complete hard disk failure could also be a lifesaver.

In any way you chose to use 3PDS, there are a few things to know before starting to write software. First, Intel AMT has 192 KB[2] of flash space available. This space must be shared between all applications that want to make use of it and so, Intel AMT includes a space arbitration system of sorts, to make sure no single application is getting greedy.

Because the way by which local applications read and write to 3PDS is very different on AMT 1.x[3] compared to AMT 2.x and beyond, it is generally accepted for applications to only support 3PDS in AMT 2.x and beyond.

The 3PDS space is allocated to applications in pages of 4 KB. A single block of space can be composed of one or more pages of flash memory. When allocating and writing into a block, the unused space is simply not written into. When reading back the block, the unused space can contain leftover data. As a result, it's important that an application zero out the leftover space or make

---

2   Intel® AMT 1.x only has 96 KB of 3PDS space available.

3   Intel® AMT 1.x uses the Intel MEI driver to locally read and write to 3PDS. These 3PDS Intel MEI commands are not supported in Intel AMT 2.x and beyond which uses EOI/WS-Management through LMS instead.

sure to indicate how much data has actually been stored in the beginning of the block to make reading back the data easier. Once a block is allocated, the entire block must be read or written. It is not possible for software to write into only a portion of the block without rewriting the entire block.

Since 3PDS is flash storage, it not as fast as regular memory. As a result, it's generally recommended to start reading or writing to 3PDS on a separate thread and the larger the block, the longer it will take to read or write. Because of the limited space and slower speed, compressing the data before storing it into 3PDS is highly recommended. For example: the GZIP compression methods available in Microsoft .NET makes this very easy.

One of the biggest mistakes developers and administrators make when using 3PDS is to assume that 3PDS is freely accessible like a file system and the Microsoft Windows registry. Before starting to use 3PDS, users must have a good understanding of the 3PDS allocation system. Even if Intel AMT is provisioned and accessible, if not set up by the administrator first, it can't be accessed locally at all.

3PDS Allocation System

In order to properly use 3PDS, the administrative console must first set up 3PDS correctly. This operation can only be performed remotely. It can't be done locally, even if the administrator username and password is known.

First, the administrator must set up to four "Enterprises." These are top level administrative domains; if a computer is owned and operated by a single entry, there should generally be only one enterprise. With Intel, we would use the string "Intel" or "Intel IT" as an enterprise name. Having many different enterprise strings means that a single computer can be administered by different entities without conflict. Without at least one enterprise, no data can be stored into 3PDS.

Next, 3PDS has a list of partner vendors and applications. By default this list is populated with a few well known industry management software vendors. The partner list can be deleted and/or changed by the remote administrator. The partner list limits the maximum amount of flash pages that can be allocated by a single application. If an application is not on this list, it is limited by a separate non-partner global setting. This setting is generally set to 2 pages or 8 KB. The partner and non-partner settings may allow for more than the total 192 KB of available flash space to be used, but this is okay since it's unlikely that all of the applications will each use all of their maximum allowed space.

Once the enterprises, partner table, and non-partner settings are all set, allocation, deletion, reading and writing of blocks can then start. Before performing any of these operations to blocks locally or remotely, the software must first register to 3PDS. This is a separate step from the Intel AMT connection with the username and password, which must always be done first. The 3PDS registration is performed using the `RegisterApplication` call. It must include the enterprise, vendor name, application name, and a unique identifier for this instance of the software. Once registered, each created block is be tagged with the information of the owner who created the block. This information is used to calculate allocation limits and determine who has read and write access to this block. Each block in 3PDS has the following attributes:

- Enterprise (string)
- Application Vendor (string)
- Application Name (string)
- Block Name (string)
- Owner (GUID)
- Number of 4-KB pages
- Permissions set
- Visibility (visible or hidden)

Block permissions allow the application to set who has the rights to read and write into this block, based on their own 3PDS registration. For example, this block can be set to be read by anyone who is registered with the same vendor name.

When the block visibility is set to false, only the owner of this block can see it. As a result, only an application that registers with the same enterprise, vendor, application, and GUID will be able to see this block.

Probably the best way to learn about this is to use Intel AMT Commander remotely and Intel AMT Outpost locally to get hands-on experience with these settings. The Manageability DTK also provides a set of tutorial videos that walk you through the steps of using 3PDS. As users get more familiar with how 3PDS works, we often get this following question: If registration is needed to read and write blocks for a given vendor and application, why is it the Intel AMT Commander can see reads and writes of all of the blocks in 3PDS regardless of the owner?

Intel AMT Commander will first enumerate all of the enterprises, vendors and applications that have been registered into 3PDS. It will then *register as each of them*, registering as many times as it needs, using the software UUID of all zeros. This trick allows Commander to gain access to most of the blocks in 3PDS. Still, this trick has its limits. If a local application sets a block to be hidden, Commander will no longer see it. Also, a local application can set block permissions to allow only the owner of the block to read and write the block, effectively locking Commander out.

Is it not possible to register both locally and remotely using the same enterprise, vendors, application, and UUID. This is why Commander will always use a GUID of all zeros[4] and Intel AMT Outpost by default uses a GUID of all zeros and a 1 at the end[5]. If a UUID is used locally, it later can't be used remotely and vice-versa. Any attempt will result in an error.

At this point, we want to dispel myths about 3DPS that come up from time to time. Intel AMT never looks at or interprets the 3PDS data. As a result, you can't put code into 3PDS and have Intel AMT execute it. Intel AMT will also never read or write data or results into 3PDS unless it's instructed to do so by local or remote software. If the data stored into 3PDS is highly sensitive and should not be read by other applications, the application must encrypt the data itself. 3PDS should not be considered to be a security storage area like the storage area provided by tamper-resistant modules.

To conclude with 3PDS, you may be thinking of placing an MP3 file into 3PDS so that you can stream music while your computer is off! The 192 KB space limitation would severely limit that type of usage, but it was a good idea while it lasted. Other ideas include placing instructions into 3DPS that could be read and executed by an OS agent the next time the computer is booted up. You could also push results such as "the backup is complete" or "finished computing this weather simulation" into 3PDS just before putting the computer to sleep. Regardless of what you chose to do with 3PDS, it is one of the Intel AMT features with many opportunities for innovation.

---

4   Intel® AMT Commander always uses {00000000-0000-0000-0000-000000000000}

5   Intel® AMT Outpost uses by default {00000000-0000-0000-0000-000000000001}

Summary

In this chapter we reviewed how to scan, connect, and gather data about a computer using Intel AMT. When done correctly, a management console should be able to handle connections to previously unknown computers regardless of the Intel AMT version or communication standard used and correctly acquire information about this computer. Discovery is also a required step before moving into the two following chapters where Intel AMT will be used to actively protect and heal a computer remotely.

Chapter **9**

Healing the Platforms

Everyone has a doctor in him or her; we just have to help it in its work. The natural healing force within each one of us is the greatest force in getting well. Our food should be our medicine. Our medicine should be our food. But to eat when you are sick is to feed your sickness.

—Hippocrates (460 BC–377 BC)

Fixing problems with computers is big business and expensive. Because of the many possible problems a computer can run into, getting the right people and knowhow at the right place at the right time can be a problem. The costs increase when one also includes expense of the downtime of an employee. Intel® Active Management Technology (Intel AMT) makes it easier for a wider array of problems to be fixed remotely.

In general, organizations who want to perform remote repairs should start by installing software solutions that specialize in doing just that. Often this type of software will allow a remote administrator to see and even take control of the user's computer remotely, upload files, download files, apply patches, and much more. Intel AMT does not replace such software; it enhances it.

Repair software operates within the operating system it is trying to fix. This is okay if the problem is minor, but is of no help when the operating system itself is the problem, or worse, the problem is completely outside the operating system, such as a wrong BIOS setting that boots up the wrong hard disk. This is where Intel AMT becomes essential.

In this chapter we cover how Intel AMT can assist in making remote repairs. The two main features we discuss are remote IDE and Serial-over-LAN. We show how these two features can be used separately or together to remotely diagnose and repair the systems.

Remoted IDE (IDE-R)

Simply put, this feature allows a remote administrator to install or "mount" a virtual disk drive on an Intel AMT computer and optionally instruct the computer to boot into this remote drive. It could be argued that IDE-R is the most powerful feature of Intel AMT, since it allows a remote administrator to take over a computer completely, regardless of its state. Before getting into what can be done with IDE-R, it is necessary to talk about how IDE-R works in detail to better understand its power and limitations.

Intel AMT IDE-R is a simple switch that can be turned on and off. By default it is off, but when turned on, Intel AMT creates two new plug-and-play (PnP) virtual devices that are visible by the operating system. These two devices are a standard floppy disk drive and a standard CD-ROM drive, as shown in Figure 9.1.

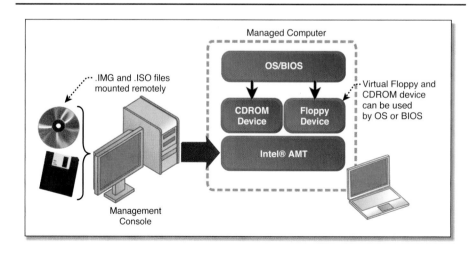

Figure 9.1   IDE-Redirection in Intel® AMT

The virtual floppy device, within Microsoft DOS or Microsoft Windows, will be visible as A: or if such a drive already exists B:. The floppy disk device is generally a read/write device, but may be read only in some cases. This device is generally 1.44 megabytes in size, but by using a small trick, it can be made much larger, up to 1 gigabyte or more.

The virtual CD-ROM device in Microsoft operating systems takes on the next available drive letter (for example, E: or F:). This device is always read only and has a maximum size of a standard CD-ROM, about 700 megabytes.

When IDE-R is activated, Intel AMT will present both of these new PnP devices to the operating system. There is no way to present just one or the other; both devices are either enabled or disabled even if the administrator will only be using one of them. Also, once activated, all IDE operations on both these devices are relayed through the network to the management console. The management console will then handle all of the IDE commands just like a hard disk does when it's connected to an IDE or SATA port within a computer.

Once enabled, a user can go to the device manager in Microsoft Windows and click on "Scan Plug-and-Plug devices" to have both devices show up in the Microsoft Windows file explorer, at which point both drives work like any other drive. As we will see later, the administrator can force a reboot of the computer with Intel AMT with a forced boot onto either one of the IDE-R devices.

IDE-R Protocol

Unlike most of the usual communications between a management console and Intel AMT, which use HTTP requests and responses on TCP port 16992 (or 16994 if TLS is used), IDE-R uses a proprietary binary protocol on port 16993 (or 16995 if TLS is used). The details of the protocol are not published by Intel, but Intel does provide a library called "IMRSDK" that implements the binary protocol and all its functionality.

Only one management console can connect and activate an IDE-R session at any given time and the binary protocol takes care of authentication and possibly encryption if TLS is used. The same credentials used for other Intel AMT operations are also used for IDE-R. It's also important to note that unlike HTTP, when using a username and password with IDE-R, both the username and password are sent in the clear over the network unless TLS is used. As a result of this, it is highly recommended that Intel AMT be used in TLS mode before an IDE-R session be attempted.

IDE-R Speed

On a fast network, both the IDE-R floppy and CD-ROM will operate at about CDROM 2x to 4x speeds or about 300 to 600kb/sec. These numbers vary depending on the network and Intel AMT version. Because IDE-R has many round trips, the speed of IDE-R goes down quickly as network latency goes up. Using IDE-R over a slower network connection such as a DSL modem could cause a remote OS boot to go from a few minutes on a fast network to hours. This is because while IDE-R is very powerful, it's also very simple and not compressed or optimized for slow network connections.

Booting a Recovery OS

A recovery OS is an operating system that is intended to only be booted up when there is a problem with the computer. Many recovery operating systems are available online based on Linux, and more recently Microsoft has started offering Microsoft WinPE (Microsoft Windows Pre-boot Environment) and Microsoft WinRE (Microsoft Windows Recovery Environment). All of these operating systems are lightweight and can be booted up remotely using IDE-R.

Often administrators will customize their own version of a recovery OS to automatically call back home and run a set of diagnostics on the computer. Complete backup and restore solutions like Norton[†] Ghost can also be booted up using IDE-R. Administrators should customize recovery OS boot images so that when booted up, they perform a set of recovery operations automatically. If interactions are required between the recovery OS and the administrator, these can be handled in a limited way using serial-over-LAN covered in the following section.

Serial-over-LAN (SOL)

The serial-over-LAN port allows a management console to send a receive data over the network to a virtual serial port on the computer with Intel AMT. Serial-over-LAN is one of the most interesting features of Intel AMT. This section describes what this serial port is and how it works.

When purchasing a computer with Intel AMT, users will notice that the computer comes with an extra serial port, as shown in Figure 9.2. This port is always enabled and there is no external connector for it.

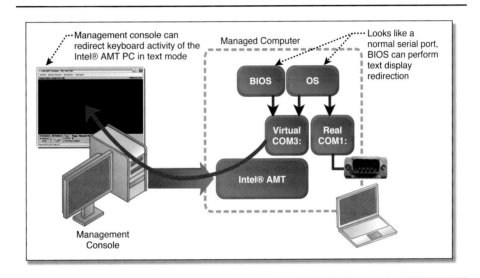

Figure 9.2   Serial-over-LAN (SOL)

In Microsoft Windows, this extra COM port requires a separate device driver. Actually, it is a small .INF file that instructs Microsoft Windows to use its own standard serial driver for this PCI serial device, as shown in Figure 9.3. Outside of the OS, the BIOS can use this port and no driver is required.

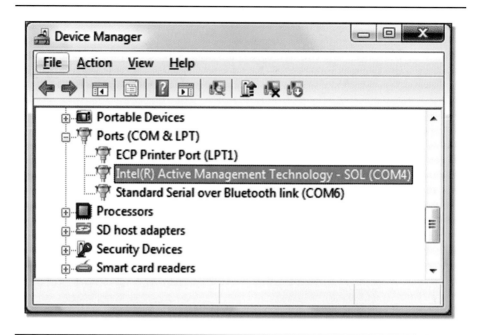

Figure 9.3   The SOL Device Driver in Microsoft Windows

Like any serial port, applications can open the port and send data to it. Intel AMT will forward the data to the connected management console. At most one management console can connect to the serial-over-LAN feature and if no console is connected sent data is simply ignored.

Serial-over-LAN Protocol

Much like IDE-R, Serial-over-LAN communication occurs using a proprietary binary protocol and with the same ports as IDE-R: 16993 or 16995 if TLS is used. Like IDE-R, specifics of this protocol are not public. A negotiation is performed at the start of the connection telling Intel AMT if this is going to be a serial-over-LAN or IDE-R session. At most one serial-over-LAN and one IDE-R session can occur, but they don't need to come from the same management console.

Like IDE-R, SOL is authenticated using the same username and password or Kerberos credentials used to authenticate with Intel AMT for other operations. The same security warning also applies here: serial-over-LAN sessions that do not use TLS will send the username and password in plain text on the network. It is therefore recommended to always make sure TLS is in use before attempting to open a serial-over-LAN session.

Serial-over-LAN Speed

Serial-over-LAN is mostly limited by the speed of the serial port. The standard COM port setting for SOL is: "115200, N, 8, 1" or 115200 bits/sec, no parity, 8 bit and 1 stop bit. These settings are set in Intel AMT and can rarely be changed. Applications making use of this virtual port should make sure to use these settings.

With the exception of dial-up, 115kb/sec is much slower than most networks. Even if Intel AMT can handle much faster data rates, the serial port speed limits the data rate between Intel AMT and the BIOS or OS.

BIOS Using Serial-over-LAN

There are two possible users for this serial port, applications that run in the OS and the BIOS itself. On computers with Intel AMT, a serial-over-LAN redirection switch is present in the BIOS and is turned off by default. When turned on, the BIOS attempts to redirect text characters into the serial port and take characters received from the serial port and emulate keyboard input, as shown in Figure 9.4.

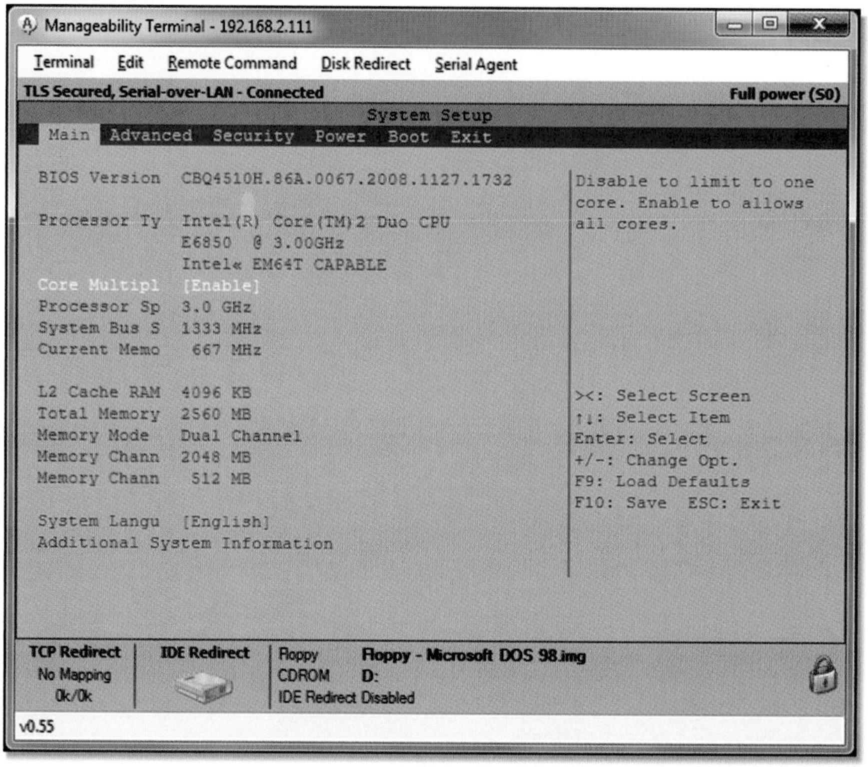

Figure 9.4   BIOS Text Display Redirection

This feature only works when the display is set to 80 by 25 text mode. This is the display mode that is used when first starting the computer and when entering the BIOS setup screens or booting up Microsoft DOS. The exact way the text display is captured and sent to the serial port varies from one BIOS vendor to another, but in general VT100 encoding is used to send cursor position and color attributes in the serial port. Some BIOS vendors have BIOS settings to allow the user to change how the display is encoded to the serial port.

We talked about the BIOS display redirection switch, but have not talked about how to turn it on or off. This switch is controlled by the RemoteControl method of the remote control EOI/SOAP service, and can only be turned on upon remote reboot of the computer with Intel AMT. The switch is turned back off by default upon the next reboot.

Examples:

Remote reset without BIOS text redirection.
```
RemoteControl(0x10, 0x157, 0x00, 0x0000, 0x00, 0x00);
```

Remote reset with BIOS text redirection.
```
RemoteControl(0x10, 0x157, 0x00, 0x0000, 0x00, 0x01);
```

Remote reset to BIOS setup with text redirection.
```
RemoteControl(0x10, 0x157, 0xC1, 0x0008, 0x00, 0x01);
```

Remote reset to IDE-R floppy with text redirection.
```
RemoteControl(0x10, 0x157, 0xC1, 0x0001, 0x00, 0x01);
```

Remote reset to IDE-R CDROM with text redirection.
```
RemoteControl(0x10, 0x157, 0xC1, 0x0101, 0x00, 0x01);
```

As we can see from these examples, BIOS test redirection can be used in many situations. The last two examples combine using BIOS text redirection with remote IDE-R. This is especially interesting if the administrative console is remotely booting a Microsoft DOS floppy disk and wants the BIOS to redirect the command prompt back to the administrator, as shown in Figure 9.5.

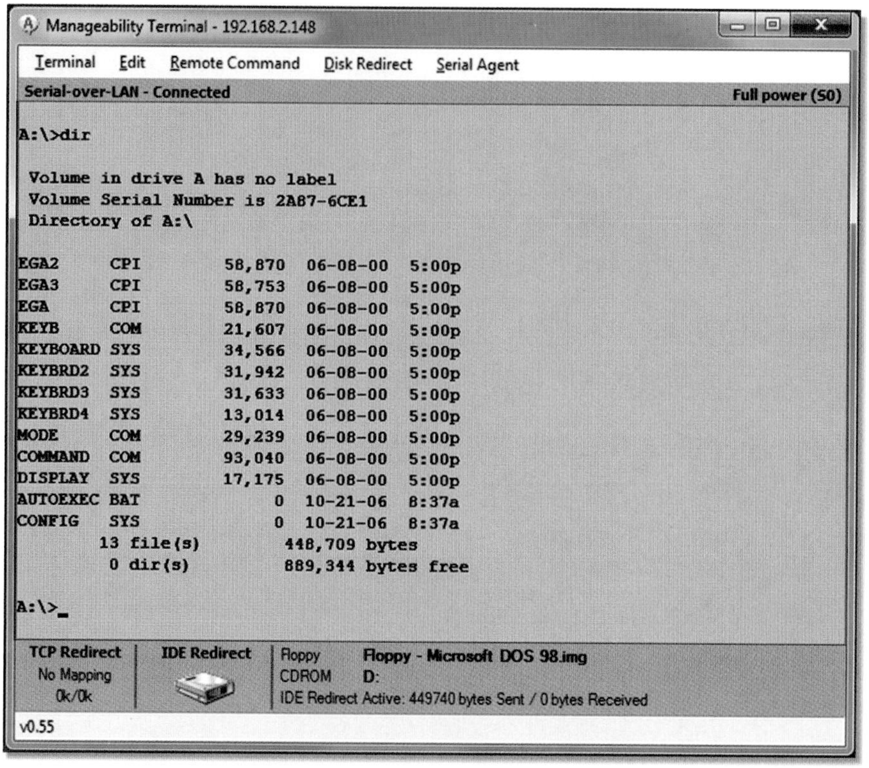

```
A) Manageability Terminal - 192.168.2.148                               _  □  X

Terminal   Edit   Remote Command   Disk Redirect   Serial Agent
Serial-over-LAN - Connected                                     Full power (S0)

A:\>dir

 Volume in drive A has no label
 Volume Serial Number is 2A87-6CE1
 Directory of A:\

EGA2     CPI     58,870  06-08-00  5:00p
EGA3     CPI     58,753  06-08-00  5:00p
EGA      CPI     58,870  06-08-00  5:00p
KEYB     COM     21,607  06-08-00  5:00p
KEYBOARD SYS     34,566  06-08-00  5:00p
KEYBRD2  SYS     31,942  06-08-00  5:00p
KEYBRD3  SYS     31,633  06-08-00  5:00p
KEYBRD4  SYS     13,014  06-08-00  5:00p
MODE     COM     29,239  06-08-00  5:00p
COMMAND  COM     93,040  06-08-00  5:00p
DISPLAY  SYS     17,175  06-08-00  5:00p
AUTOEXEC BAT          0  10-21-06  8:37a
CONFIG   SYS          0  10-21-06  8:37a
        13 file(s)       448,709 bytes
         0 dir(s)        889,344 bytes free

A:\>_

 TCP Redirect   IDE Redirect   Floppy    Floppy - Microsoft DOS 98.img
  No Mapping                    CDROM     D:
   0k/0k                        IDE Redirect Active: 449740 bytes Sent / 0 bytes Received
 v0.55
```

Figure 9.5   Redirected Microsoft MS-DOS Screen

OS Applications Using Serial-over-LAN

The second possible use of the serial-over-LAN port after the BIOS is OS level applications. Only one application may open the serial-over-LAN port at any given time and send data to the management console. It is generally accepted that such applications send VT100 encoded serial data just like the BIOS. This allows the remote administrator to use the same terminal software for both BIOS display redirection and controlling serial applications.

So why would an OS level application want to communicate with a management console using a slow serial port when network sockets would be much faster? Because this serial port bypasses the OS network stack and communicates with the management console using the Intel AMT network stack instead. If the OS network stack is not working or completely disabled, this serial port will still work. Also, an application using this serial port can be assured to be communicating with an authorized administrator since Intel AMT will perform the authentication before letting a management console send and receive data to this serial port.

When running a variation of Linux, it is common for administrators to run a new shell and pipe the input and output to the serial-over-LAN port. This way, once the OS is running an administrator can log into a terminal session using serial-over-LAN even if the OS network stack is not working. In Microsoft Windows, software like Intel AMT Outpost that is part of the Manageability DTK will offer the administrator many remote services through the serial port.

One other possible use of this serial port is for kernel debuggers that can route debugging data to a serial port. Using Intel AMT as a serial port for this type of usage is beyond network management, but a perfectly acceptable usage.

When building an application that runs on an Intel AMT computer and binds to the Intel AMT SOL serial port, it is not possible to know when a management console connects or disconnects from the serial port.

Also, there is no way for an application to tell which Intel AMT user is currently connected to the serial port. If needed, applications running in the OS must perform their own access control over the serial port. All an application can be assured of is that one of the users authorized to connect to Intel AMT may be connected to the serial port, but you cannot know which one.

Building a Serial-over-LAN Terminal

We talked about how the BIOS and applications can send VT100 data to a management terminal using the Intel AMT serial port. This section covers the art of building and using a terminal on the console side. It is an art because so many things can and do go wrong.

First, the management console terminal must have a display size of 80 characters wide and 25 characters high. Terminals intended to be used with modems often have 24 characters high, which causes problems.

Second, different BIOS vendors have different key mappings for F1 to F12 keys. Since these keys are often used in the BIOS screens and the mapping varies, a terminal should allow the administrator to quickly change from one mapping to another.

Table 9.1 The Three Common Fx Key Mappings that Serial-over-LAN Terminals Should Support

Key	Mapping 1	Mapping 2	Mapping 3
F1	ESC + [+ O + P	ESC + 1	ESC + O + P
F2	ESC + [+ O + Q	ESC + 2	ESC + O + Q
F3	ESC + [+ O + w	ESC + 3	ESC + O + R
F4	ESC + [+ O + x	ESC + 4	ESC + O + S
F5	ESC + [+ O + t	ESC + 5	ESC + O + T
F6	ESC + [+ O + u	ESC + 6	ESC + O + U
F7	ESC + [+ O + q	ESC + 7	ESC + O + V
F8	ESC + [+ O + r	ESC + 8	ESC + O + W
F9	ESC + [+ O + p	ESC + 9	ESC + O + X
F10	ESC + [+ O + M	ESC + 0	ESC + O + Y
F11	Not Defined	ESC + !	ESC + O + Z
F12	Not Defined	ESC + @	ESC + O + [

This first mapping is often use by Intel BIOS and because F11 and F12 keys are not defined in this mapping, administrators can't start the boot device selection menu when booting; this would require the F12 key.

The second mapping is used by HP BIOS. It is interesting because most users can type hit the Escape key followed by 1 for F1, so explicit terminal support is not required but recommended.

The third mapping seems to be supported by many other BIOS vendors because freely available terminals such as Putty[1] support this mapping by default.

Because an administrator may be managing many computers from different vendors with different BIOS support, an ideal serial-over-LAN terminal should support all three mappings and allow switching between them.

---

1 Putty is freely available for download at: http://www.putty.org.

Lastly, a good serial-over-LAN terminal must support all of the possible VT100 escape codes correctly. Not implementing this correctly will likely result in the screen not looking quite right in some situations.

Table 9.2 List of Common VT100 Escape Sequences

Sequence	Description
ESC + [+ 2 + J	Clear Screen
ESC + [+ (y) + ; + (x) + H	Move cursor to (x), (y) coordinates. Upper left of the screen is (1,1). X and Y should never be zero.
ESC + [+ (a1) + ; + (a2) + m	Set display attributes. 0 = Reset attributes 1 = Bright, 2 = Dim 7 = Reverse, 27 = No reverse 30 to 39 = Foreground colors 40 to 49 = Background colors 90 to 99 = Bright foreground colors 100 to 109 = Bright background colors
ESC + [+ (c) + K	c = 0 or omitted, start at cursor and erase rest of line. c = 1, erase from start of line until cursor c = 2, erase entire line
ESC + [+ h	Enable line wrap
ESC + [+ l	Disable line wrap

If a developer wants to use a standard terminal like Putty or Microsoft Windows XP HyperTerminal, these terminals can't connect directly to Intel AMT. The protocol is proprietary and authentication is required. Using these standard terminals is not recommended, but someone can use this by building a small serial relay application and using the raw TCP feature that both Putty and HyperTerminal support, as shown in Figure 9.6

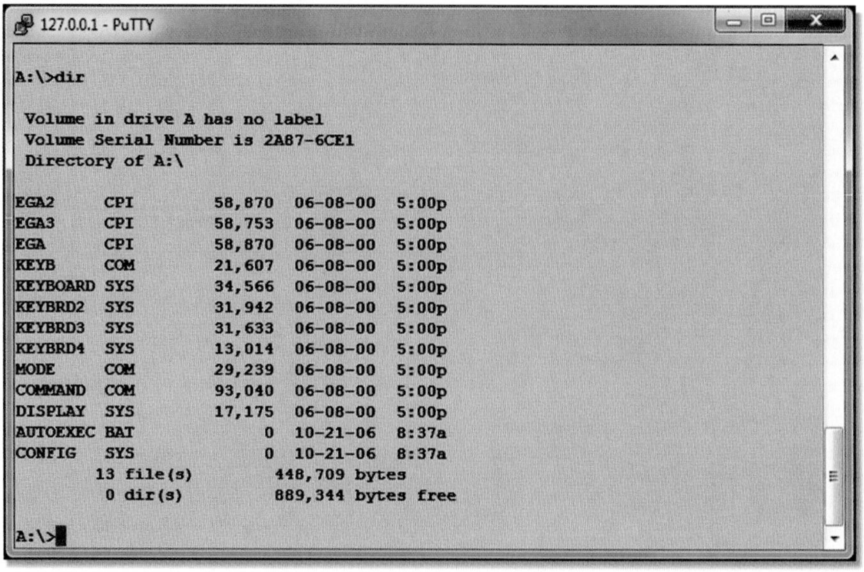

```
127.0.0.1 - PuTTY

A:\>dir

 Volume in drive A has no label
 Volume Serial Number is 2A87-6CE1
 Directory of A:\

EGA2        CPI        58,870   06-08-00   5:00p
EGA3        CPI        58,753   06-08-00   5:00p
EGA         CPI        58,870   06-08-00   5:00p
KEYB        COM        21,607   06-08-00   5:00p
KEYBOARD    SYS        34,566   06-08-00   5:00p
KEYBRD2     SYS        31,942   06-08-00   5:00p
KEYBRD3     SYS        31,633   06-08-00   5:00p
KEYBRD4     SYS        13,014   06-08-00   5:00p
MODE        COM        29,239   06-08-00   5:00p
COMMAND     COM        93,040   06-08-00   5:00p
DISPLAY     SYS        17,175   06-08-00   5:00p
AUTOEXEC    BAT             0   10-21-06   8:37a
CONFIG      SYS             0   10-21-06   8:37a
         13 file(s)         448,709 bytes
          0 dir(s)          889,344 bytes free

A:\>
```

Figure 9.6   Using a Standard Terminal

Of course, the best way to go is to use a terminal that was built from the ground up to support serial-over-LAN, such as IAmtTerm.exe that comes with source code in the Manageability DTK. Such a terminal also has the benefit of having support power state monitoring, remote reboot, and IDE redirection all on the same user interface.

Advanced Uses of Serial-over-LAN

Earlier in this chapter, we talked about how OS-resident applications could open and use the Intel AMT serial port to send and receive data from the administrative console and that it is generally recommended for applications to assume that the management console is running a VT100 terminal and so VT100 escape codes should be used.

If the same software developer builds console and agent software located on either side of the serial connection, extra nonstandard escape codes can be defined to greatly enhance the features offered by VT100. Of course, care should be taken to remain VT100-compatible in case one side or the other does not support these extra escape codes.

The Manageability DTK's terminal and agent software do exactly that to enhance the features supported over the serial port while remaining backward-compatible. Some of these features include uploading and downloading files, obtaining a list of running processes, starting and stopping processes, browsing the file system, enabling and disabling device drivers, and forwarding TCP connections over the serial port.

All of these extended features are very useful if the operating system's network stack is not working, or when you need to boot a recovery OS and want to make more tools available than the ones offered by a command prompt.

Probably the most powerful extended serial feature of the DTK is TCP connection forwarding over the serial port. This feature forwards a local console port to a remote port on the computer with Intel AMT, with the terminal and the agent acting as middle-men, relaying the data, as shown in Figure 9.7.

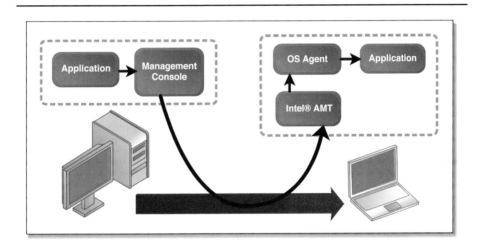

Figure 9.7   TCP-over-SOL, Using Intel® AMT Out-of-Band Channel to Carry TCP Traffic

Probably the most impressive demonstration of this feature involves performing a remote display session using VNC or Microsoft RDP over the serial port. The demonstration starts by disabling all of the network adapters on the computer with Intel AMT. Going to a command prompt and typing "IPCONFIG" proves that the operating system has no IP address. In reality, the Intel AMT network stack is still running and a serial-over-LAN connection to the OS agent on the Intel AMT computer is still possible.

Using the TCP-over-SOL feature, the administrator can still take control over the computer's display and mouse remotely and even fix and re-enable the network adapter in the OS. Details on how to do this are explained in the Manageability DTK serial-over-LAN white paper and tutorial video.

Summary

This chapter covered IDE redirection and serial-over-LAN, two of the most powerful features of Intel AMT and two features that allow an administrator to take action over a remote computer in order to diagnose problems and fix them. IDE-R redirection allows an administrator to bring diagnostic and repair tools to a troubled computer, and serial-over-LAN allows the administrator to have control over these tools even if the OS network driver is not loaded or not functional. A proper combination of software and Intel AMT hardware support results in unprecedented new possibilities for remotely fixing problems that would otherwise have required hands-on access to the computer.

Chapter 10

Protecting the Platforms

Painting: The art of protecting flat surfaces from the weather and exposing them to the critic.

—Ambrose Bierce (1842–1914)

When it comes to the cost of keeping computers in good working order, there is almost nothing worse than rogue software such as a computer virus to create immeasurable loss of productivity. In this chapter we will go over the Intel® Active Management Technology (Intel AMT) features that are intended to protect the computer and network from software attacks.

Much like repairing computers as discussed in the previous chapter, effective protection of computers and the network is best done with a combination of software- and hardware-based solutions. Many software-only solutions exist today, but they can all be themselves victims of attacks because they run within the operating system they are attempting to defend.

Paring software solutions with Intel AMT, a hardware module that can be trusted regardless of the operating system, forms a much more solid network protection story. The three features covered in this chapter are:

- System defense - hardware packet filtering
- Agent presence - software monitoring
- Heuristic filters - network attack detection

Each of these features work with each other and with software to provide an extra layer of network defense.

System Defense

Starting with Intel AMT 2.0, Intel introduced the system defense feature, which is mostly a feature of the new Gigabit Ethernet adapter built onto the platform. This new onboard gigabit network adapter can perform shallow packet header inspection and filtering at gigabit speeds. Each time a packet is sent or received by the network interface, it is matched against a set of filters; the action associated with the first filter to match the packet will be performed. If no filter is matched, a specified default action is taken.

This simple hardware traffic matching engine built right into the Intel Gigabit adapter is at the core of the Intel System Defense feature. All the administrators need to do is to use Intel AMT to program the filters on the network adapter. Intel AMT provides a secure and authenticated path for the network administrator to set or clear these filters.

Network Filters

Filters are the basic entities that are placed in the gigabit adapter that network packets are matched against. Each filter is composed of the following information:

- **Name** – A human readable name for the filter that is at most 16 characters in length.

- **Direction** – A flag indicating if inbound or outbound traffic is to be matched. If traffic much be matched in both directions, two filters must be created.

- **Profile** – Action to be taken can be one of these: allow the packet through, limit this type of packet to a set number per second, or drop the packet. Regardless of the action taken, the packet can also be counted, incrementing one of the hardware counters in the network adapter.

- **Log when triggered** – Log an event in the event log and possibly send an alert when this filter is triggered for the first time.

■ **Type** – The type of filter. There are 7 possible filter types:

- Ethernet

- IPv4, IPv4/UDP, IPv4/TCP

- IPv6, IPv6/UDP, IPv6/TCP

    Each of these filter types has a set of additional parameters that must be filled in to perform proper matching.

The detail of how a filter is defined is best described in the Intel AMT SDK, as shown in Figure 10.1. We should note that the definition of a filter varies a little depending if EOI/SOAP or WS-Management is used to communicate with Intel AMT.

Figure 10.1 Setting Up a Filter to Count Outgoing ICMP Packets

When defining a filter, a common issue involves the confusion over the traffic direction. In Intel AMT Commander, the Direction dropdown list at the top indicates if this filter looks at traffic going in or out of the Ethernet adapter. Further down, in the IPv4 traffic header information, there is a second direction field. This second field indicates which IP address to look at, IPv4 source or target address. The target or outgoing IPv4 address is the address of the other computer on the network. The source or incoming IPv4 address is the address of this local Intel AMT computer. The source (local) and target (remote) address are used the same way, regardless of packet direction.

In general, 16 or more filters can be active in each traffic direction on the Ethernet adapter at any given time. The precise number depends on the version of Intel AMT.

Network Policies

Once network filters are defined and set up in Intel AMT, they must then be added into a System Defense policy, which is a group of zero or more filters as shown in Figure 10.2. Filters on their own can't be enabled on the hardware; they must be part of a policy and only one System Defense policy can be active at any given time.

A policy also includes three default filters that indicate what to do when none of the network filters match a packet.

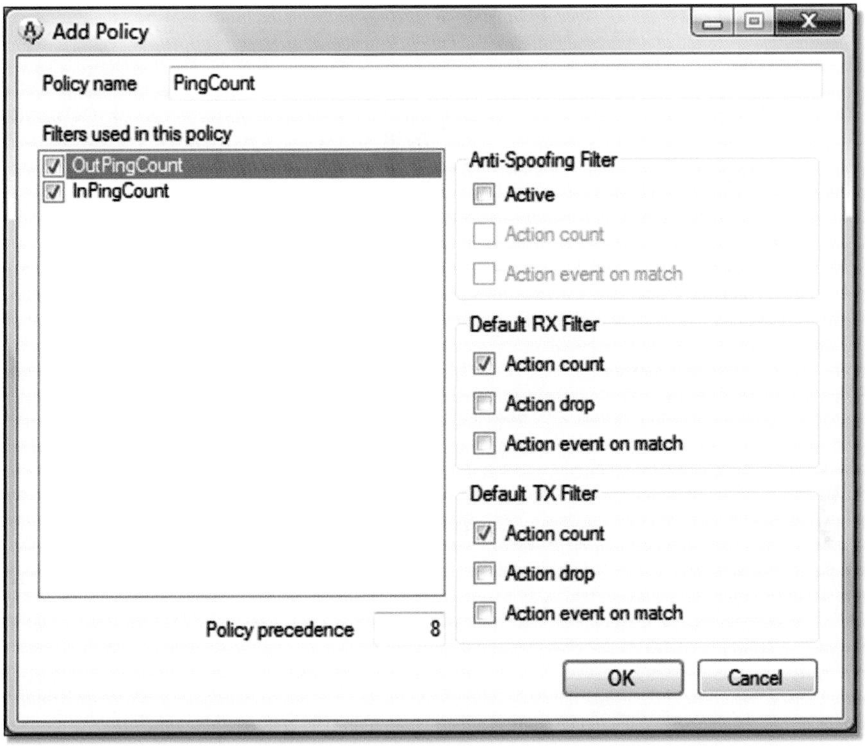

Figure 10.2 Intel® AMT Commander Window for Adding a New System Defense
Policy

As shown in the example in Figure 10.3, an administrator creates two network filters for counting ICMP packets, one inbound and one outbound. A
policy is then created that includes both these filters and sets the default action
to count the packets. Once this policy is made active on the network interface,
Intel AMT will start counting ICMP packets both inbound and outbound
and all packets that don't match the filters both inbound and outbound.

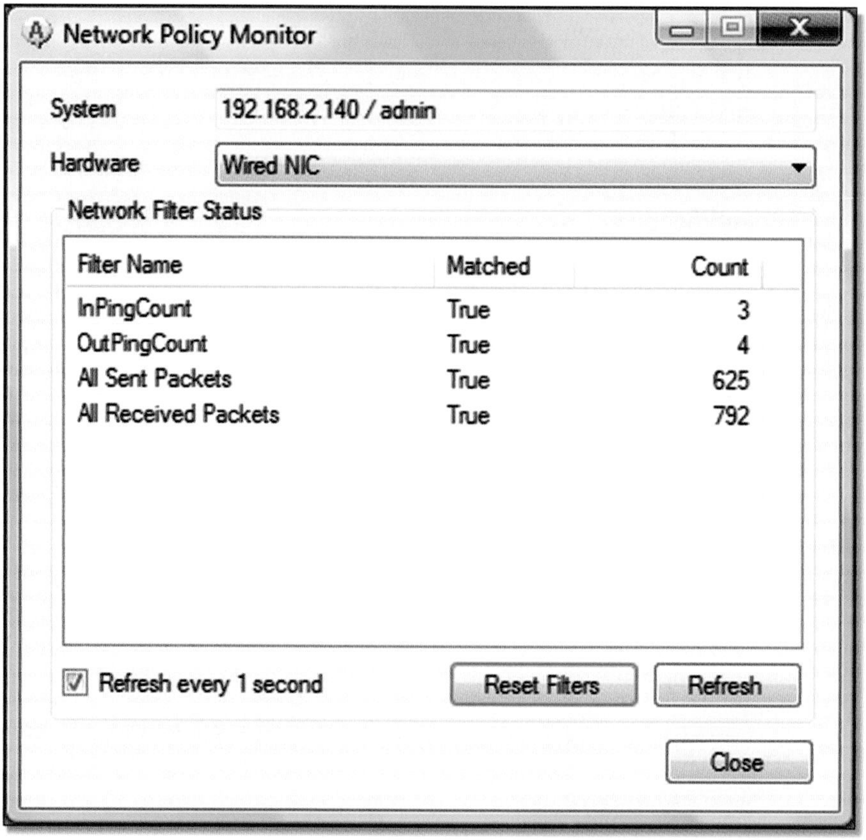

Figure 10.3 Intel® AMT Commander Screen Showing System Defense Traffic Counters

Because of how Intel System Defense policies can be defined, it is possible to limit traffic on a given port, IP address, or subnet by placing a Pass-through filters for the allowed inbound and outbound traffic and place a Drop All default action on the policy. This way, if none of the filters are matched, the packet is simply dropped. This can be very useful in situations where a computer has been compromised and the administrator wants to severely limit the other network nodes a computer can communicate with.

It is important to note that System Defense filters and policies never apply to Intel AMT traffic. It is not possible for example to block Intel AMT port 16992 using a System Defense filter. In fact, Intel AMT traffic would not even be counted or processed in any way. This means that it is possible to add a new policy with no filters and a default action of Drop All on both send and receive to deny all packets from going to the operating system. Still, Intel AMT and features such as Serial-over-LAN and IDE redirect would still work properly.

Anti-Spoofing Filter

When setting up a new System Defense policy, each policy comes with three default filters, the default transmit, default receive, and anti-spoofing filters. The anti-spoofing filter only looks at outbound packets and checks to see that the sender IP address matches the IP address of Intel AMT.

In other words, if the OS attempts to send a packet on the network that have a return address that does not match the real IP address on the Intel AMT computer, the anti-spoofing filter will catch it. As of Intel AMT 5.0, only IPv4 packets are looked at.

Spoofing an IP address is a typical way to attack another computer while trying to mask the real source of the attack. In general, it's a good idea to block such packets. There are rare occasions, especially on servers that are multi-home, for which this filter would not be desirable. For work desktops and laptops, making use of the anti-spoofing filter is a good idea.

Rate Throttling Filter

A little known feature of Intel AMT System Defense is the rate throttling filter support. To use this feature, simply create a usual filter such as an outgoing UDP match all filter, set the filter profile to Rate Throttling, and set a rate of 10 packets per second. Add this filter as part of a policy and activate the policy.

At this point, no more than 10 packets per second can leave the computer at any time, and surplus packets will be discarded. Someone can test this feature using the Intel AMT Net Traffic tool. This time, run Intel AMT Net Traffic on two computers, the computer using Intel AMT and another one on the network, as shown in Figure 10.4

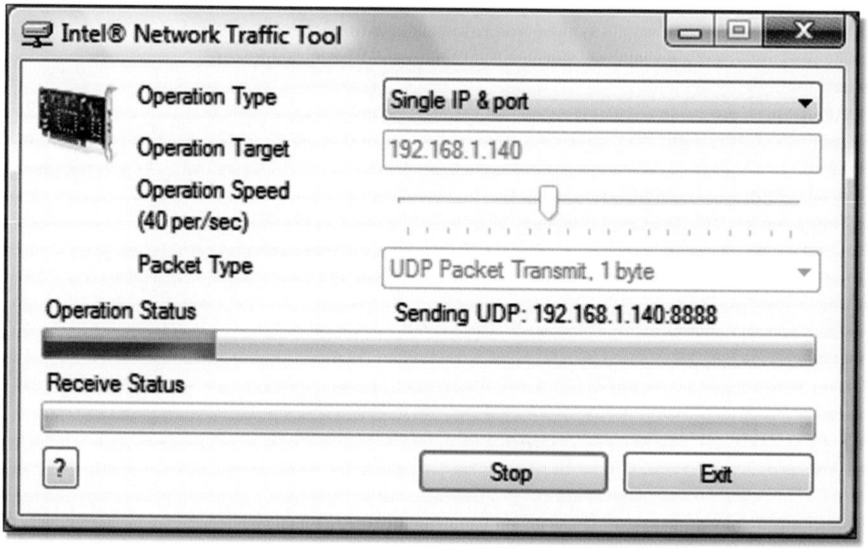

Figure 10.4 Intel® Network Traffic Tool Set Up to Send Packets to a Single Target IP Address

By setting the Intel Network Traffic Tool to send packets at a rate of 40 packets per second and the filters limiting it to 10 packets per second, the result will be very clear on the computer receiving the packets. Intel AMT Commander can be used to activate and deactivate the System Defense filter to see the difference in received packets.

Rate throttling packets can be very useful in preventing unwanted network flooding. It can be used to limit packets sent to a single IP or port, all packets or subnet. Inbound rate throttling can be used to protect running OS applications from packet floods.

Heuristic Filter

Starting with Intel AMT 3.0, Intel introduced a new feature called the heuristic filter to help defend the network. Viruses can cause wide spread damage on computer systems. In the late 1990s there were stories in the media of viruses causing complete network shutdowns and large corporations would tell employees walking in the office in the morning to stay off computers. These rapidly propagating viruses created a great deal of damage and lost productivity. With Intel AMT 3.x and AMT 5.x, Intel has attempted to provide a new defense against IP address scanning viruses, called heuristic filters.

With this new feature, Intel AMT monitors outgoing network traffic and attempt to detect a IP address scanning pattern and stop it. To be clear, this feature is not a defense against viruses; rather, it blocks the Intel AMT computer from attacking other computers on the network.

At the hardware level, the gigabit Ethernet interface sends a sample of the outgoing traffic to Intel AMT for analysis. Intel AMT only gets a sub-sample because at gigabit speeds, Intel AMT management engine is not sufficiently fast to handle all that traffic. Within that sample, Intel AMT attempts to look for interesting events such as opening a TCP connection or sending a UDP packet to a new IP address. Most of these interesting events are fairly typical and should not be of concern. However, if the frequency of the interesting events rises above a threshold set by an administrator, a potential attack is detected and Intel AMT can take action. In Figure 10.5, Manageability Commander is monitoring the state of the heuristic filter in an Intel AMT 3.0 computer.

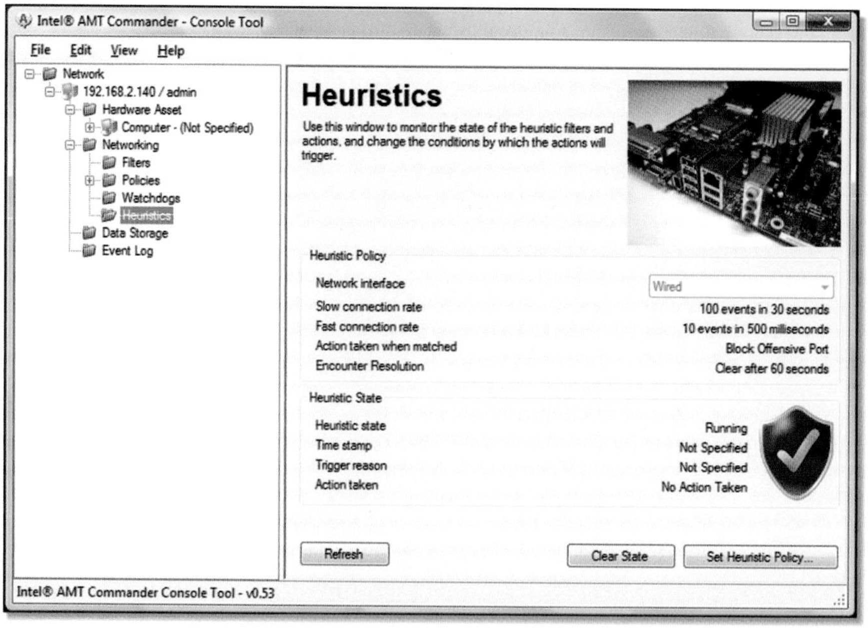

Figure 10.5 Monitoring the State of Heuristic Filters

Heuristic Policy

The heuristic filter feature is enabled and set up by the network administrator. The feature must be set up and enabled with triggering thresholds and actions to be taken once the filter is activated.

Intel AMT Commander provides an easy way to set up heuristic filter policies and actions as shown in Figure 10.6. Again, this feature is only available on Intel AMT 3.x and 5.x, so Intel AMT Commander will not display this feature when connected to other versions of Intel AMT.

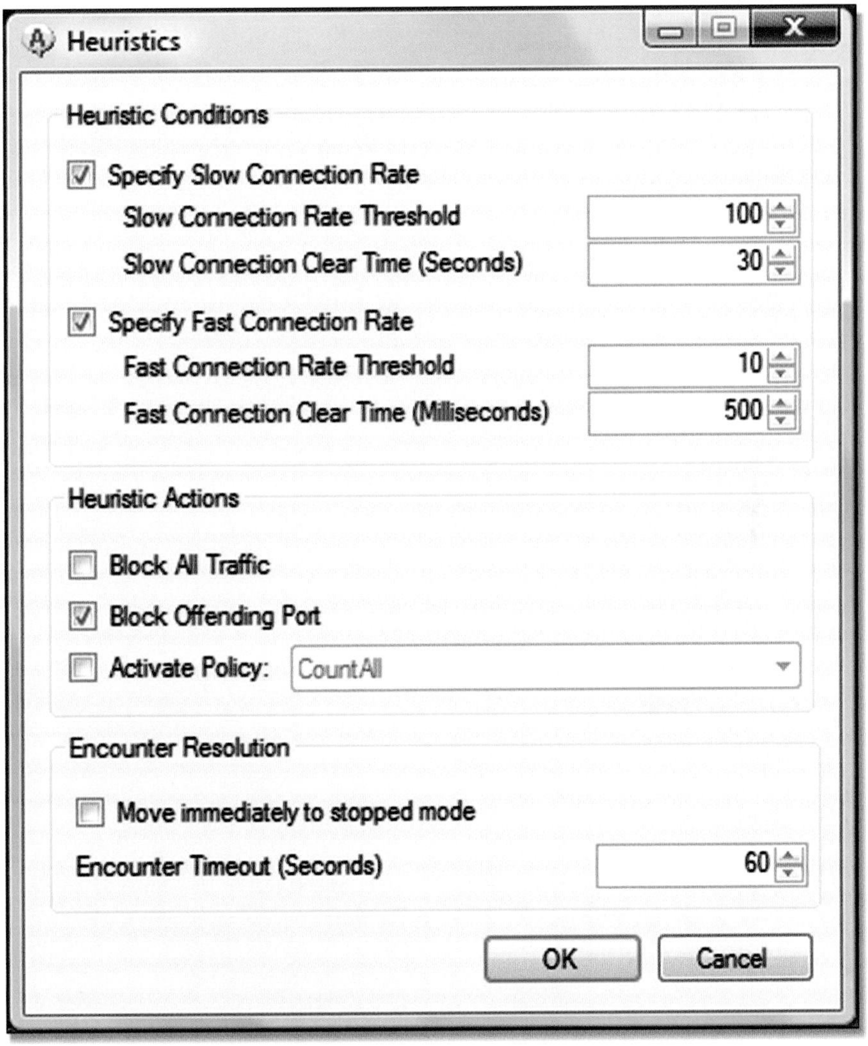

Figure 10.6 Intel® AMT Commander Heuristic Policy Setup

The Intel AMT Commander dialog box is separated into three parts. The heuristic conditions at the top are what will cause the heuristic filter to trigger. The administrator can set up to two thresholds, a slow and a fast one. The slow threshold will count for a given number of interesting events between 1 and 50 seconds. The fast counter count events between 10 to 1000 milliseconds. Two counters allow an administrator more flexibility in setting heuristic policy trigger. The generally recommended values are 100 events in 30 seconds or 10 events in 500 milliseconds. This recommendation comes from looking at previous IP address–scanning viruses.

Once the heuristic trigger is set up, the administrator must specify what action to take. The choices are to block all network traffic, block the offending outgoing port only, and/or enable a specified System Defense policy.

Lastly, the administrator can opt to keep the resulting action permanent, or allow it to expire after a certain time. If the action is permanent, the administrator will have to reset the heuristic filter manually.

Heuristic Filter Demonstration

In an attempt to demonstrate heuristic filters in real life, the Intel AMT DTK provides a tool called Intel AMT Net Traffic as shown in Figure 10.7.

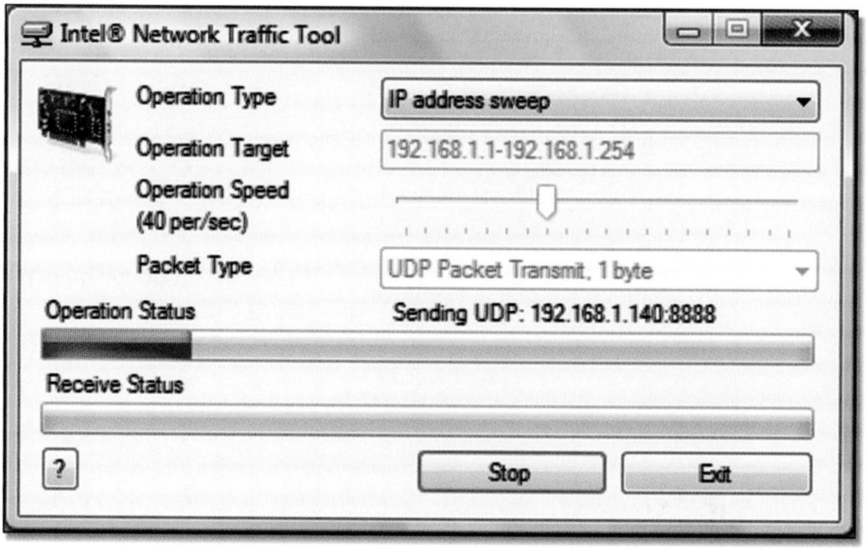

Figure 10.7 Intel® AMT Network Traffic Tool

It's a small traffic generation tool that can be used to artificially trigger the heuristic filter. Once the heuristic policy is set up and active, run this tool on the computer with Intel AMT and perform an IP address sweep using a range of IP addresses outside the local network subnet.

Why scan outside the local subnet? It so happens that Microsoft Windows will block outgoing traffic within the subnet to IP addresses that don't exist. As a result of this existing filter in the Microsoft operating system, Intel AMT will never see any unusual events within the local subnet.

Intel AMT Commander is built to poll the state of the heuristic filter every 5 seconds when the UI is looking at the heuristic state, so starting the IP address sweep should result in a displayed change in the state without a few seconds.

Heuristic Filter Limitations

It is important to also know the limitations of the heuristic filter feature. The Intel AMT heuristic filter should not be used as a replacement for OS-level firewall and virus protection software.

Since there is only one heuristic filter and it no longer works once triggered, if the resulting action is to block the offending port only it is possible for another attack on a different port to work. In other words, someone could trigger the heuristic filter using one outbound port and then, while the heuristic filter is not looking anymore, launch an IP address port scan on a different outbound port.

On the other hand, if the action taken is to block all ports, it may be possible to cause a denial of service attack, using Intel AMT to stop all work on this computer.

Another limitation of the heuristic filter has to do with how it analyzes the interesting events. Someone playing around with the Intel Net Traffic Tool will notice that if both the target IP address and port change during the scan, the heuristic filter no longer triggers.

Agent Presence

Proper management of a computer must include management based on both hardware and software. With agent presence, Intel AMT attempts to serve as a trusted entity that can help monitor running applications in the operating system. This is done by creating what is called a *watchdog GUID* in Intel AMT and then having an OS application register and perform a "heartbeat" on that GUID at regular intervals.

This way, Intel AMT can report to the management console the registration and heartbeat state of a given GUID, indicating to the administrator that an OS-level application is running correctly.

To get started, the administrative console must first create a watchdog as shown in Figure 10.8. This is done by calling the ConsoleWatchdogCreate method that is part of the AgentWatchdogRemote SOAP service[1].

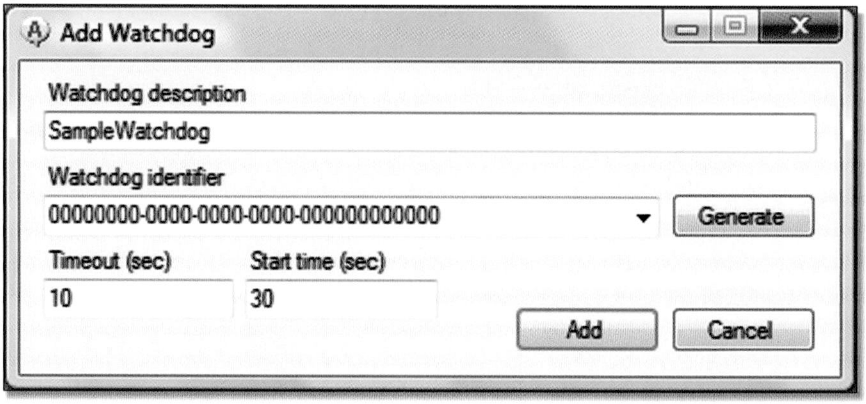

Figure 10.8 Intel® AMT Commander Window for Adding an Agent Presence Watchdog

A watchdog must specify a name, GUID, heartbeat time, and start time as shown in Figure 10.9. The human-readable name is only used to help the administrator track this watchdog. The watchdog GUID is important and should uniquely identify an application. The timeout is the maximum amount of time an application has to perform a heartbeat. Beyond this time, something wrong is assumed to have occurred to the application such as an unexpected error and closure. Lastly, the start time is the maximum time expected between the power up of the computer and the start of this application. If a computer is booted up and the application is never loaded, this start time will pass and something incorrect is assumed to have happened. For example, something must have prevented the application from starting up.

Once a watchdog is added to Intel AMT, it can have one of five states:

1   See the Intel AMT SDK for a complete list of methods and services.

- **Not Started** – Occurs when the watchdog was just added or the computer was just powered on and the watchdog is waiting the start up amount of time specified by the administrator.

- **Stopped** – The OS application performed a correct exit.

- **Running** – The application is correctly running.

- **Expired** – The application was expected to be running, but has not reported. Either the application did not start, or it stopped unexpectedly.

- **Suspended** – The computer is in an Sx sleep state and OS-level applications are not currently running.

A watchdog can change state at any time. The state of a watchdog can be polled by a management console, but these states will be especially useful when looking at performing automatic actions based on state transitions.

Figure 10.9 Intel® AMT Commander Displaying a Watchdog State

Application Heartbeat

Once a watchdog is created by the management console, it's time to run software that will perform the heartbeat of the watchdog GUID. This software must run on the computer with Intel AMT with an MEI driver and Local Manageability Service (LMS) that are working correctly.

First, the local software must authenticate to the LMS using HTTP or HTTPS and then use the following methods on the AgentWatchdogLocal service:

- **AgentWatchdogRegister** – Register to start performing heartbeats on a watchdog. The registration call will provide the application with the maximum time internal for the watchdog.

- **AgentWatchdogHeartbeat** – Perform a heartbeat on a watchdog; this must be called periodically after registration is made.

- **AgentWatchdogShutdown** – Stop performing heartbeats on a watchdog; must be called before existing the application.

These three methods are simple and allow the application to report to Intel AMT it's proper running state. The registration to a watchdog will also provide the application with a sequence number that must be incremented and used everytime the application performs a heartbeat or shuts down the agent. This sequence number prevents other applications from easily spoofing the heartbeat.

For people who want to try performing agent registration and heartbeat for demonstration's sake, the Intel AMT DTK includes an application called Intel AMT Outpost. This agent tool, shown in Figure 10.10, includes agent presence support.

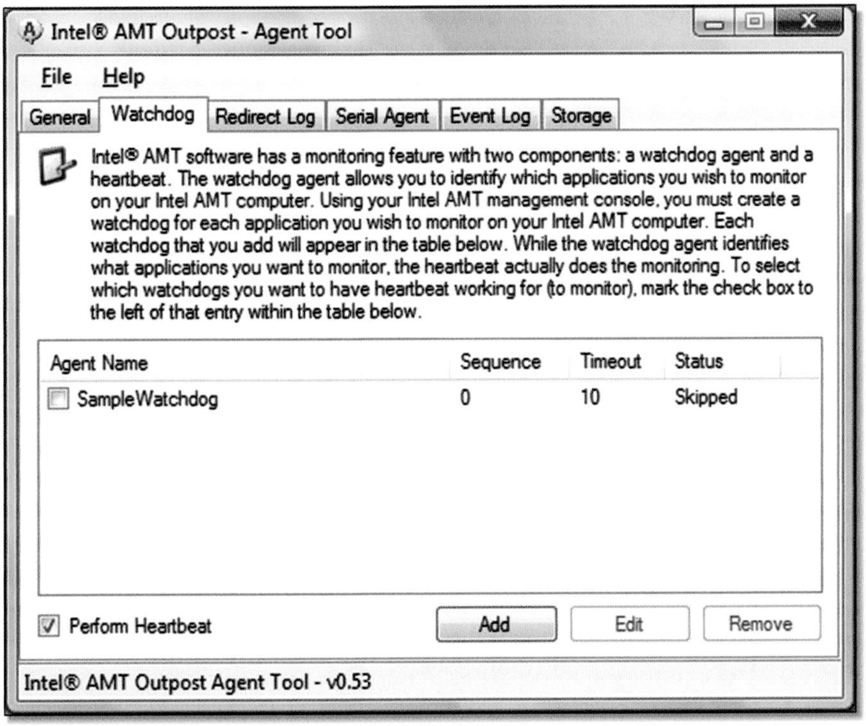

Figure 10.10 Intel® AMT Outpost Used to Perform Agent Presence Operations

Intel AMT Outpost allows a user to add watchdog GUIDs and perform correct registration and heartbeat by checking the box next to the watchdog. A user can also set up Outpost to perform heartbeat when a given process such as Notepad is running. This is very useful for demonstrations. Ultimately, critical applications such as corporate agents, anti-virus applications, and firewall applications should select and publish a GUID on which they will attempt to perform heartbeat whenever possible. It is also important for software vendors to publish a way for administrators to provide a username and password for the software to locally log in to Intel AMT. Administrators should create a local-only account for the purpose of performing heartbeats.

Taking Action

Now that we know how to create a new watchdog agent remotely and perform local heartbeat on it, it's time to see what we can do with the watchdog state information.

Intel AMT provides for each watchdog agent a way to attach an action to a state transition. For example, an administrator can specify that whenever a firewall GUID changes to the expired state, an event is logged into the Intel AMT event log and a 'Block All' System Defense policy is activated. When the firewall software goes back online, the System Defense policy can be disabled.

The administrator can set up a rule that states "when going from any state to the expired state, activate the agent presence policy and log the event to the event log." Causing the event to be logged will also cause a network alert to be sent to management consoles if they are subscribed to receive events. In Figure 10.11, we see the dialog box used by Intel AMT Commander to set up such a rule.

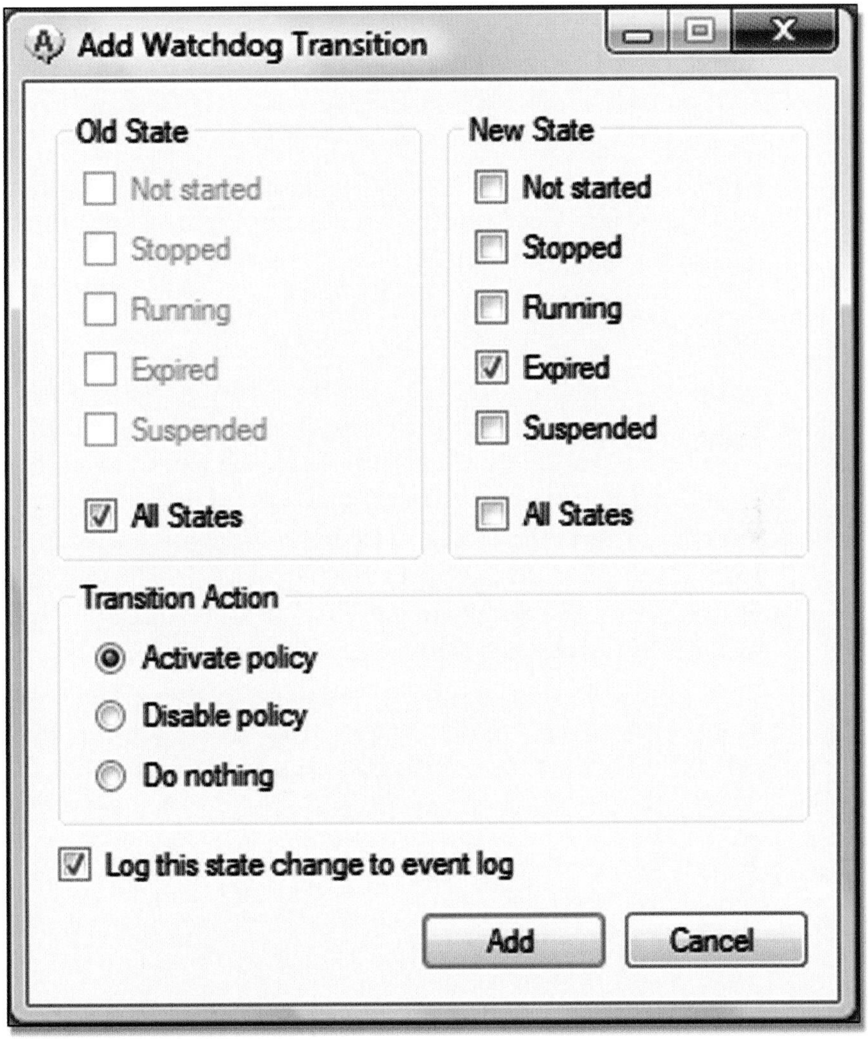

Figure 10.11 Intel® AMT Commander Window for Configuring an Action Based on a State Transition

A limitation of agent presence actions is that only one system defense policy can be set to be activated per network interface (one for wired, one for wireless). Once selected, the circuit breaker policy will be enabled when a change in transition occurs.

Any transition can be set to disable the current system defense policy, regardless of what the currently active policy is. You can disable the current one, but you can only enable a single set policy.

One way to get around this limitation is for a management console to actively receive the network alert indicating that a state transition has occurred and manually activate or disable a system defense policy. This active approach is more flexible, but requires the computer to be connected on the managed network. For laptops, having Intel AMT activate a policy on its own is much more useful since it will work regardless of where the laptop is.

Summary

Using a combination of software and hardware is the best way to effectively protect a network of computers from attack. This chapter covered the three Intel AMT system protection features. System defense and heuristic filters can be used right away, without the need of any specialized software running on each PC. Agent presence support should be added to mission critical software to help monitor their correct operation and make sure to take appropriate action if it is not the case. In the end, making correct use of these features can save lots of time and money the next time an unexpected attack occurs.

Chapter 11

Connecting and Communicating with Intel® Active Management Technology

Disconnecting from change does not recapture the past. It loses the future.
— Kathleen Norris, *O Magazine*, January 2004

Once all of the features of Intel® Active Management Technology (Intel AMT) are understood, it's time to understand how to access them. Connectivity to Intel AMT is a large and important topic. Since Intel AMT uses out-of-band connectivity and a set of strong security measures along with many protocols, a good understanding of this topic is necessary in order to successfully use Intel AMT. Connectivity to Intel AMT is defined in detail in the Intel AMT SDK. This chapter provides an overview of the connectivity features, security features, and protocols used to communicate with Intel AMT. We will also look at connectivity from a software developer's point of view. When writing Intel AMT software, developers may want to support a wide range of Intel AMT versions and simplify as much as possible the process of connecting to Intel AMT. This chapter includes ideas for how to simplify the connection process and how to make the most of every version of Intel AMT going as far back as Intel AMT 1.0. This chapter assumes that Intel AMT has already been provisioned.

Connection

Intel asked and obtained from the Internet Assigned Numbers Authority (IANA) a set of reserved TCP ports for Intel AMT. These are TCP ports 16992 through 16995 and are intended to be used only with Intel AMT. Obtaining these reserved ports is important since Intel AMT will steal these ports from under the operating system.

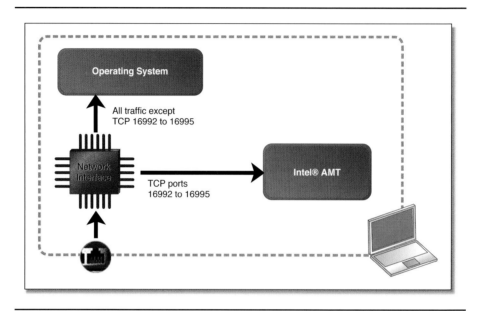

Figure 11.1 Operating System Gets All Traffic Except TCP Port 16992 to 16995

When Intel AMT is enabled in DHCP mode, inbound TCP connections to ports 16992 through 16995 are rerouted to Intel AMT using a hardware filter in the Ethernet adapter. As a result, if an application listens to port 16992 through 16995, it will never receive any inbound TCP connection.

On most versions of Intel AMT, if set to static IP mode, Intel AMT uses a separate MAC address and IP address for out-of-band communication. As a result, inbound TCP connections on ports 16992 through 16995 on the operating system's IP address will still work correctly.

We should also note that an application listening on TCP ports 16992 through 16995 could still receive TCP connections from other network adapters that are not enabled with Intel AMT and from the local OS loopback adapter.

Port Usages

Now that we know how Intel AMT makes use of four special inbound ports, let's look at function each of these ports performs.

- 16992 – HTTP traffic
- 16993 – TLS secured HTTPS traffic
- 16994 – Serial-over-LAN and IDE Redirect
- 16995 – TLS Secured Serial-over-LAN and IDE Redirect

Ports 16992 and 16993 are identical except that on 16993, Transport Layer Security (TLS) must first be negotiated before useful traffic can flow. The same applies to 16994 and 16995, which are also identical except for TLS.

With Intel AMT, only TCP ports 16992/16994 are used when TLS is not configured; ports 16993/16995 are used when TLS is in use. A management console does not have a choice to use TLS or not. If TLS is configured on a given computer with Intel AMT, any attempts to connect to 16992 or 16994 will fail. The reverse is also true, if TLS is not configured, management consoles can't connect to ports 16993/16995.

The TLS protocol used with the secure communications with Intel AMT is the same TLS protocol used all over the Internet and is also built into most web browsers. When an administrator is attempting to access the Intel AMT Web page, it can do so with the following URL in any web browser:

Without TLS:

```
http://computername:16992
```

With TLS:

```
https://computername:16993
```

In all cases, once a secure TLS session is negotiated, the useful network traffic is the same as the non-TLS equivalent port.

The same TLS versus non-TLS usage also applies to ports 16994 and 16995 but because these ports use a proprietary binary protocol, special software[1] must be used to access these ports.

---

[1] The IMRSDK.dll library included in the Intel® AMT SDK is specifically intended to make use of port 16993 or 16995 for Serial-over-LAN and IDE Redirect services.

Authentication and Authorization

Once Intel AMT is set up, two of the four Intel AMT management ports are usually open and ready to receive connections from a management console. TCP connections on these ports can occur at any time. Before accepting any command from a management console, Intel AMT must first authenticate that the management console is authorized to perform such an operation. The authorization phase determines who the administrator is, and the authorization phase determines if this individual has appropriate rights to perform this action.

Authentication and authorization are probably the two single most critical operations for Intel AMT. Since some of the management features that are possible using Intel AMT could lead to computer data loss, it's important that only permitted administrators be allowed to perform management operations. Intel AMT uses an authentication system called HTTP-Digest[2] or Kerberos[3] used within the HTTP protocol. At a high level and without TLS, the steps are as follows:

■ Receive a TCP/HTTP connection of port 16992.

■ Use HTTP-Digest or Kerberos to authenticate the user.

■ If the user is not in the Intel AMT user table, reject the connection.

■ If the user does not have privileges to perform this operation, reject the operation.

■ Perform the management operation.

With TLS, steps are added to the beginning of the session.

■ Receive a TCP/HTTPS connection of port 16993.

■ Intel AMT sends its own certificate to the console for validation.

■ If policy requires, Intel AMT requests and checks that the console has a valid and trusted certificate.

■ Use HTTP-Digest or Kerberos to authenticate the user.

■ If the user is not in the Intel AMT user table, reject the connection.

---

2   Defined in RFC 2617.

3   Defined in RFC 4120.

- If the user does not have privileges to perform this operation, reject the operation.
- Perform the management operation.

The steps with TLS and without TLS are the same except that with TLS, there is an additional layer of security at the start of the session. Also with TLS, the entire session is fully encrypted, making it impossible for anyone else to listen in on the network conversion.

Ports 16994 and 16995 used for Serial-over-LAN and IDE Redirection use exactly the same steps but use a proprietary binary protocol instead of HTTP. If TLS is not used, password-based authentication on port 16994 will result in the password being sent in the clear on the network. This is why it's highly recommended that TLS always be used when performing serial-over-LAN or IDE Redirect operations.

Environment Detection

Even with all of the security care, authentication and authorization steps taken by Intel AMT, the simple fact that there are open ports waiting for outbound connections makes it possible for an external party to attempt an attack on Intel AMT. If a corporate user were connected on a hotel network, someone in a different room could scan the network for open Intel AMT ports and attempt to log into Intel AMT by guessing the password. Sometimes, just knowing that Intel AMT is present and active on a computer is sufficient to make it a target for other attacks or theft. This scenario is especially relevant for mobile platforms.

In order to protect from this and other types of attacks, Intel AMT 2.5 and higher include a feature called environment detection. The goal of this feature is to close all Intel AMT inbound ports when the computer is determined to be outside the corporate network. During provisioning, Intel AMT can set up one to four domain suffixes. For example: "intel.com" or "openamt.org" would both be valid values. Once set and activated, Intel AMT will only open inbound ports when it gets a DHCP address that ends with one of the known suffixes. In our example: "oregon.intel.com" would be okay, but "intel2.com" would not match and the ports would be closed.

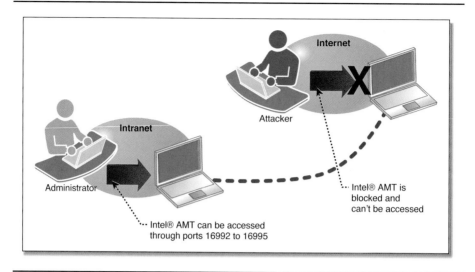

Figure 11.2 Computer Moving from Inside to Outside; Environment Detection Blocks Intel® AMT When Outside the Intranet

Proper use of the environment detection can restrict or completely eliminate the possibility of outsiders attempting to attach Intel AMT.

Intel® AMT VPN Flag

If a computer is connected to a network that is outside the managed corporate network and the environment detection feature is blocking inbound ports, it is still technically possible for an administrator to communicate with Intel AMT. When outside the corporate network, most corporations use virtual private network (VPN) software to allow a computer to join back into the corporate network using a secured connection.

Intel AMT 2.5 and above support an additional feature we will call the VPN flag. When provisioning Intel AMT, this flag can be set to enabled or disabled[4]. If enabled, Intel AMT will accept connections from an administration console through a VPN.

---

4   Oddly, the VPN flag can be set but its current value can't be read back. Provisioning servers or consoles should simply set to VPN flag to the intended value.

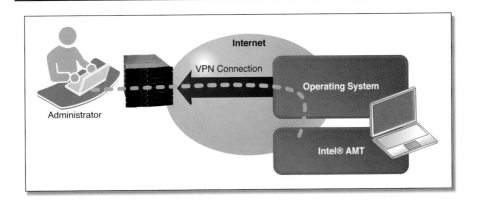

Figure 11.3 Intel® AMT Traffic over VPN

Since VPN software runs within the operating system, the management console would be connected to Intel AMT using an in-band channel. If for example the console reboots the computer remotely, connectivity would be lost. Using this feature is still interesting to configure and obtain monitoring data for Intel AMT, but it should not be used to attempt remote repair.

Starting with Intel AMT 4.0, a new client-initiated connection feature allows Intel AMT to communicate directly with a management console. This feature is covered in Chapter 12, "Internet Platform Management."

Local Host Access

In order for Intel AMT to function correctly, both remote applications such as management consoles and local applications such as agents need to communicate with Intel AMT.

As we indicated earlier in this chapter, Intel AMT intercepts TCP ports 16992 through 16995 for outside communications, but this only works when the network traffic comes from outside the computer and is rerouted to Intel AMT by the network interface. For communication with local applications, a completely different data path is used. Called the Intel Management Engine Interface (Intel MEI), it was also known as the Host Embedded Controller Interface (HECI). These days, Intel uses the name Intel MEI, but HECI may still be found in older documents.

Intel MEI is a driver that has a direct local communication path with Intel AMT. It does not use the operating system network stack; instead it's a direct set of request/response messages that Intel AMT understands. Local applications can use the Intel MEI driver to make a limited set of requests to Intel AMT. These requests are limited, but they don't need any authentication. They include such requests as: "What version of Intel AMT?" and "Is Intel AMT provisioned?" The Intel MEI driver can also route network packets to Intel AMT. Intel provides a background Microsoft Windows service called Local Management Service (LMS).

Both the Intel MEI driver and LMS are provided as part of the software drivers included with a platform. For Intel motherboards, users can find the latest version of the software on support.intel.com. For other vendor's platforms, go to that vendor's support Web site.

As shown in Figure 11.4, the LMS listens on ports 16992 and 19663 of the local computer and routes network traffic to Intel AMT using the Intel MEI. It's tempting to think that once Intel MEI and LMS are properly installed and running, the local port 16992/16993 are exactly equivalent to the same ports accessed from outside the computer, but this is not the case. There are significant differences in how Intel AMT handles local and remote traffic. First, the well known user friendly Web page is not available locally. As a result, pointing a browser to http://localhost:16992 or https://localhost:16993 on the local computer will result in a blank page. One of the biggest differences between local and remote interfaces is the Intel AMT functionality that is available.

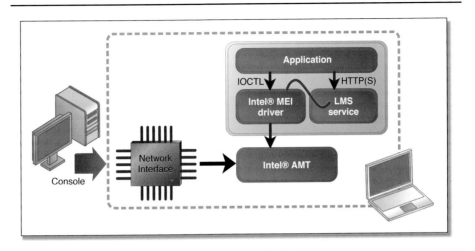

Figure 11.4 Local Management Service (LMS) Using the Intel® MEI Driver to Send Traffic to Intel® AMT

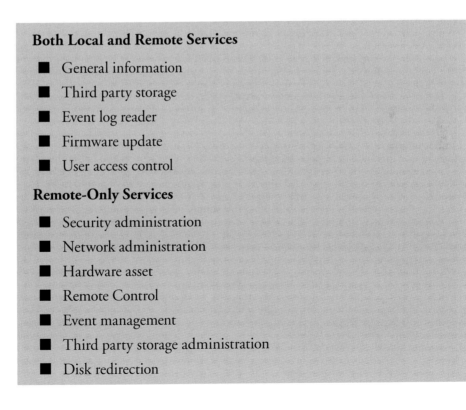

Both Local and Remote Services

■ General information

■ Third party storage

■ Event log reader

■ Firmware update

■ User access control

Remote-Only Services

■ Security administration

■ Network administration

■ Hardware asset

■ Remote Control

■ Event management

■ Third party storage administration

■ Disk redirection

Remote-Only Services (Continued)

- Remote agent presence
- System Defense
- Network time
- Wireless administration
- Endpoint access control administration
- Audit log
- Remote access

Local-Only Services

- Local agent presence
- Endpoint access control
- Local user notification

A decision was made when designing Intel AMT to restrict access to local services because applications running within the operating system are not trusted. In fact, they are being managed by Intel AMT. By restricting local access to services, we also limit the possibility of rogue applications trying to attack Intel AMT using the local interface.

Access to services provided to the local interface still requires that the local application authenticate to Intel AMT using the same authentication and authorization that is used for the remote interface. The same HTTP digest and optional TLS protocols can used to authenticate and possibly secure the session. Local users must still provide a username and password or Kerberos authentication to use local services. Even if the local user authenticates using the Intel AMT administrator credentials, only local services will be available.

When setting up Intel AMT, it's generally a good idea to create one or more separate, local-only user accounts within Intel AMT. This is because locally running applications may not store the account password properly. If not configured properly, a local user could find an Intel AMT username and password in the local Microsoft Windows registry and use it from a different computer to gain access to Intel AMT remote features. This is why it's especially important not to use a separate local-only account.

By separating the local and remote Intel AMT interfaces and user accounts, we create a separation between what is being managed and who is managing. It is also worth nothing that serial-over-LAN and IDE redirection services, along with ports 16993 and 16995, are not available locally.

Implementation of the VPN Flag

Earlier in this chapter, we covered the VPN flag feature and its benefits. Some readers may be wondering about the relationship between LMS listening on local ports and the VPN flag feature. When a management console connects to Intel AMT through a VPN, it will actually connect to the local LMS port and not the external Intel AMT port. As a result, the console should have access to the limited features offered by the local interface.

If the VPN flag is turned on, Intel AMT will start offering all of the remote services to the local interface only if the packets have a source address that is not a local IP address.

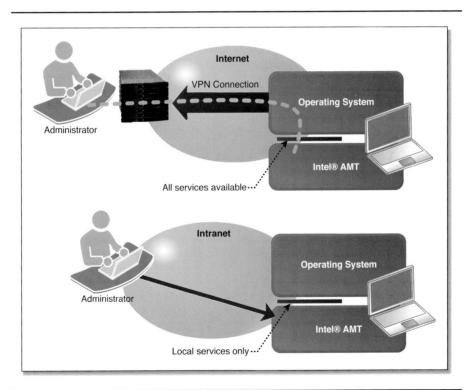

Figure 11.5 VPN Flag Enabled, Local and Remote

In other words, when the VPN flag is enabled, connections that originate from outside the local platform to LMS will be offered all of the remote services. Connections coming from the local loopback interface will still only have access to the limited set of local services.

The VPN flag feature preserves the limitation of the local interface while allowing management consoles to access all of the services and feature of Intel AMT when connecting through a VPN.

Summary

Connectivity to Intel AMT is as easy as connecting to any normal web server on the Internet. As with any web server, security considerations are very important. As we saw in this chapter, Intel AMT provides very robust authentication and privacy, along with an extra layer of protection when the computer is connected on a foreign network. The limited access to Intel AMT features through the local LMS interface/Intel ME interface makes it more difficult for local application to try to cause problems.

A good understanding of Intel AMT connectivity both locally and remotely is crucial for developers building both consoles and local agents that best take advantage of the features offered by Intel AMT.

In the next chapter, we will cover another connectivity option that is new with Intel AMT 4.0 and builds upon the concepts that we covered in this chapter.

Chapter 12

Internet Platform Management

The Internet is like alcohol in some sense. It accentuates what you would do anyway. If you want to be a loner, you can be more alone. If you want to connect, it makes it easier to connect.

— Esther Dyson, Interview in *Time Magazine*, October 2005

We have covered a wide array of Intel® Active Management Technology (Intel AMT) features, but until now all of the benefits of Intel AMT were only available to computers connected on a managed network. In this chapter we cover a new feature available starting with Intel AMT 4.0 called Client Initiated Remote Access (Fast Call for Help). Fast Call for Help is a secure VPN-like connection initiated from Intel AMT to a management server. Once the Fast Call for Help connection is established, this tunnel can be used to communicate with Intel AMT. Fast Call for Help opens a new world of possibilities for remote computer management since, for the first time on commonly available computers, the platform itself can securely connect back to a management server over the Internet. This is especially important with laptops that are often moved and connected to random networks and behind NAT routers. Having laptops move around is no longer an obstacle to using hardware-based network manageability.

This chapter first covers the environment detection feature of Intel AMT, which is important to understand and use Fast Call for Help. After that, we will talk about the Fast Call for Help protocol, how the Fast Call for Help connection is configured, triggered, and authenticated.

Environment Detection

Before going into Fast Call for Help itself, we must first review a feature that was first introduced with Intel AMT 2.5. At the time, having Intel AMT TCP ports open for connection, even if authentication was securely checked, was still a security issue. Imagine someone connecting a laptop with Intel AMT to a hotel room network and having someone in a different room scanning, finding, and attempting to attack the Intel AMT ports on the computer.

To counter the possibility of such an attack, the environment detection feature was added. It is configured with up to four home DNS suffixes and when the computer performs a DNS request, if the response indicates that the computer is in one of the home networks, the Intel AMT ports are open. Otherwise they are closed. Figure 12.1 shows how this works.

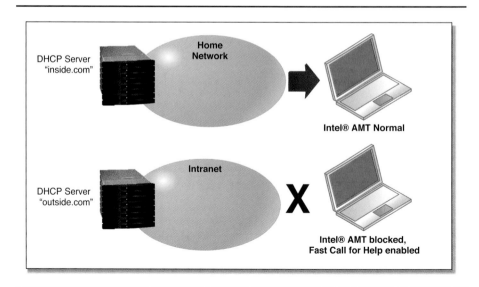

Figure 12.1 Environment Detection Turned On and Off. When On, Blocks All Intel® AMT Traffic.

Starting with Intel AMT 4.0, the same environment detection exists with a new twist. Instead of just blocking the inbound Intel AMT ports, the new Intel Fast Call for Help feature is enabled and the platform can now call home when policy requires. Figure 12.2 shows how the computer calls home and the administrator can access Intel AMT capabilities through a common server.

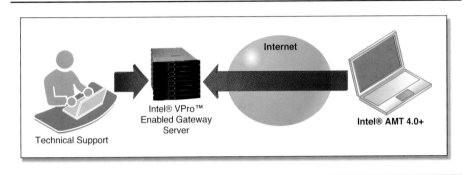

Figure 12.2 Intel® Fast Call for Help Used Over the Internet to Contact the Corporate Server

It is important to understand that Intel AMT 4.0 works exactly like previous versions of Intel AMT when the computer is connected to the native corporate network, the network of the organization to which the computer belongs.. This chapter covers Fast Call for Help, which is only active when the computer is detected to be outside the native corporate network. It's important because many people just starting out will forget to setup the environment detection feature correctly.

Manageability Commander, part of the Manageability DTK, can be used to set up the environment detection policies for a given computer. When trying this for the first time, it may be a good idea to first prepare two simple home routers with two different DHCP network names, one could be "inside. net" and the other "outside.net". Intel AMT would then be configured with "inside.net" as being part of the home network. With this setup ready, the Intel AMT computer can be moved from one network to the other.

Intel® Fast Call for Help Protocol

Intel Fast Call for Help is a TCP-based connection to a known and trusted administration server. The connection is always secured using TLS; this is true even if the computer with Intel AMT is configured in small business mode. Inside this TLS session is a binary protocol that is inspired but not compatible with the well known SSH port forwarding protocol.

As shown in Figure 12.3, the Intel AMT TCP ports (16992 to 16995) are forwarded through this tunneling connection but otherwise are used just like they would be used if Fast Call for Help connection was not in use. In addition, the same SNMP trap network alerts and WS-Management event notifications coming from Intel AMT are also forwarded through this tunnel connection.

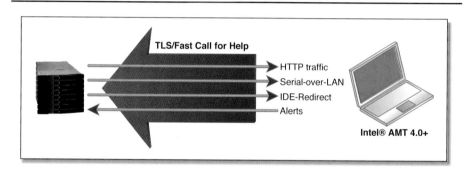

Figure 12.3 HTTP, SOL, IDE-R, and Network Alerts through the TLS Secured Fast Call for Help Tunnel

If the computer with Intel AMT is configured in enterprise mode with TLS enabled, the tunnel will then have two levels of TLS security. Figure 12.4 shows how the Fast Call for Help tunnel will be protected by TLS and will carry TLS secured HTTP, Serial-over-LAN, and IDE redirect traffic. The double security may seem a bit much, but since both levels of TLS authenticate different things, they are both useful. The TLS secured tunnel session authenticates the computers with Intel AMT and Intel vPro Technology enabled gateway. The inner TLS secured sessions authenticate individual Intel AMT users.

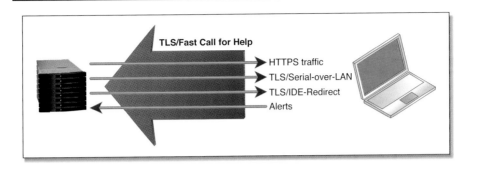

Figure 12.4 TLS Is also Used within the TLS Secured Intel Fast Call For Help Tunnel. TLS Is Applied Twice.

Intel Fast Call for Help connections are always outgoing connections and connect what is called an Intel vPro Technology enabled gateway. An Intel vPro Technology enabled gateway is a server or router that receives and processes Fast Call for Help connections. The Intel AMT SDK provides such software as reference, but for real deployments organizations should contact one of many vendors that have a product quality version of an Intel vPro Technology enabled gateway. In the Intel AMT SDK, the reference gateway software is called the Management Presence Server (MPS). Regardless of the version of the gateway that is used, in large organizations should be installed in the network DMZ, between the firewalls that separate a corporate network from the Internet. Figure 12.5 shows the reference MP Server installed in the corporate DMZ.

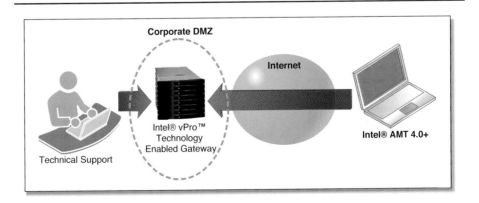

Figure 12.5 Intel® vPro™ Technology Enabled Gateway within the Corporate DMZ

An Intel vPro Technology enabled gateway acts as an intermediary between the management console and computers enabled with Intel AMT that are outside the intranet, routing management traffic within the Intel Fast Call for Help connection.

Intel® Fast Call for Help Policies

Since an Intel Fast Call for Help connection requires a new layer of authentication to verify both that the computer is managed by this server and that the management server is in fact the real one and not a fake. Fast Call for Help connections are also initiated by the computer with Intel AMT. Both the new authentication and connection triggers need to be configured by configuring the Fast Call for Help policies. In this section, we look at how the tunnel connection is triggered and authenticated and how to set up a computer with Intel AMT to use this feature.

Connection Triggers

A Fast Call for Help connection can be initiated in one of three ways. As shown in Figure 12.6, these three ways are: user initiated, periodic timer, or network alert. The policy can be set up to use any combination of these three connection triggers.

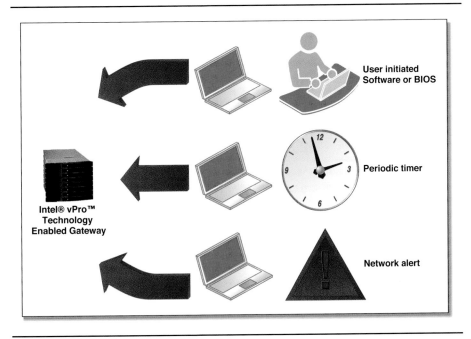

Figure 12.6 Three Connection Trigger Types

Using software like Manageability Commander or Intel SCS, an administrator can change policies. In Manageability Commander shown in Figure 12.7, we can connect to the computer with Intel AMT in the Management Engine tab and hit the Configuration button next to the Remote Management line. This will bring up the Fast Call for Help policy configuration dialog.

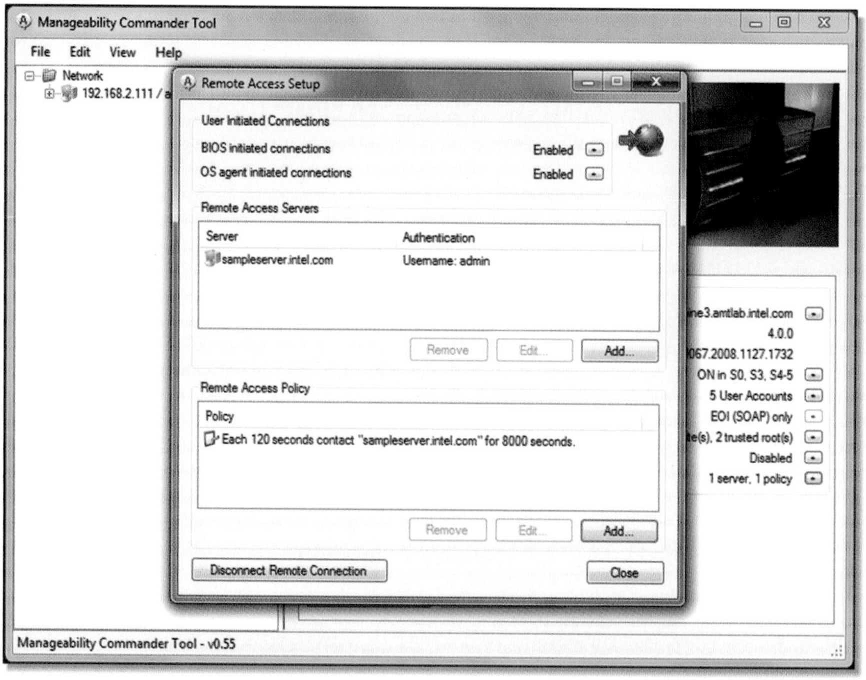

Figure 12.7 Fast Call for Help Policy in Manageability Commander

At the top of the screen, the administrator can control if the BIOS or OS tunnel connection initiation is allowed. In the middle of the screen is the configuration of the Intel vPro Technology enabled gateways, the servers that receive the Fast Call for Help connections. Lastly at the bottom of the screen is the connection action to perform for each of the three possible types of connection trigger. You can specify for each of the possible triggers to what server to connection to and specify a backup server if the primary one is not available.

The user initiated trigger can take one of two forms: the user can initiate Fast Call for Help from the BIOS or from the OS. The administrator has policy control to allow the user to initiate Fast Call for Help and allow or deny Fast Call for Help connections initiated by the BIOS or OS. Depending on the computer with Intel AMT, Fast Call for Help could also be user triggered using a combination of keyboard keys or a hardware button. Regardless of how the user actually opts to trigger the Fast Call for Help connection, the way this works is that BIOS-initiated Fast Call for Help connections are connections that are initiated before the operating system is booted. Once the operating system is allowed to boot, any user triggered Fast Call for Help connection is considered to be initiated by the OS.

When looking at what Fast Call for Help policies are possible, we can also take note that Fast Call for Help is useful for both taking care of user problems and for passive monitoring of platforms. The main focus is often on the repair aspect of Fast Call for Help—a user gets into trouble and initiates a Fast Call for Help connection to ask for help. However, in most cases Fast Call for Help can be initiated every day using a periodic timer policy so that administrators have an opportunity to monitor the platforms' state and location from time to time.

Fast Call for Help Network Routing

Because Fast Call for Help connections are always initiated by the computer with Intel AMT, the management connection can work even if the computer is connected behind a network address translator (NAT). Figure 12.8 shows how the connection passes through standard routers.

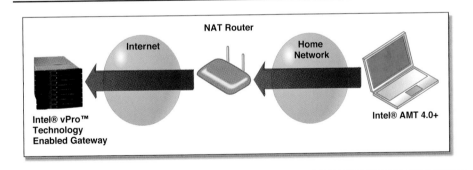

Figure 12.8 Intel® AMT behind a NAT Router

This setup is very common in home networks where the home is only assigned a single IP address and the home router translates private home addresses into global addresses. In such a setup outbound connections work, but inbound connections are difficult or sometimes impossible. By using Fast Call for Help, Intel AMT gets around the NAT problems and so connecting the computer to most networks and launching a Fast Call for Help connection will work.

There are, however, limitations to Fast Call for Help. Outgoing Fast Call for Help connections can only be made on network interfaces that are connected to Intel AMT. So, like the rest of the Intel AMT features, adding a new USB network interface will not work. Also with Intel AMT 4.0, Fast Call for Help is only available on the wired interface and not wireless. So even if Intel AMT is correctly configured to work over wireless, Fast Call for Help will not work unless the wired Ethernet adapter is connected. Lastly, if the network has some type of access control on it, such as a redirected Web page that requires the user to accept a license agreement, PPPoE, PPPoA, 802.1x or any other authentication limitation, Intel AMT will not be able to use the network.

If a policy causes a Fast Call for Help connection be initiated but the network is not available, Intel AMT will try to connect three times before failing.

If for any reason the Fast Call for Help tunnel is unexpectedly disconnected, Intel AMT will attempt to reconnect automatically. This is why the Intel vPro Technology enabled gateway will not simply close the Fast Call for Help connection once it's done. To properly close a Fast Call for Help connection, a management console must call the "CloseRemoteAccessConnection" method on the RemoteAccessAdmin SOAP service. Calling this method causes Intel AMT to correctly disconnect the Fast Call for Help connection on its end.

Fast Call for Help Security and Authentication

Since Fast Call for Help is mostly used for connections over the Internet, security is a prime concern. Because Fast Call for Help is only enabled when outside the managed network and when Intel AMT inbound ports are all closed, Intel AMT itself is much less vulnerable to attack. In Figure 12.9, we review the authentication process. When a Fast Call for Help connection is established, TLS protocol negotiation starts first. This is exactly like the often used HTTPS protocol. TLS will first request and validate the Intel vPro Technology enabled gateway certificate. The MP Server certificate must be signed by a trusted root certificate, so setting up Fast Call for Help will require placing a valid trusted root certificate in the Intel AMT trusted certificate store.

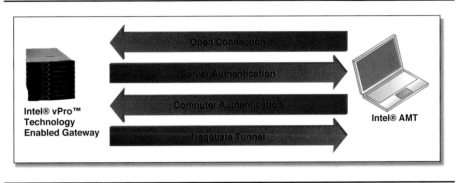

Figure 12.9 Overview of the Authentication Process

Once the Intel vPro Technology enabled gateway is connected, Intel AMT must now authenticate to the gateway. Figure 12.10 shows the two authentication systems supported by Intel AMT, either a certificate of its own or a username and password. It's important not to confuse the username and password used to authenticate Fast Call for Help with the Intel AMT user accounts. They are completely different. The Fast Call for Help uses a completely different set of credentials to authenticate the Fast Call for Help tunnel. Once established, the management console must authenticate through the tunnel to Intel AMT using a standard user account.

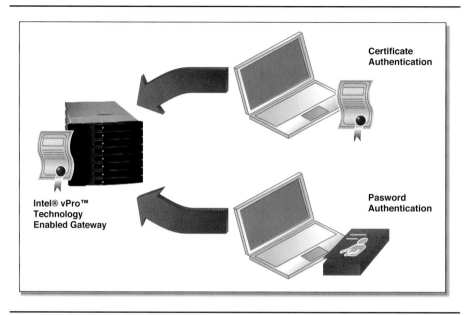

Figure 12.10 Intel® AMT Supports Both Certificate and Username/Password Authentication.

Fast Call for Help Connection

Once a Fast Call for Help connection is established between Intel AMT and the Intel vPro Technology enabled gateway, the management console must get to work. It would be very interesting for the management console to know why the Fast Call for Help connection was established in the first place, what trigger (User/Timer/Alert) caused the Fast Call for Help connection to be initiated. This information would be useful because if the user initiated the Fast Call for Help connection, help is probably required. On the other hand, if a network alert or periodic timer initiated the Fast Call for Help tunnel, the management console can probably just gather information about the platform or take action depending on the severity of the event.

As it stands with Intel AMT 4.0, there is no easy way for the Intel vPro Technology enabled gateway or the management console to know exactly why an Intel AMT computer as established the Fast Call for Help connection, but this section will examine this question.

As of Intel AMT 4.0, Fast Call for Help policies allow up to four Intel vPro Technology enabled gateways to be configured and each trigger policy (User/Timer/Alert) allows each trigger to specify a primary and a backup Intel vPro Technology enabled gateway. Once connected, Intel AMT will not communicate with the MPS server until one of the three triggers causes the connection to be established. Figure 12.11 shows a sample policy. If a policy were set up where each trigger connects to a different MPS server, we would know which trigger caused the connection. Of course, this would require setting up a minimum of three Intel vPro Technology enabled gateways. We also know that if a Fast Call for Help connection is established because of a network alert or timer and the user causes Fast Call for Help to initiate a connection, the current Fast Call for Help session is closed and will be reconnected on the MPS server that is set for user initiated Fast Call for Help sessions.

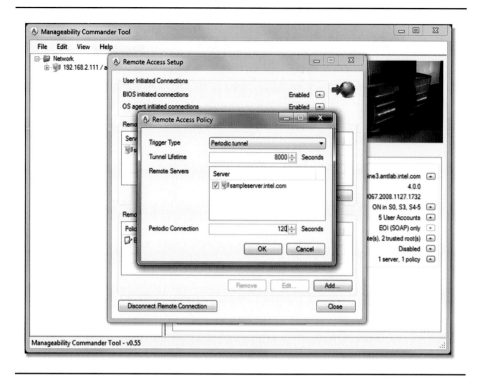

Figure 12.11 Typical Fast Call for Help Policy in Manageability Commander

Even if all the Fast Call for Help trigger policies are set to connect to the same Intel vPro Technology enabled gateway, you can still determine what caused the Fast Call for Help connection to be established in the first place. If the user manually initiates the Fast Call for Help connection, an event is also stored in the event log. A management console can read the event log and see that this event was placed in the log a short time ago and conclude that the user needs help.

If a network alert initiated the Fast Call for Help connection, that network alert will immediately be sent through the Fast Call for Help tunnel to the management console upon Fast Call for Help connection.

If the connection is due to the Fast Call for Help periodic timer policy, the event log will be clear of user help request events and no network alerts will be sent through the Fast Call for Help tunnel.

Intel® vPro™ Technology Enabled Gateway

The Intel vPro Technology enabled gateway that is included in the Intel AMT SDK is certainly not the only one; it is only provided as a reference. Vendors are encouraged to build their own to best suit their own product needs.

This section will take a quick look at the Intel vPro Technology enabled gateway that is included in the Intel AMT SDK, called MPS for Management Presence Server. It's important to understand its overall architecture before attempting to install it. Figure 12.12 shows the basic components once installed.

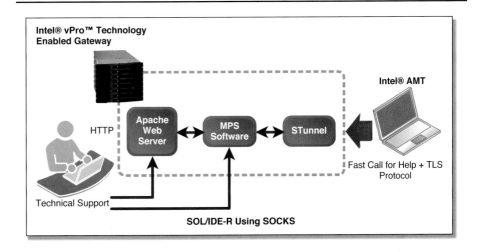

Figure 12.12 The Three Components of the Reference MPS Server Included in the Intel ®AMT SDK

The Intel vPro Technology enabled gateway included in the Intel AMT SDK is really three parts. First, an open source application called STunnel[1] receives the connection, performs certificate-related authentication, and forwards a non-secured connection to the MP Server proper. Second, MPS performs a conversion of Fast Call for Help traffic into the SOCKS protocol. Lastly, the Apache[2] web server acts as the middleman between HTTP requests made by the management console and SOCKS protocol required by the MP Server.

---

1   Stunnel is available at http://www.stunnel.org/

2   Apache web server is available at http://www.apache.org/

In order to perform serial-over-LAN and IDE redirect sessions, the console must be able to communicate using the SOCKS protocol directly. Figure 12.13 shows both HTTP and SOCKS protocols being used towards the server.

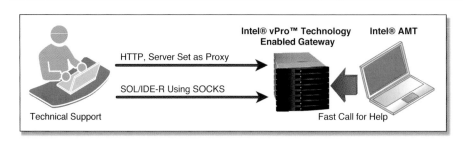

Figure 12.13 HTTP/SOL/IDER Used with Intel® vPro™ Technology Enabled Gateway

In order to simplify the task of adding SOCKS support to management consoles, SOCKS support was added to the IMRSDK.dll library. Management consoles will have to be slightly modified to support the new SOCKS support in this library.

Management consoles must also be modified to support sending HTTP management traffic to the Apache server just as if it were a proxy.

The Intel AMT SDK MPS can also be set up to send WS-Eventing alerts what a Fast Call for Help connection is established or dropped. Configuration to receive such events involves modifying the MPS configuration file. Figure 12.14 shows the server relaying network alerts to the administrator.

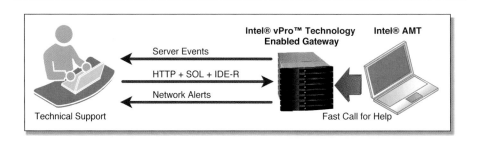

Figure 12.14 Intel® vPro™ Technology Enabled Gateway Events Inform the Console of Newly Connected and Disconnected Fast Call for Help Connections

There is currently no way to change the MPS event subscriber list on the fly or order to add or remove subscribers and no way to query MPS to list all existing connections. Of course, this is only a limitation of the reference Intel vPro Technology enabled gateway that is provided with the Intel AMT SDK. A different vendor's implementation can be made with much more functionality.

Manageability DTK and Fast Call for Help

The Manageability Developer Tool Kit (DTK) includes tools and features to help users test Fast Call for Help. Manageability Connector shown in Figure 12.15 is a simple tool that runs on the computer with Intel AMT and shows the current state of the platform environment detection, the Fast Call for Help connection and allows a user to trigger and disconnect the Fast Call for Help tunnel.

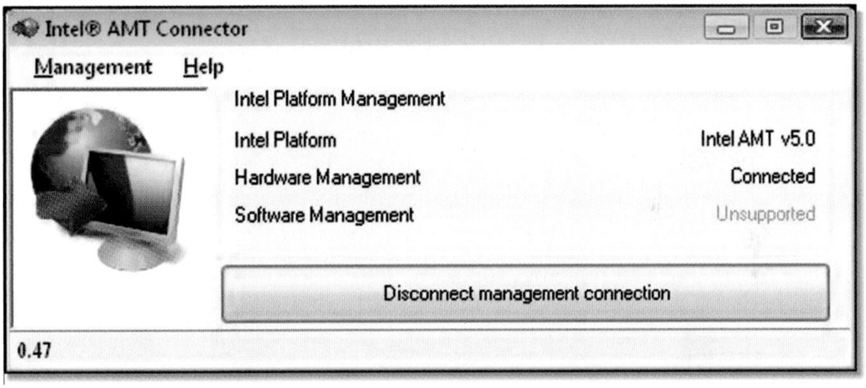

Figure 12.15 Manageability Connector

Users can also mix SDK and DTK tools, using Manageability Commander and Connector with the Intel AMT SDK's Intel vPro Technology enabled gateway. This is ideal when developing, installing, or testing the Fast Call for Help feature.

Fast Call for Help Network Speed

Management consoles will find that management operations through a Fast Call for Help tunnel and over the Internet are considerably slower than when performed on a fast local network without Fast Call for Help. Even if the Internet network connection used is relatively fast, the added latency, added processing work, and addition of an MP Server middleman will slow things down.

This slowdown will especially be felt when many network round trips are required and IDE redirect is going to feel this slowdown the most. The IDE redirect protocol relays data that is commonly transported over short and very fast wires inside a computer. Since IDE redirect makes many round trips; network administrators may opt to attempt to minimize the use of IDE-R over Fast Call for Help. One way to do this is to provide a recovery OS on the computer's hard disk or on a CD-ROM or flash drive.

Another consideration is that management consoles don't always use the HTTP protocol efficiently. Management software that open and close a HTTP session for each SOAP or WS-Management call may see a significant impact on performance. In the next section we explore exactly such a situation.

Fast Call for Help Considerations

Management consoles will be increasingly using WS-Management as the management protocol of choice for communicating with Intel AMT. For developers working on Microsoft Windows, an often used solution for quickly building WS-Management–compatible software is to use Microsoft WinRM[3] (Windows Remote Management). This is an ActiveX object that performs WS-Management operations on the network. Using WinRM works fine normally but developers will run into a problem when using WinRM with the Intel vPro Technology-enabled gateway provided in the SDK. Since the Intel AMT SDK Intel vPro Technology-enabled gateway acts like an HTTP proxy, developers will have to instruct WinRM to use the Intel vPro Technology-enabled gateway as an HTTP proxy. One way to do this is to use the "ProxyConfig" command line, but this is a global setting and will change how all applications using WinRM behave.

---

3   Microsoft† Windows XP requires a download. Look for "WS-Management v1.1" on the download section of the Microsoft Web site.

A possible solution for developers is not to use WinRM and instead try Openwsman[4] or use the C# WS-Management library that is built into the Manageability DTK[5]. Both these libraries will allow developers to target each WS-Management requests to a specific proxy or no proxy at all depending on what needs to be done.

Another benefit of using either OpenWSMAN or the Manageability DTK WS-Management stacks is speed. Both of these stacks support HTTP/1.1 pipelining that allows many requests and responses to be performed on a single HTTP connection. Microsoft WinRM will open and close an HTTP session for each WS-Management call that is performed resulting in many more network round trips and significantly reduced speeds.

Summary

In a world of increasingly mobile computing, being able to use the features offered by Intel AMT over the Internet on mobile devices is very valuable. All of the value of Intel AMT we have seen in previous chapters from monitoring and asset tracking to remote repair is not available over the Internet. Some companies are working on removing the notion of a trusted network altogether, and assuming that all computers are always connected on an un-trusted network. In such an organization, all computers, both desktops and laptops, would use Fast Call for Help all the time.

Moving forward, Fast Call for Help makes Intel AMT not only a great hardware-based manageability solution but is sometimes the only one that can be deployed and truly work.

---

4   Openwsman is available at: http://www.openwsman.org

5   Look for the WsManDIrectClient.cs file in the Intel® AMT DTK

Chapter 13

Intel® Active Management Technology in Small and Medium-sized Business

I do not fear computers. I fear the lack of them.

— Isaac Asimov (1920–1992)

If you have a computer enabled with Intel® Active Management Technology (Intel AMT) and want to just get started, you can "get your hands dirty" with this chapter and start using Intel AMT features with the freely available Manageability Developer Tool Kit (DTK). First, go to the following Web site, download and install the tools.

```
http://www.intel.com/software/amt-dtk
```

These tools are available freely with source code. For this chapter, only the binary versions of the tools are needed. Before starting, Intel AMT will need to be set up since new computers come with Intel AMT turned off. Appendix A demonstrates how to get into the BIOS or Intel MEBX screen at boot time and set up Intel AMT for the first time. Additionally, one should check that Intel AMT can be accessed using the built-in web server. To do this, use any web browser on a different computer and type in the following URL:

```
http://computername:16992/
```

Here "computername" must be replaced with the name or IP address of the computer with Intel AMT. It's important to note that this must be done from a different computer on the same network. Attempting to access the Intel AMT Web page from the same computer will not work. Figure 13.1 shows a sample network setup for Intel AMT and management console.

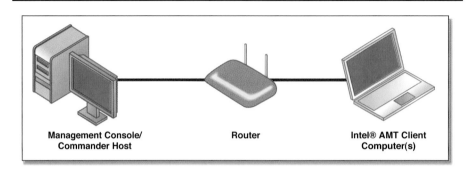

| Management Console/ | Router | Intel® AMT Client |
| Commander Host | | Computer(s) |

Figure 13.1 Simple Intel® AMT Network Setup

The computer that will serve as the management console does not have to support Intel AMT, but if the console does support Intel AMT, it will not be able to manage itself, only others. Once we have one or more computers with Intel AMT set up and ready to go, it's time to install the Intel Manageability Developer Tool Kit (DTK).

Installation

The DTK must be installed on Microsoft Windows XP or Microsoft Windows Vista; both 32-bit and 64-bit platforms are supported. The DTK also requires Microsoft .NET; make sure you have the latest version. It includes console and agent software so it's useful to install the DTK on both the console computer and all computers with Intel AMT. Start by launching the installer and accepting the user license. The installer file will generally have the name:

```
Manageability_Developer_Tool_Kit_<version>.msi
```

During the installation you will be prompted to install management tools, remote agents and other tools, as shown in Figure 13.2. In general, if installing on a computer that supports Intel AMT, select remote agents; otherwise, this option need not be selected since remote agents only work on computers with Intel AMT.

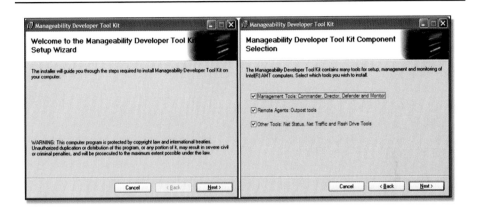

Figure 13.2 Manageability DTK Installation Screens

Once completed, a set of new tools will be installed on the Start menu, under All Programs and Manageability Developer Tool Kit. Depending on the options selected in the installation, up to four main applications will be installed, which are described in the following sections.

Manageability Commander Tool

This is a sample Intel AMT management console and probably the most useful tool of this software package. Commander is built to make use of all major Intel AMT features and so serves as a great demonstration and development tool.

Manageability Network Defense Tool

This is a simplified version of the Commander tool. It's more limited, but resembles more closely what an easy-to-use Intel AMT tool would look like.

Manageability Director Tool

This is a simple setup and configuration tool. It can be used by advanced users to set up Intel AMT with full certificate security and reset Intel AMT to factory defaults.

Manageability Outpost Tool

This is an Intel AMT agent that can only run correctly on computers with Intel AMT enabled. It will log into Intel AMT using the local Intel Management Engine Interface (Intel MEI) and provide most of the functions that are available through this interface. Generally, Outpost should always run in the background and provides the console with many more management features if it's running.

Manageability Commander

Let's get started by running Manageability Commander (Commander). Again, this console application can't run on the computer that's being managed; it must run on a different computer running on the same network. When entering Commander for the first time, no managed computers are listed. We need to add computers we are going to manage. To do this, we can manually add them or scan the network for computers that support Intel AMT.

To add a known computer, click File→Add→Add Intel AMT Computer.… The dialog box shown in Figure 13.3 prompts you for the address, username, and password of the Intel AMT computer.

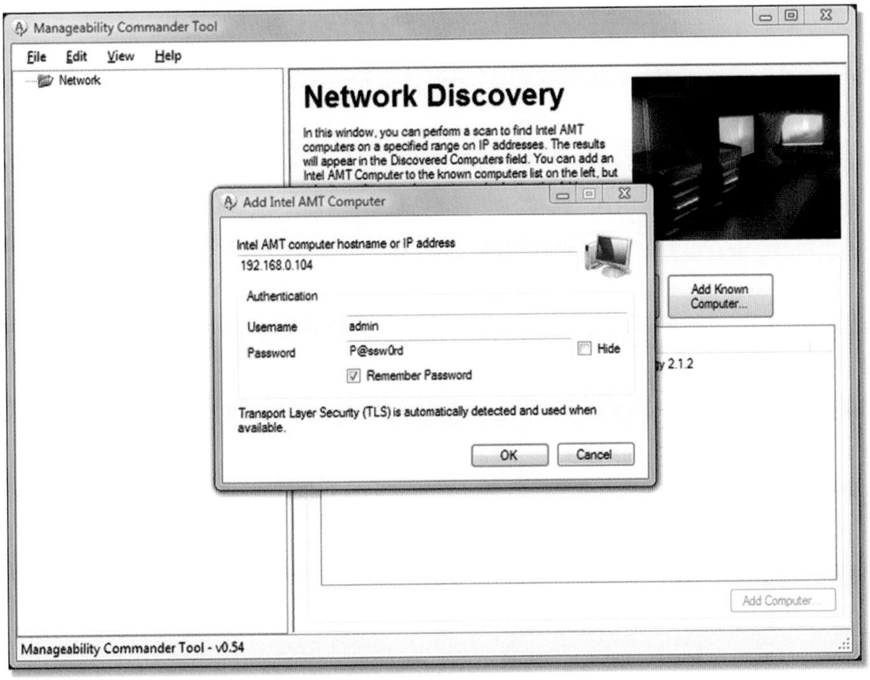

Figure 13.3 Manageability Commander Prompting for a New Intel® AMT Computer

Additionally, Commander can scan the network for Intel AMT computers. While in the Network Discovery screen, enter the starting and ending IP address and press the Start button. As shown in Figure 13.4, as each computer is found, it will be added to the Discovered Computers list.

When possible, Commander tries to gather data about the computer that was found. Without knowing the username and password to log into Intel AMT, Commander can only discover whether transport layer security (TLS) is being used, and when TLS is not in use, which version of Intel AMT is supported. When a computer is discovered, it must still be added to the list of managed computers. To do this, select a discovered computer and click Add Computer. A dialog box will prompt you for a username and password.

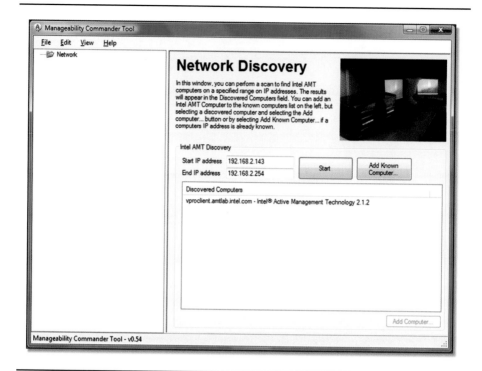

Figure 13.4 Manageability Commander Finds One Computer After Performing a Limited Network Scan

For each computer that is discovered, repeat the process of selecting it and adding it to the list of managed computers on the left tree view. It's possible to add the same computer more than once. This is especially useful if Intel AMT is configured with more than one user account. For now, only the administrator account with the username "admin" can be used.

Connecting

Once one or more computers have been added to the left side of the Commander tool, its time to connect to them and start performing management operations. As shown in Figure 13.5, select a computer on the left side tree view and press the connect button.

Tip	You can also connect to a computer by right-clicking on its name and selecting the Connect option, or by double-clicking the computer's name in the left side tree view.

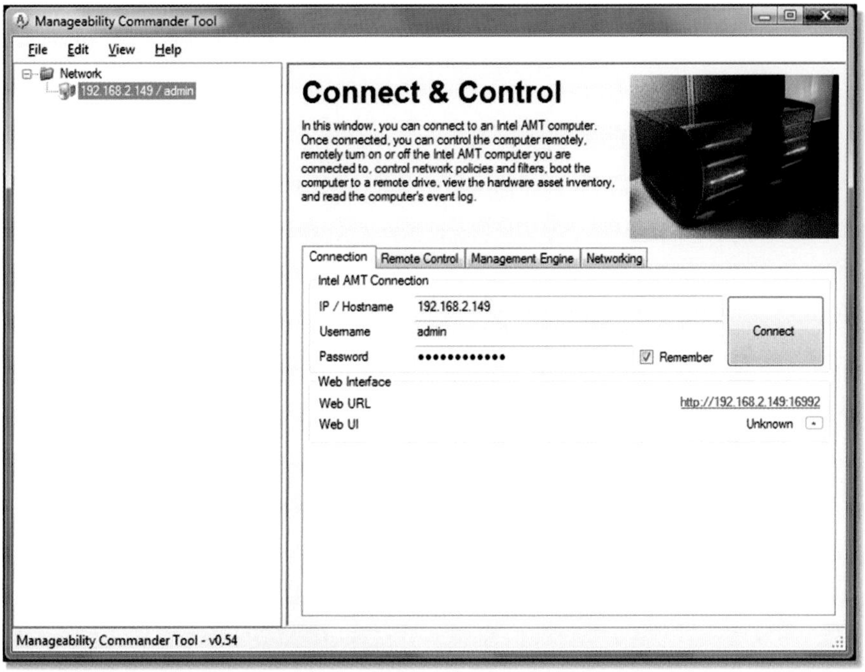

Figure 13.5 Selecting and Connecting to an Intel® AMT Computer

When Commander connects to an Intel AMT computer, it will immediately acquire most of the state information from Intel AMT. For the first few seconds, Commander will fill up the tree view with information as it arrives. By acquiring most of the state when first connecting, the user interface is much faster, but may contain stale information. The "Clear Web Service Cache" and "Fetch Web Service Cache" options on the File menu can be used to force Commander to reload its state cache, but using these is rarely needed. Many management consoles can connect to Intel AMT at any given time and the changes made by one management console may not be reflected in the other consoles unless the cache is cleared.

If there is any problem connecting to the Intel AMT computer, remove the computer and add it again, double-checking the hostname, username, and password. Also make sure that the Intel AMT Web page is accessible and Intel AMT setup as been completed as described in Appendix A.

Now that we have connected Manageability Commander to Intel AMT, we can start management operations. Feel free to open and browse the connected computer and explore the tree view on the left side of the screen.

Remote Display

Now it's time to remotely manage the computer using the Serial-over-LAN feature of Intel AMT. Select the computer on the left side and go to the Remote Control tab as shown in Figure 13.6.

Figure 13.6 Manageability Commander Redirection and Control Screen

Here, we can make sure that the Serial-over-LAN, IDE-Redirect, and redirection ports are all enabled. The redirection port is 16994 without TLS and 16995 with TLS security. If the redirection port is disabled, management consoles can't use the Serial-over-LAN or IDE-Redirect features. Now we click Take Control to open the terminal window.

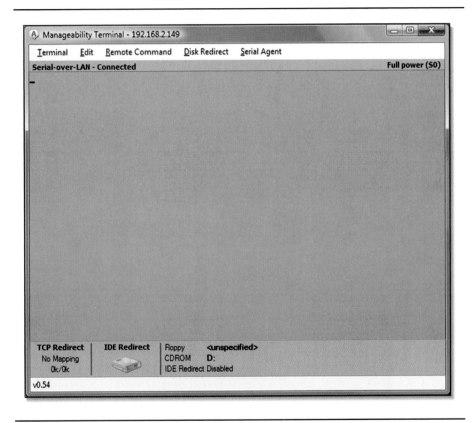

Figure 13.7 Manageability Commander VT100 Terminal Window

Figure 13.7 shows the VT100 terminal window. This terminal is just like the terminals used years ago with modems. It has a fixed number of 25 text lines and an 80-character width. This terminal view was built from the ground up for use with Intel AMT. On the top status bar, we see the terminal connection state of the upper left and the computer's power state on the upper right. The power state is polled every few seconds, but this polling can be turned off by clicking on the power state indicator. The bottom status bar is mostly dedicated to displaying IDE-Redirect state. To use IDE-Redirect, select the Disk Direct menu at the top of the terminal.

From this screen, we can use the Remote Control menu to perform remote power control on the Intel AMT computer. Let's select Remote Reboot to BIOS setup in the remote control menu.

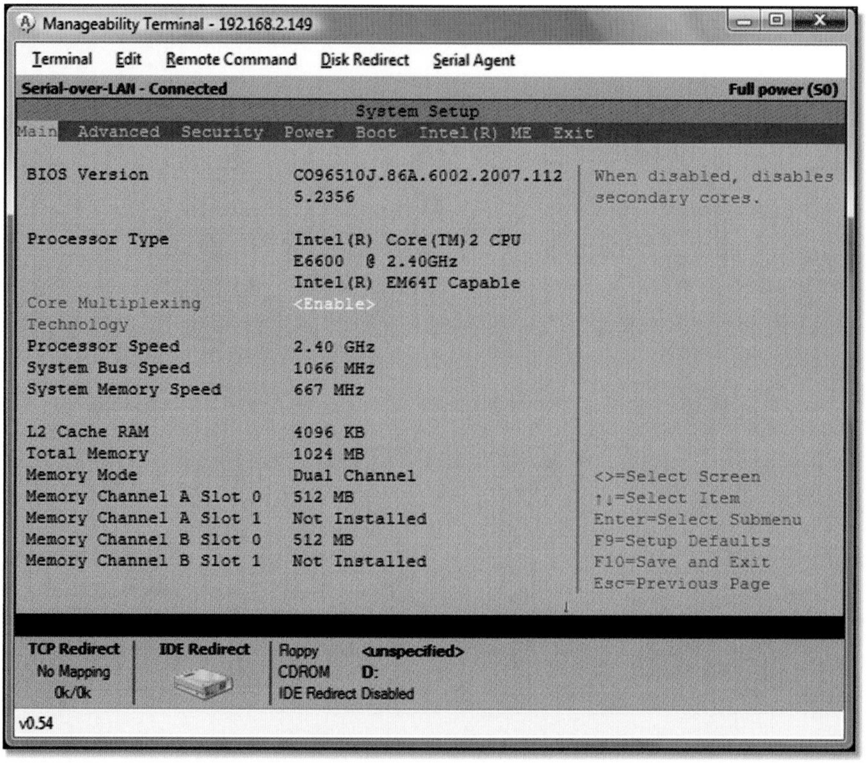

Figure 13.8 Remote BIOS Management Using Manageability Commander

The managed computer will abruptly reboot and after a few seconds, the computer's BIOS screen will show up on the terminal window as shown in Figure 13.8. At this point, the administrator can remotely navigate the BIOS screens and change the necessary settings. The F1 to F12 keys have different values depending on the BIOS, if the function keys don't work correctly, try going into the Terminal menu and select a different key translation from the Special Key Translation sub-menu. There are three possible translations and one of them will usually work.

The remote control menu allows easy access to most of the commonly used remote control operations, but the Custom Command option at the bottom of the remote control menu allows for all possible remote operations a computer can support. For example, on some computers, it's possible to enter the BIOS and lock the local user's keyboard.

Now, let's perform a normal reboot and have the managed computer boot into Microsoft Windows. Since the computer is now in graphics mode, the terminal will be blank and remote management operations are normally not possible using Serial-over-LAN when the operation system is running, but there is a way around this problem.

On the Intel AMT computer, install and run Manageability Outpost. This is an agent tool that usually runs as a background service, but can also run as an application. Once Outpost is running, select the Serial Agent tab and make sure the checkbox is enabled as shown in Figure 13.9.

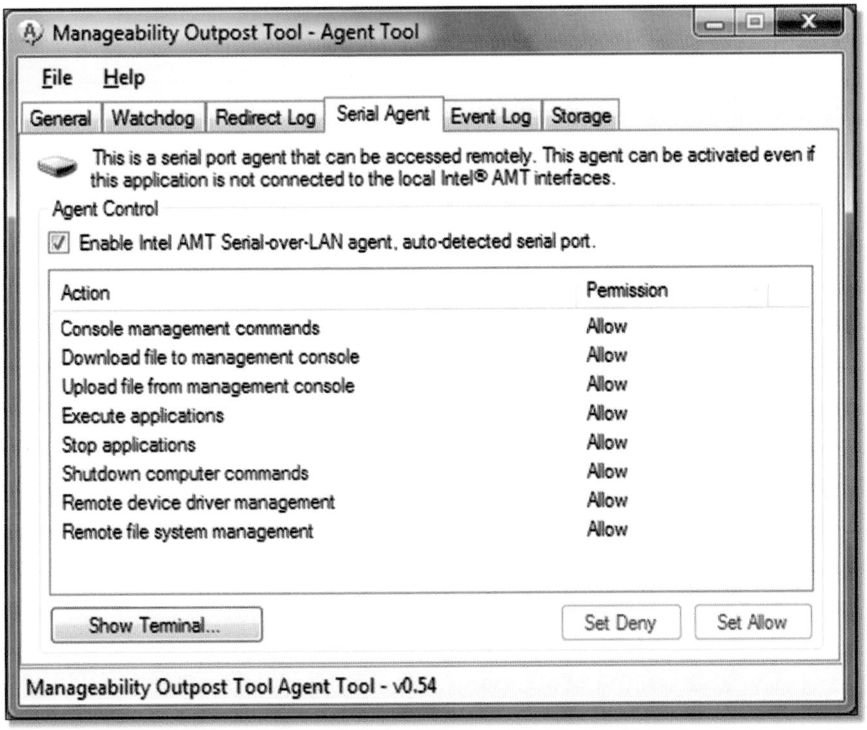

Figure 13.9 Manageability Outpost Serial Agent Is Enabled

When enabled, Outpost automatically finds the Intel AMT serial port and offers a remote management command prompt. The privacy controls in Figure 13.9 allow the local user to block some remote management operations.

As soon as Outpost is started, it will display a welcome screen to the remote administrator as shown in Figure 13.10. If the remote terminal is connected after Outpost runs, the administrator can cause the welcome screen to reappear at any time using the reverse apostrophe key (`). It's the key located above the TAB and left of the 1 key on US-English keyboards.

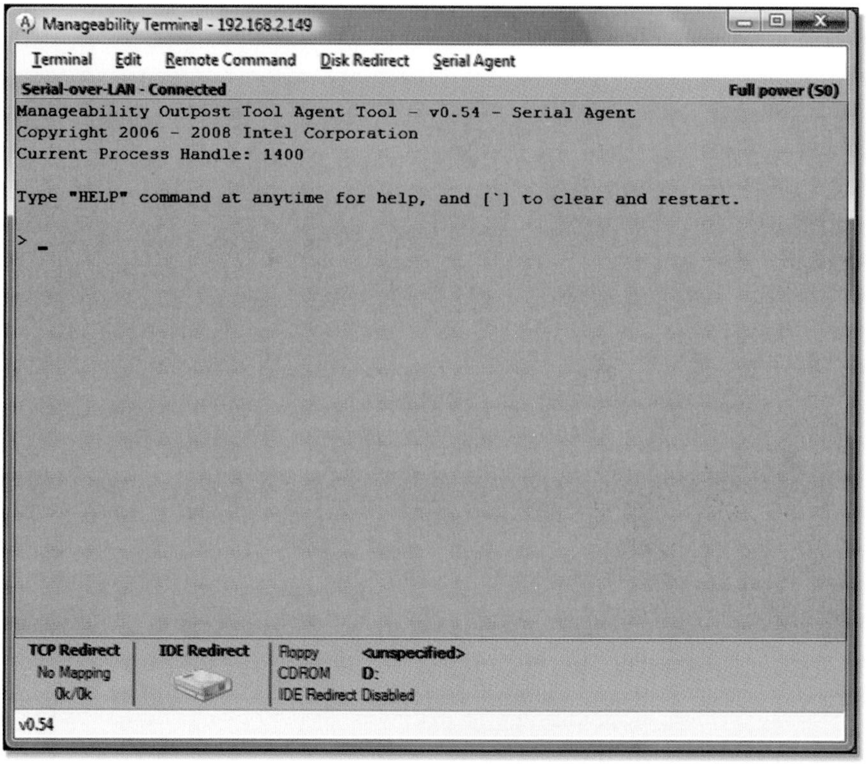

Figure 13.10 Manageability Outpost Command Prompt on the Administrator's Terminal

At this point, the administrator can type the `help` command and start remotely managing the computer. Commander and Outpost are also built to talk to each other in a special way. When both Commander and Outpost are running, all the options in the Serial Agent menu above the terminal become active. Instead of enumerating, starting, and stopping processes using the command prompt, the Serial Agent menu includes a Process Monitor window that is much easier to use.

Now that we can remotely manage a computer using Commander and Outpost, we go on to the managed computer and disable all of the network drivers. Open a command prompt on the managed computer and type `ipconfig` to confirm that the Intel AMT computer has no IP address. Then, notice that Commander and Outpost still work. This is because Intel AMT has its own connectivity via an embedded network stack, separate from the operating system.

It's also possible to redirect TCP connections over Serial-over-LAN using the TCP Port Redirector in the Serial Agent menu. One good usage of this feature is to perform a VNC connection to a computer that has no working network stack. For instructions on how to do this, consult the tutorial video and user guide on the Manageability Developer Tool Kit Web site[1].

Intel® System Defense

Starting with Intel AMT 2.0, the administrator can manage a set of hardware network filters on each Intel AMT computer; this feature is called Intel® System Defense. Commander allows the administrator to add, remove, view, and activate network policies and filters. First, let's run the Manageability Net Status tool on the Intel AMT computer. This is a normal PING tool, no different from the PING command, but was built to be more user- and camera-friendly for onstage demonstrations.

In Figure 13.11, we elected to ping our own local router and the progress bars are moving to the right as traffic is being sent and received correctly. We will now attempt to use Commander to add a hardware filter to block this stream of packets. In Figure 13.12, we select the Policies folder and click Create New Policy.

---

1   http://www.intel.com/software/amt-dtk

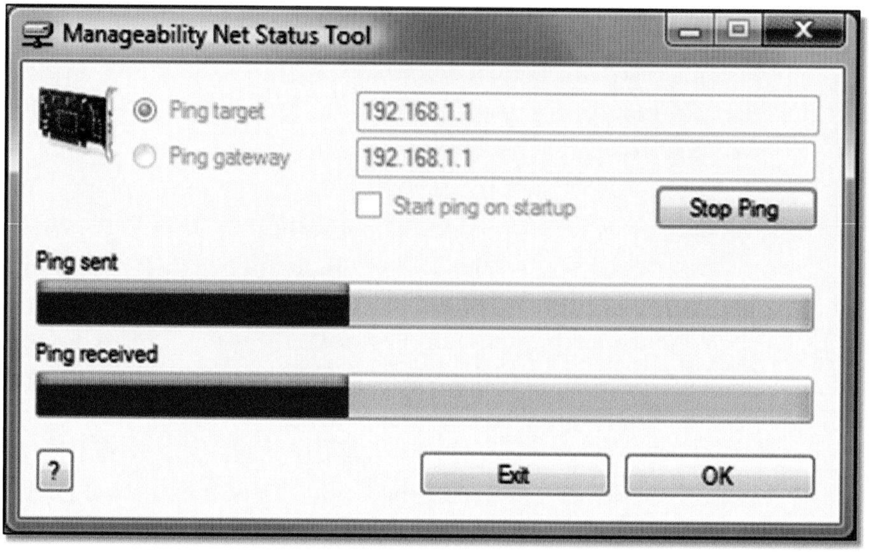

Figure 13.11 Manageability Net Status Tool Sending and Receiving Ping Packets

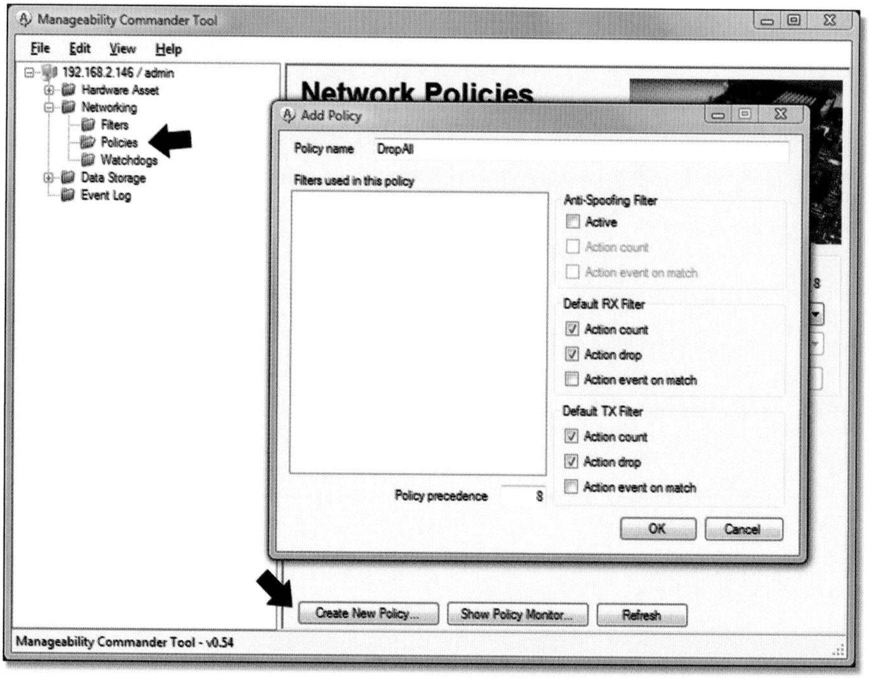

Figure 13.12 Adding a Network Policy with Commander

With Intel AMT, the administrator can create network filters and none, one, or many filters can be part of a network policy. Only one network policy can be active at any give time. In this first example, we create a policy with no filters. Packets are compared against all filters in the policy and if none of them match, the default action is performed. In our case, we will simply select drop and count defaults for both transmit and receive, we will call this policy "DropAll". Press OK to add this new policy to Intel AMT. At this point, the newly created policy is present in Intel AMT but not active.

To activate a network policy, select it in the tree view and press the activation button on the lower right of the screen, as shown in Figure 13.13. The preferred way to enable and disable a policy is to right-click the policy in the tree view and select it to enable or disable it. Once the policy is enabled, all traffic to and from the operating system will be dropped. The Net Status tool we started earlier will show that PING traffic is no longer getting a response. Right-clicking the policy and disabling it will cause the traffic to resume normally.

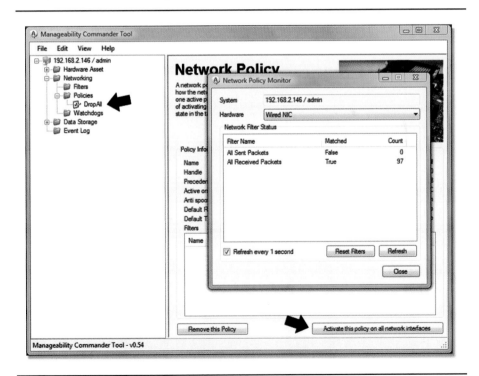

Figure 13.13 Activating a Network Policy and Viewing the Results

In Commander, we can also right-click a policy and select "Show Policy Monitor…" to display a window that will poll the Intel AMT network policy state and hardware counters. We can use this to see how much traffic is being dropped.

Once we understand how network policies work, we can add network filters to our policies. Select the Filters folder in Commander and click Create New Filter. In Figure 13.14, we have an example of a filter that will only count and drop inbound PING traffic.

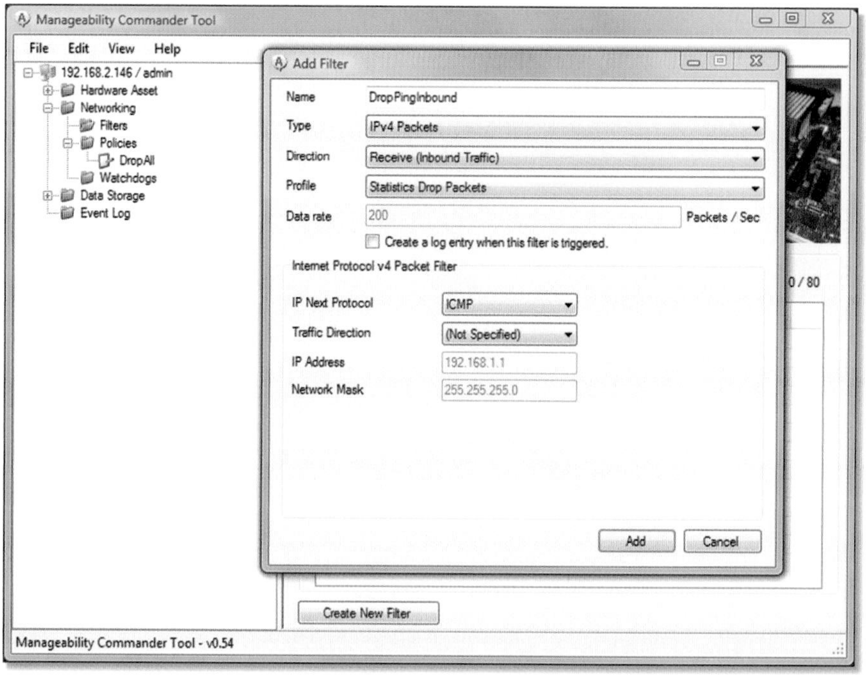

Figure 13.14 Adding a Filter to Block Only Inbound PING Traffic

Once we have created this filter, we can create a new policy that includes this new filter. Figure 13.15 shows how to do this. In this new policy, we will also select to count packets that don't match any filter as our default action. This allows us to see more counters in the policy monitor window.

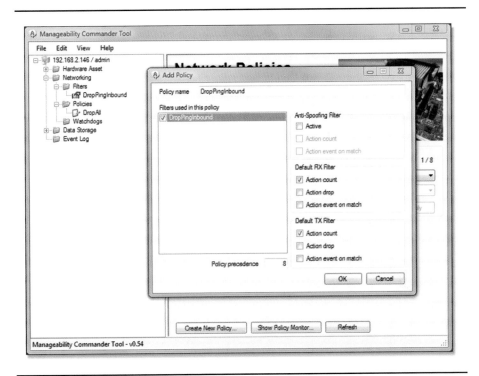

Figure 13.15 A Policy That Drops Only Inbound PING Packets

Summary

In this chapter we got hands-on experience with Intel AMT for the first time covering two of the main features of Intel AMT: Serial-over-LAN and Intel System Defense. The Manageability Developer Tool Kit (DTK) is a good starting point for people experimenting with Intel AMT for the first time or wanting to check the state of Intel AMT in the field. Users are encouraged to play around with Commander and Outpost. An extended user's guide and many tutorial videos are available on the Manageability Developer Tool Kit Web site, the same site where these tools can be downloaded.

Chapter 14

Securing Intel® Active Management Technology from Attacks

After an access cover has been secured by 16 hold-down screws, it will be discovered that the gasket has been omitted.

—De la Lastra's Corollary

The Internet is full of malware and malicious people. Any new technology is under constant threat to be attacked by adversaries for fun, fame, and profit. As a target, Intel® Active Management Technology (Intel AMT) is no different. The attackers could operate remotely and communicate with Intel AMT over the wired or wireless network interfaces. Alternatively the attacker could also operate locally by physically operating the Intel AMT computer, or by placing some malicious program in the computer's operating system that operates on behalf of the attacker. This chapter explains the details of the security protections designed into Intel AMT. These protections ensure that Intel AMT is well guarded from attacks by malicious entities (people or programs) operating remotely or locally.

However, providing robust security in any system often comes at a cost. This cost is usually in terms of reduced convenience and ease of use in using the system. This chapter also describes the tradeoffs between security and ease of use of the Intel AMT computer. It describes the various choices available to an IT architect in configuring Intel AMT such that it best suits the deployment environment, both from ease of use and security perspectives.

Threats to an Intel® AMT Computer

The previous chapters covered the unique and powerful set of security and remote management capabilities offered to the IT manager by Intel AMT. However, just like most other powerful capabilities in any system, the bad guys can and will attempt to misuse Intel AMT to attack the computer. The extent of damage caused depends on the nature of the attack. For example, it could be something relatively less severe such as causing nuisance to the end user of the computer, or something more serious such as disabling some of the security protections offered by Intel AMT.

Before going over the security protections designed into Intel AMT to defend and protect against the bad guys, it is useful to understand the threats the bad guys pose to a computer equipped with Intel AMT. Several of these attacks also apply to all computers in general.

Local Attacks

Attacks can be remote or local. A local attack to a computer means that the attacker has physical access to the computer having control of its keyboard, mouse, network connection, USB and serial ports, power button, and so on. Such an attack could take place when the user has left a computer unattended (such as when gone for lunch, or during nights if the computer is a desktop computer that the user cannot carry home at night). Of course, such an attack is one of the most powerful forms of attack, but requires the attacker to bypass many other hurdles such as the building security system, or security guards, video surveillance, and so on. A more likely scenario is that the attacker is a rogue insider. Several assumptions can be made regarding the motivations of the attacker, and the constraints under which the attacker is operating, as follows.

The attacker may simply steal the computer and walk away with it, assuming it's a laptop or a small form-factor desktop model, and not bound to the wall by a steel cable. Or he may just open the computer chassis and steal the hard disk. This assumes that the attacker is after the currently stored data on the disk, and does not worry about the discovery of the attack, since in such cases the attack will be detected pretty soon. The attacker may adopt a stealthier approach such as copying some important files from the computer's disk onto his USB flash drive. This requires the attacker to bypass the computer's login or unlock mechanisms such as BIOS password, hard-disk password, operating system or unlock password, thereby making the attack difficult.

The attacker may also be interested in installing backdoors on the computer allowing him to have subsequent access to the computer remotely. The attacker can do so by accessing the computer's disk and placing some malicious programs on the disk. This also requires the attacker to bypass the computer's login or unlock mechanisms. It also requires the malicious program to be of a nature that this undetectable by the anti-virus and anti-spyware tools installed on the computer, thereby further increasing the difficulty of the attack.

An even more invasive and hard-hitting form of local attack is possible when the attacker opens the chassis of the computer and does something really bad to the computer's hardware. Examples include installing a wireless transmitter for keystrokes, replacing the existing BIOS with a malicious version of the BIOS, replacing the firmware of Intel AMT with a malicious or modified version of the firmware, or using a hardware flash reader (available at Radio Shack for a few hundred dollars) to read sensitive data off the Intel AMT flash device. Of course, the assumption is that the attacker has access to the required tools and the time needed (with no one watching or walking by) to mount such an attack. These attacks are therefore much harder and complex, but still possible, and need to be defended against.

Several of these attack scenarios apply to Intel AMT, and the defense and protection mechanisms Intel AMT provides to protect against these attacks is the subject of this chapter. Some of the attack scenarios do not apply to Intel AMT. For example, if an attacker simply walks away with the hard disk of the computer, Intel AMT cannot prevent the data falling into the attacker's hands.

Remote Attacks

Remote attacks far outnumber local attacks because of their very nature of being mounted remotely and not requiring the attacker to be physically vulnerable at the time of conducting the attack. Remote attacks are more complex to mount due to the reduced attack surface relative to local attacks, since the remote attacks have to be mounted over the wired or wireless network connections. Following are some remote attacks that an attacker may try to mount against Intel AMT computers. Subsequently we will see how the protections designed into Intel AMT prevent these attacks.

Man in the Middle

The attacker may try to snoop the communication flowing over the network between Intel AMT and the management console. Some types of transactions between Intel AMT the management console involve some sensitive information such as security settings. Snooping can allow the attacker to have knowledge of such information. Using more complex mechanisms, the attacker may also try to intercept the communication and modify the information as it flows over the network. Such an attack can cause Intel AMT to act upon commands that were not sent by the management console but instead were sent by the attacker.

Injecting Malicious Host Software

The attacker may try to load and execute some malicious code in the host operating system. An attacker can try to inject code into the operating system space remotely in several ways. Sending malicious code via email, browser activity, and exploiting an unpatched vulnerability in the kernel are just a few examples. Once the attacker has successfully loaded his code and the code begins execution, then the code can communicate with Intel AMT in that computer using the local communication mechanisms—Intel Management Engine Interface (Intel MEI) or LMS, explained in earlier chapters—and try to attack or compromise the Intel AMT code executing in the memory of the computer, or try to attack the nonvolatile memory that stores the Intel AMT code.

Impersonation and Privilege Elevation

The attacker may try to impersonate the legitimate system administrator of Intel AMT to carry out operations within Intel AMT that would normally be allowed only by the system administrator. Password guessing, online or offline dictionary attacks, and password cracking are some ways to do this. Replaying old transactions (such as sending old network packets captured off the network) may also result in impersonation.

Typical usage of Intel AMT requires multiple system administrators to have access to various command sets in Intel AMT. For example, a security system administrator may have access to the commands that control the System Defense settings, whereas a system discovery administrator may have access to the commands for hardware asset discovery. A system discovery administrator may try to elevate his privileges to execute System Defense related commands with the malicious intention of disabling the System Defense capability of the computer.

Runtime Attacks by Exploiting Vulnerabilities

The attacker may try to exploit runtime vulnerabilities in the code of Intel AMT. Such known vulnerabilities may exist in unpatched code on computers. For example, there may be a specific vulnerability in the code of Intel AMT that can be exploited by sending a malformed network packet. Some of the common classes of attacks that exploit vulnerabilities in all types of software and firmware are buffer overflow attacks, stack attacks, and code injection. See http://en.wikipedia.org/wiki/Category:Security_exploits for details on various types of exploits.

Denial of Service

If the security protections are strong, the attacker may not be able to steal confidential information, or actively damage the computer by sending unauthorized commands. Still, an attacker may be able to do just enough so as to cause of a Denial of Service, the service in this case being Intel AMT. Examples are where an attacker can send a malformed command to Intel AMT causing it to crash. Or an attacker may alter the network settings in the routers so that Intel AMT becomes unreachable by the management consoles. Such attacks also have the capacity to cause indirect damage to the user. For example, if an Intel AMT computer cannot be contacted by the management console to perform a critical virus patch update, then the computer is at risk if the particular virus in question is at large.

Rogue Insider

Rogue insider attacks are less common than any of the aforementioned attacks, but if they occur, the consequences are catastrophic. A rogue insider is a corrupt trusted person having legitimate access rights to the system. The unique problem in this scenario is that any security measures designed into the system are ineffective by definition. There are several motivations for a trusted insider to become corrupt. Disgruntled or revengeful employees, bribed employees, or underpaid employees trying to make an extra buck by selling company secrets, and ideologically motivated employees all fall under this category. An irony of such an attack is that a trusted system administrator can easily mount the attack and also escape undetected by covering his trails. Some published case studies have revealed that rogue insiders have only been caught after a long time since they became corrupt. Often the reason for their capture has been because the corrupt employee became lazy and careless after some time, and committed some stupid mistakes that alerted others.

The following sections of this chapter and the next chapter describe the specific protections designed into Intel AMT to prevent the classes of attack described above.

Intel® AMT Process and Memory Isolation

The firmware of Intel AMT executes on the Intel Management Engine (Intel ME) in the chipset. The Intel ME, as discussed in Chapter 7, is a separate processing engine from the main CPU that executes the operating system such as Windows or Linux. Therefore, the processes running on the Intel ME are completely isolated from the main CPU and there is no direct path of process communication between the main CPU and Intel ME processes (except the Intel Management Engine Interface or Intel MEI as described in Chapter 7). The Intel MEI is very limited and provides a very specific communication channel between software in the main OS and Intel ME firmware processes such as Intel AMT.

The memory that the Intel ME firmware uses is also isolated by the chipset hardware from access by the main CPU. The chipset isolates the Intel ME memory using the UMA (Unified Memory Architecture) mechanism.

Attempts by any piece of software in the main OS to directly access the Intel ME memory is blocked by the chipset hardware.

Process and memory isolation for firmware executing in the Intel ME provides the bulk of security protection to Intel AMT from malicious software residing in the main OS. This allows the critical functionality in Intel AMT to execute unhindered, regardless of the presence of malware in the main OS space.

Intel® AMT Nonvolatile Storage Isolation

The nonvolatile storage of Intel AMT is the place where the code and data for Intel AMT is stored. In the currently shipping generations, this is a piece of NOR flash, controlled by an SPI flash controller located in the I/O Controller Hub or ICH, also known as the Southbridge. The same nonvolatile storage also stores the BIOS code and other pieces of data, such as the data used by the Gigabit Ethernet controller (GbE). Therefore, several pieces of hardware on the platform have some form of access to this nonvolatile storage. It is required that the Intel AMT code and data is not accessible by the BIOS or the GbE.

To facilitate this protection, the Intel AMT flash device is partitioned into multiple logical regions such as BIOS, Intel ME, GbE, and the Flash Descriptor, as shown in Figure 14.1. The ICH hardware defines owners for each of these regions, and defines an identifier for each owner. The owners in this case are pieces of hardware located on the platform having some sort of access to the nonvolatile storage, such as the Host CPU, Intel ME, and GbE. The ICH hardware uses the Flash Descriptor to support read/write access per owner for each region defined. At platform power on, the ICH hardware reads the Flash Descriptor data structures (located at offset 0 of the nonvolatile flash), and enforces the access control. So those region boundaries cannot be moved, nor can an unauthorized owner read/write to various regions of the flash. For example, the Intel ME cannot read/write into the BIOS region and vice versa (if the Flash Descriptor is set that way). The Flash Descriptor is itself read/write protected from all other region masters. This is the standard operating mode providing the required security for various regions of the nonvolatile flash storage device.

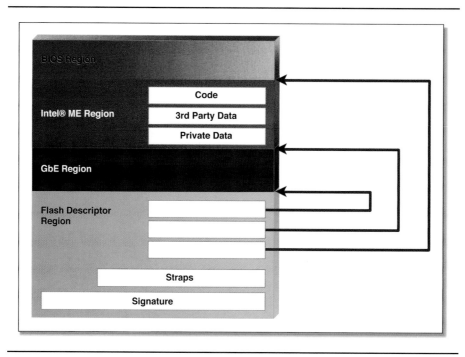

Figure 14.1 Intel® ME SPI Flash Partitions

The main purpose of the Flash Descriptor is to describe the various regions the flash device is divided into, and the different owners that can access the various regions and their read/write security permissions. Each master has direct read access only to its region. However, write access has to be explicitly granted, and is available via a hardware interface.

There is a pin (called Security Override Strap pin) in the ICH, which if set allows read/write access to the entire flash device by anyone. This is primarily provided for initial manufacturing and testing, and later on for facilitating programming or reprogramming the flash in case of service returns scenarios where, for example, the flash got corrupted for some reason. Therefore, if a malicious entity were to gain physical access to the platform, he could open the chassis of the computer and set the Override Strap, and cause a platform reset. He would then be able to gain read/write access on the complete flash part. The malicious entity could then modify the Flash Descriptor to grant itself read/write access to sensitive portions of the flash (such as the BIOS boot block), and subsequently access those sensitive portions on the flash, thereby compromising the security of the system.

However, even by mounting a physically invasive attack such as opening the computer chassis and setting the security override strap pin as mentioned above, an attacker cannot compromise the security of Intel AMT. The attacker can load a maliciously modified copy of the Intel AMT firmware on the flash device, but this copy of the firmware will not execute because the firmware signature is invalidated. The attacker cannot read sensitive information from the flash device either because all the sensitive information is secured using the blob service protection. These protection mechanisms are explained in the following sections.

Firmware Security

One of the major concerns in using software that is generally available, such as that which is available over the Internet, is the uncertainty regarding the trustworthiness of a piece of code published in this manner. There are two issues that must be addressed to make users trust the software:

- *Ensuring authenticity,* that is, assuring users that they know where the code came from

- *Ensuring integrity,* that is, verifying that the code wasn't tampered with since its publication or in transit

The use of digital signatures on the code assures recipients that the code does indeed came from the specified source.

Digital signatures are created using a public-key signature algorithm such as the RSA public-key cipher. In practice however, public-key algorithms are often too inefficient for signing long pieces of data (which is code in this case). To save time, digital signature protocols use a cryptographic digest, which is a one-way hash of the code. The hash is signed instead of the code itself. Both the hashing and digital signature algorithms are agreed upon beforehand.

Here is a summary of the process:

1. A one-way cryptographic hash of the code is produced using a standard hashing algorithm such as SHA-1 or SHA-256.

2. The hash is encrypted with the private key of the signer. The encrypted hash is the digital signature of the signer on the code.

3. The code and the digital signature (encrypted hash) are transmitted to the recipient.

4. The recipient produces a one-way hash of the code using the same cryptographic hashing algorithm.

5. Using the digital signature algorithm, the recipient decrypts the signed hash with the signer's public key.

6. If the signed hash matches the hash computed by the recipient, the signature is valid and the code is intact.

When software (code) is associated with a publisher's unique signature, distributing software over insecure media (such as the Internet) is no longer an unsafe or anonymous activity. Digital signatures ensure trust (authenticity of origin and integrity) on the code.

A good discussion on code signing is available at [9].

Intel® AMT Firmware Signing Process

Intel signs the firmware code for Intel AMT using the principles of digital code signing technology as explained above. This ensures that the only code that is executed by the Intel ME is the one that is produced and digitally signed by Intel. To provide end-to-end integrity and data origin authentication for firmware images and manifests, the Code Signing System located at Intel's secure facilities generates and stores a set of asymmetric Firmware Signing Keys (FWSK). These keys are used to generate digital signatures for manifests, as shown in Figure 14.2. The public key corresponding to the private key used to generate the manifest digital signature is placed in the manifest. Manifest digital signatures are generated using the RSA algorithm with modulus lengths of 2048 bits.

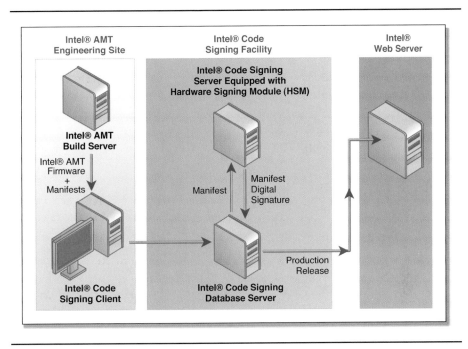

Figure 14.2 Intel Firmware Signing Process

A SHA-1 hash of the public portion of the FWSK key is placed in Intel AMT system ROM. This provides a root-of-trust embedded in the chipset hardware that defeats flash substitution attacks. Therefore, an attacker cannot succeed in running a copy of Intel AMT firmware that is not signed by Intel by copying such a firmware image directly on the flash. To successfully do this, the attacker would also have to modify the public portion of the FWSK key in the ROM, which is not possible.

Asymmetric keys based on the RSA algorithm are used to eliminate the need to create system or platform unique firmware images and manifests. And because only public keys (no secrets) are stored in the Intel AMT hardware, the integrity and data origin authentication protection mechanisms for firmware cannot be compromised by a hardware attack on any single Intel AMT system.

Once a production release of new Intel AMT firmware images and manifests has been placed on its external Web site by Intel, customers such as OEMs, Enterprise IT departments, and other SMB customers can receive these updates either from Intel or from their own OEM Web sites, as shown in Figure 14.3. A Google search for Intel AMT firmware will reveal several links to OEM Web sites to obtain the Intel AMT firmware downloads. Some OEMs bundle the Intel AMT firmware image along with their BIOS images for downloading purposes.

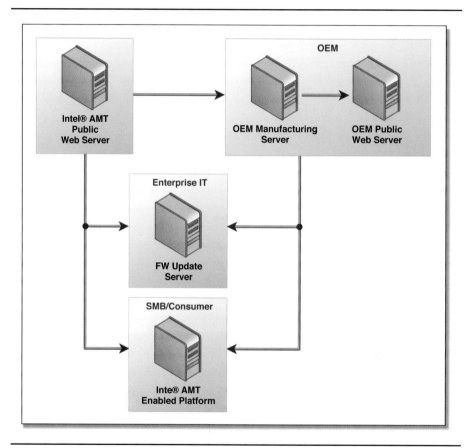

Figure 14.3 Firmware Distribution Flow

Intel® AMT Firmware Update Mechanism

Intel AMT provides a mechanism to update its firmware image. This is a very important aspect to maintain the security of the Intel AMT subsystem. The availability of a robust and secure firmware update mechanism ensures that there is a way to apply patches to the Intel AMT firmware. The patches could be for bug-fixes related to security, reliability, or the patches could contain new functionality that enhances the security of the Intel AMT subsystem. This section describes the mechanism by which Intel AMT firmware gets updated in a reliable and secure manner.

The firmware update can be done via the local interface or network interface. The local interface allows an application running in the main OS to communicate with Intel AMT and update its firmware image. Similarly a remote application can also communicate with Intel AMT and update its firmware image over the network interface. An ISV could also design a mechanism to remotely update Intel AMT's firmware remotely over the local interface by using a local agent in the main OS.

One of the problems that can occur during the firmware update process is that power to the computer can be lost (as in the case of a faulty power supply or interrupted power supply). In such a case we do not want the system to be stuck with a partial image of the firmware, thereby making it totally useless.

To mitigate this problem, the firmware image in Intel AMT nonvolatile flash memory is partitioned into two parts: a code area and a recovery area. The code area stores the main firmware image of Intel AMT, which has the firmware update application in it. The recovery area stores a small firmware application—the recovery application. These two areas of flash are never updated concurrently. Only if the update to one area is successful is the other area is updated. This ensures that there is always a working copy of a firmware update application or recovery application. The recovery application can be restarted in the event of a power failure to recover the firmware image, resulting in power-loss tolerance. All firmware needed for receiving the image and validating its integrity so as to enable standalone operation of the local recovery process is partitioned into the recovery area. The extra space in UMA is used to upload the new image, which is validated completely before being saved to flash memory. In the event of power failure or other problems, recovery code boots the next time allowing local, but not remote, recovery to take place.

The Firmware Update application in an Intel AMT subsystem operates as a service. The service listens for an incoming message originating from internal host or network client telling Intel AMT to begin an immediate firmware update across the interface specified in the message. Dual functionality of this kind ensures that Intel AMT systems can obtain the latest firmware update on their own. Alternately, when necessary, an administrator can target a specific Intel AMT system for immediate update. The Firmware Update application preserves current firmware image settings, such as OEM-provisioned data, user configured settings and date, and policy settings, enabling roll-back to a previous firmware version. Whenever firmware is written to the Intel AMT flash device, all other Intel AMT system applications are shut down and brought to a halt. Intel AMT firmware can be updated through network interfaces when the platform is connected locally in the Enterprise in S0 and S*x* states. Update can also occur in S0 through the internal host interface where both the host OS and the Intel AMT systems are operational.

Intel® AMT BIOS Security

Intel AMT has its own BIOS component that is integrated with the system BIOS. The Intel AMT BIOS component is a part of the overall Intel ME BIOS component, which is called Intel ME BIOS Extension (Intel MEBX), as explained in Chapter 7. The Intel AMT BIOS component offers several BIOS level interfaces to configure certain Intel AMT settings from the BIOS. Access to the Intel AMT BIOS screen is allowed only after providing the Intel AMT admin password. Intel AMT requires that one input the Intel AMT administrator password before proceeding to the Intel AMT BIOS screen. Figure 14.4 shows the Intel AMT BIOS password request screen. Once the correct password is provided, the MEBx proceeds to Intel AMT BIOS configuration screens.

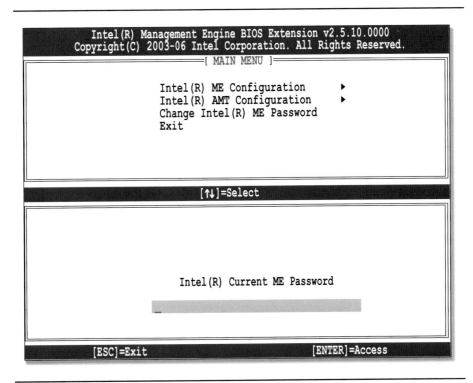

Figure 14.4 Intel® AMT BIOS Password Request Screenshot

After the Intel AMT admin password authentication is successful, the Intel AMT firmware allows the Intel MEBX to call into it via the Intel ME Interface (Intel MEI). For the Intel MEBX to communicate with Intel AMT firmware over the Intel MEI, no more security protection is required. This stage of availability of Intel AMT functions is called the pre-boot interface. After the Intel MEBX completes its job, it passes back control to the BIOS. After the BIOS completes its execution, it signals this event to the Intel AMT firmware. At this point, the Intel AMT firmware closes the pre-boot interface and enables the post-boot interface. The post-boot interface of Intel AMT is the one that is available over the Intel MEI to the host operating system, or over the network interface to management consoles. The post-boot interface to the host OS via the LMS route or to the management console requires authentication in the form of either HTTP Digest or Kerberos based HTTP Negotiate (discussed later in this chapter). Also, the Intel AMT firmware could be configured to mandate the use of the TLS protocol between the host operating system or management console and the Intel AMT firmware, for additional protection.

As is evident from this explanation, Intel AMT enforces a higher bar of security requirements for the post-boot interface as compared to the pre-boot interface. The post-boot security requirements must meet a higher bar because the operating system or the network infrastructure has a much wider and more exploited attack surface than the BIOS. Hence, Intel AMT invests a much higher degree of trust in the BIOS than the operating system and the network, or software running in the operating system or on the network (agents, consoles, applications, services, drivers, and so on).

Securing the Communication with Intel® AMT

Intel AMT uses Transport Layer Security (TLS) to secure its communication over the network. This protocol prevents man-in-the-middle class of attacks by providing communication security and privacy between two end-points over the Internet and enterprise intranets. The specific benefits of using TLS are as follows:

- It supports server side and client side authentication
- It is application independent, allowing other protocols like HTTP to be transparently layered on top of it
- It is able to negotiate encryption keys as well as authenticate the server (and optionally the client) before data is exchanged by higher-level applications
- It maintains the security and integrity of the transmission channel by using encryption, authentication and message authentication codes.

The TLS protocol establishes a secure channel of communication between the client and server, and consists of two parts, server authentication and optionally client authentication. Figure 14.5 shows the sequence of transactions in the TLS protocol between the client and server. In the first part, the server sends its certificate and its cipher preferences in response to a client's request. The client then generates a master key, which it encrypts with the server's public key and transmits the encrypted master key to the server. The server recovers the master key and authenticates itself to the client by returning a message authenticated with the master key.

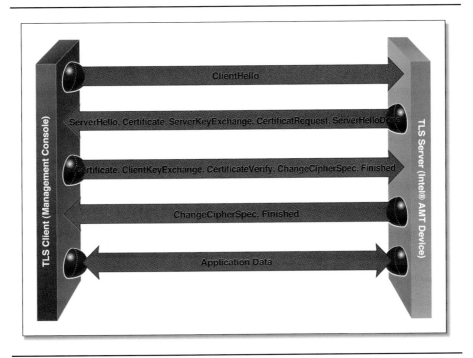

Figure 14.5 TLS Protocol Handshakes

In the optional second part, the server sends a challenge to the client. The client authenticates itself to the server by returning the client's digital signature on the challenge, as well as its public-key certificate. A variety of cryptographic algorithms are supported by TLS. Subsequently, the client and server use keys derived from the master key to encrypt and authenticate the exchange of data between themselves. This was a very short description of the TLS protocol. We did not want to spend a lot of time explaining the TLS protocol in this book. The TLS protocol specification can be found in [10] and [11]. An easier description can be found in any network security book. My favorite network security book is [1].

Intel AMT works in the TLS server mode, while applications on other devices, host or management consoles, work in the TLS client mode, and initiate communications to applications on the Intel AMT system. Intel AMT supports both the mandatory first phase of authentication (server authentication) and the optional second phase of client-side authentication.

Further authentication of the IT administrator operating the Management Console (which in turn is the TLS client) is achieved using the HTTP Digest or Kerberos authentication protocols. These protocols are described later in this chapter.

To support these applications, Intel AMT supports a minimum number of simultaneous TLS sessions. As of this writing this number was 24, but Intel's engineering team fine-tunes this number with every product generation to balance functionality and performance. TLS in the Intel AMT system contains an RSA certificate or certificate chain and the RSA private key that corresponds to the leaf certificate in the chain. The public key certificate and the private keys are used for TLS server authentication during the TLS handshake.

The cipher suites and associated certificate types and key exchange algorithms supported are listed in Table 14.1.

Table 14.1 TLS Cipher Suites in Intel® AMT

Cipher Suite	Certificate Type and Key Exchange Algorithm
TLS_RSA_WITH_NULL_SHA	RSA, X.509v3
TLS_RSA_WITH_RC4_128_SHA	RSA, X.509v3
TLS_RSA_WITH_AES_128_CBC_SHA	RSA, X.509v3

The TLS implementation uses RSA keys with modulus lengths of up to 2048 bits. The implementation supports a single certificate hierarchy with a minimum depth of two (Root and Leaf) or one (self-signed root certificates). Certificate Revocation List (CRL) is also supported to further validate Host and Intel AMT system certificates.

The TLS_RSA_WITH_AES_128_CBC_SHA cipher suite is preferred and used whenever possible. The TLS_RSA_WITH_RC4_128_SHA is used only where the AES is not available. The TLS_RSA_WITH_NULL_SHA cipher suite will only be used where regulatory requirements do not allow the use of the confidentiality.

Authentication to Intel® AMT

The HTTP protocol provides for three authentication mechanisms: the HTTP Basic authentication, the more secure HTTP Digest authentication, and the most secure HTTP Negotiate authentication (based on Kerberos). The first two mechanisms are password-based and are detailed in RFC 2617. Kerberos is based on a symmetric key system, and is based on RFC 1510. Intel AMT supports only the latter two mechanisms, HTTP Digest and HTTP Negotiate authentication mechanisms. The reason for not supporting HTTP Basic authentication is to eliminate the risks associated with this least secure mechanism of authentication.

Password-based Authentication to Intel® AMT

HTTP Basic Authentication protocol (Intel AMT does not support this) provides for a challenge-response authentication mechanism that may be used by a server to challenge a client, and by a client to provide authentication information back to the server. In this scheme, the client sends its user ID and password to the server, and the server will authorize the client only if it can validate the user ID and password. Otherwise, the server responds with an error code. The user ID and password are sent across the wire, without any encryption, which makes the basic authentication scheme inherently insecure.

The HTTP Digest Authentication scheme is more secure than the HTTP Basic Authentication Scheme, because the password is never sent from the client to the server in the clear. In the Digest Scheme, the server challenges the client with a random value (called a nonce). A valid response contains a cryptographic checksum of the username, the password, the given nonce value, and some other data. In this way, the password is sent over the wire as a hash to prevent interception and reuse. Upon receiving the response, the server computes the checksum (a cryptographic hash) using the same inputs, and compares the computed checksum with the one received from the client. If they match, then the client is authenticated.

Intel AMT uses the HTTP Digest Authentication Scheme for authentication of the client (such as the Management Console), before allowing access to the system. A challenge is sent to the client, and a response containing the digest of the password and other information, must be returned.

The Intel AMT system stores the MD5 hash of the username, password, and the HTTP realm. The HTTP realm incorporates the Intel AMT machine ID, which is unique for every system. This makes the hash value stored on every Intel AMT system unique.

Should an attacker break into the Intel AMT system's flash memory and seizes this hash value, it is of no use in attacking other Intel AMT systems, even if the passwords of those Intel AMT systems happen to be the same. The cryptographic hashing also ensures that the passwords are hard to be reverse engineered by gaining access to the hash value. The steps involved in the HTTP Digest authentication technique are detailed in Figure 14.6.

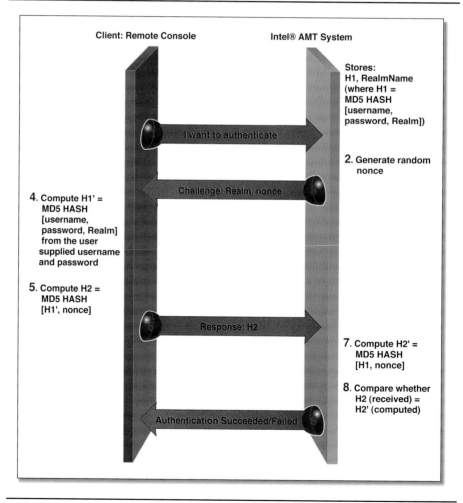

Figure 14.6 HTTP Digest Authentication

Intel AMT requires that HTTP Digest passwords used for authentication to the Intel AMT system meet the following minimum criteria:

■ Must be at least 8 characters long, and up to 32 characters long.

■ Must have at least one digit character (0, 1,…9)

■ Must have at least one special non-alphanumeric character ("!", "$", "%"). Some special characters, such as double quotes, commas, semicolons, and colons are not allowed.

■ Must contain both lowercase and uppercase Latin characters

These restrictions enforced by Intel AMT help to reduce susceptibility of passwords to offline dictionary attacks by attackers.

Kerberos Authentication to Intel® AMT

Kerberos is an authentication service developed by the Project Athena team at MIT. The first general use version was version 4. Version 5, which addressed certain shortfalls in version 4, was released in 1994. Kerberos uses secret-key technology for encryption and authentication. Unlike a public-key authentication system, Kerberos does not produce digital signatures. Instead Kerberos was designed to authenticate requests for network resources.

In a Kerberos system, there is a designated site on each network, called the Kerberos Key Distribution Center (KDC), which performs centralized key management and administrative functions. The KDC maintains a database containing the secret keys of all users and machines/servers, authenticates the identities of users, and distributes session keys to users and servers who wish to authenticate one another. Kerberos requires trust in a third party (the KDC). If the KDC is compromised, the integrity of the whole system is lost. However, Kerberos is generally considered adequate within an administrative domain or enterprise. Just as a contrast, public-key cryptography was designed precisely to avoid the necessity to trust third parties with secrets.

Kerberos also addresses a key shortcoming of the password-based HTTP Digest approach. HTTP Digest requires that each Intel AMT device be configured with at least one username and password pair. In a large enterprise with thousands of systems, it is going to require a good amount of management bandwidth to configure and manage unique username/password pairs for all the systems. This may lead to the usage of weak passwords, or common passwords on the systems. Otherwise the ISVs will be required to develop components that effectively manage passwords, without compromising the security of the enterprise.

The integration of the Kerberos protocol over HTTP for authentication to Web services, with the Windows Domain Controller acting as the KDC, is wrapped under the HTTP Negotiate protocol umbrella. HTTP Negotiate protocol allows the use of the older Windows NTLM protocol for authentication. HTTP Negotiate is essentially a wrapper protocol over Kerberos or NTLM. Intel AMT supports authentication using the Kerberos-based HTTP Negotiate protocol. Integrating the authentication framework of Intel AMT systems on the Kerberos-based HTTP Negotiate protocol provides for a standard and single-sign-on style authentication to Intel AMT. This eliminates the need for ISV applications (including the Intel AMT configuration service) to manage unique and strong username/password pairs for all Intel AMT systems. Authentication to Intel AMT thereby becomes as strong and as secure as authentication to the Windows domain; and administrators wanting to manage Intel AMT systems need only log in to the Windows domain to gain access to Intel AMT devices. Windows infrastructure is the most widely deployed in the industry today, and integration with Microsoft Windows authentication will cater to a vast majority of the IT user base.

Note | Researchers at MIT invented the Kerberos authentication protocol. The Kerberos page on the MIT Web site [2] has plenty of useful information on Kerberos. A good starting point for Kerberos documentation is [3]. My favorite is [4]. Microsoft has also developed very good documentation on Kerberos. The HTTP Negotiate Protocol is especially very nicely explained in the 3-part article [5]. Starting at [6] you can follow a gold mine of information on Microsoft Kerberos. My favorite is [7].

Following are some of the benefits derived from leveraging the Kerberos authentication that is integrated with Active Directory:

- If an IT administrator is logged into the Microsoft Windows domain using his username (that is, domain\username such as, for example usa/john) and password, then he is able to automatically authenticate (behind the scenes; without supplying any other password) to Intel AMT computers.

- An IT administrator is allowed or denied privileges to manage an Intel AMT computer based on his membership to a group in Active Directory. This will ensure that when an IT administrator is no longer supposed to manage one or more Intel AMT systems, his privileges to do so are revoked simply be removing his membership from the group in Active Directory.

- Intel AMT devices are able to ascertain the identity of the administrator attempting to gain access to the Intel AMT system, and be able to apply access control for that user. The notion is that not everyone who is successfully authenticated by Intel AMT is allowed access to all resources within Intel AMT. The authorization that a given user has is governed by an Access Control List (ACL) located within an Intel AMT device.

Let us see how the magic happens. Every Intel AMT subsystem has a unique identity (like every user and server has a unique identity) within the Kerberos domain, and is configured with a few unique Kerberos credentials (as described below) during the initial configuration process. The Intel AMT subsystem is represented as a Kerberized service and supports those portions of the Kerberos protocol that are specified for a Kerberized service. This is because Intel AMT is a service that administrators authenticate to, when they want to perform some Intel AMT actions. Specifically, the Kerberos credentials configured into Intel AMT are as follows. More details of the initial configuration process of Intel AMT are described in Chapter 17.

- Kerberos Service Principal Name (SPN). The SPN uniquely identifies the Intel AMT object's within the Kerberos domain. In Windows Active Directory, the Kerberos domain is the same as the Windows domain. The SPN takes the form HTTP/<fqdn>:<port number>, where the FQDN (Fully Qualified Domain Name) is the FQDN of Intel AMT, and the port number is the port at which Intel AMT Kerberos service runs. The port number is used to differentiate the Intel AMT Kerberos service from any other Web service running on a different port on the host operating system.

- Realm Name. This is the name of the Kerberos domain (also referred to as realm), which is the same as the Windows domain when Intel AMT is deployed with Microsoft Active Directory.

- Encryption Algorithm used by Kerberos. Usually this is RC4-HMAC.

- Kerberos Master Key for an Intel AMT subsystem. This is a unique and secret key that belongs to each Intel AMT subsystem, and is shared between the Intel AMT subsystem and the KDC.

- Clock Tolerance. This is the tolerance (usually set to a few minutes) within which the time must be synchronized between the KDC, Intel AMT and the Management Console.

With these credentials, the Intel AMT subsystem is ready to use Kerberos to authenticate administrators connecting to Intel AMT to perform Intel AMT operations. Figure 14.7 shows the Kerberos protocol at a high level. The Management Console acts as a Kerberos Client, and Intel AMT as a Kerberized Service. The Windows domain controller is the KDC in an Active Directory–based deployment. The steps shown in green in Figure 14.7 are performed by the IT administrator or the console on his behalf. Steps in red along the arrows depict the Kerberos messages that flow on the network as part of the Kerberos protocol. The steps in red towards the right of the KDC and the Intel AMT computer depict the operations performed by the KDC or Intel AMT respectively during the Kerberos authentication process. The conceptual steps that take place behind the scenes are as follows (in reality a lot more goes on, but we will leave it as an exercise for the reader to investigate the gory details).

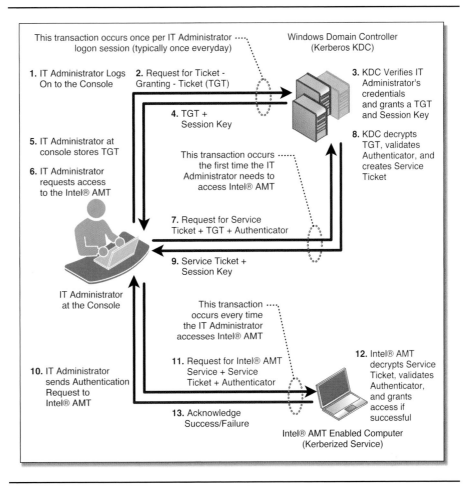

Figure 14.7 Kerberos Authentication Protocol

1. The IT administrator operating the Management Console authenticates to the Windows domain in the normal way. This gives a Ticket Granting Ticket (TGT) to the Management Console.

2. When the IT administrator wants to perform Intel AMT operations on a given Intel AMT computer, the Kerberos agent on the Management Console obtains a Kerberos ticket from the KDC for authenticating to Intel AMT.

3. The Management Console supplies this ticket to Intel AMT. It also supplies a token (called authenticator).

4. Intel AMT validates this ticket (because it is encrypted by the KDC using Intel AMT's master key). Intel AMT validates the authenticator as well (using a session key which is embedded inside the ticket). Intel AMT also validates that the time stamp inside the authenticator is recent (usually within a few minutes in the past). This prevents replay attacks.

5. At this time, Intel AMT has successfully authenticated the IT administrator. The IT administrator can now perform Intel AMT operations that this administrator is permitted to perform.

6. The ticket sent by the IT administrator contains a list of Active Directory groups that the IT administrator is a member of. Intel AMT uses this list to determine the permissions of the IT administrator when Active Directory–based Kerberos is used for authentication.

The next section describes how permissions are enforced on an authenticated IT administrator.

Access Control in Intel® AMT

Intel AMT allows access to its operations to multiple administrators. In other words, more than one IT administrator is allowed to perform operations in Intel AMT. But not all IT administrators have the exact same privileges or permissions. Intel AMT makes it possible to group IT administrators such that one group of administrators has access to one particular group of operations; another group of administrators has access to another group of operations, and so on.

Intel AMT has predefined groups of operations. Each such group of operations is called an Intel AMT Access Control Realm. Each realm has a predefined set of operations assigned to it. Some examples of realms and the operations in those realms are given in Table 14.2. Although this list is not complete, a complete list with detailed documentation can be found in the Intel AMT Software Developer's Kit.

Table 14.2 Intel® AMT Access Control Realms

Intel® AMT Access Control Realm	Sample Operations in the Realm
Security Administration	Configure additional administrators, setting their credentials and permissions, configuring TLS, Kerberos, etc.
Network Administration	Configure TCPIP parameters, host name, domain name, 802.1x parameters, etc.
Hardware Asset Information	Obtain hardware information for the computer
Remote Control	Remotely control the computer by turning it on, off, restart the computer, etc.
ISV Storage	Read and write data into the ISV storage area of Intel AMT
Redirection	Configure the Intel AMT subsystem for an IDE Redirection session
Agent Presence	Register or deregister an agent presence watchdog, send a heartbeat to Intel AMT, etc.
Network Time	Get and set the Intel AMT Protected Real Time Clock
General Information	Various kinds of read operations that most authenticated IT administrators can do such as reading the version number of Intel AMT, reading the time, reading the audit log policies, reading the audit log, read the network settings, read the capabilities available in Intel AMT, read the computer's UUID, etc.
Firmware Update	Perform a firmware update for the Intel AMT firmware
Wireless Configuration	Configure wireless profiles into Intel AMT for access via wireless interface to Intel AMT
Remote Access	Configure the Remote Access parameters such as Management Presence server address, Remote Access policies, etc.
Secure Audit Log	Configure the Audit Log settings such as auditors, audit policies, export audit logs for archival, etc.
Local User notification	Allows an agent in the host operating system to be notified of certain events inside Intel AMT

As of this writing, a maximum of 16 IT administrators is configurable in any given Intel AMT subsystem, 8 based on HTTP Digest authentication, and 8 for Kerberos-based authentication. Each administrator can be assigned to one or more Access Control Realms. There is one special IT administrator who has access to all Access Control Realms. This administrator is the Security Administrator. This administrator can add or remove more administrators to the various Access Control Realms. The complete list of permissions is stored in a structure called an Access Control List (ACL). This structure conceptually looks like the one in Figure 14.8.

HTTP Digest ACL

Username (String Value)	Hashed Password (String Value)	Realm Bitmap (R1 through Rn)								
U1	H(pwd1)	1	1	1	1	1	1	1	1	1
U2	H(pwd2)	0	1	0	0	0	1	1	1	1
U3	H(pwd3)	1	0	1	0	1	0	0	0	1
...	...	...	...	...	...	...	...	...	...	...
U8	H(pwd8)	0	0	1	1	0	1	0	0	1

Kerberos ACL

Group SID (Binary Value)	Realm Bitmap (R1 through Rn)								
SID1	1	0	0	1	1	1	1	0	1
SID2	1	0	1	1	0	0	1	1	0
SID3	0	1	1	0	1	0	0	0	1
...	...	...	...	...	...	...	...	...	...
SID8	1	0	1	1	0	1	0	1	0

Realm Bitmap Decoder: 1 = Access Allowed   0 = Access Denied

Figure 14.8 Intel® AMT ACL Structure

For IT administrators using HTTP Digest, each entry in the HTTP Digest ACL structure (depicted by each row in Figure 14.8) stores the username, hashed password, and the Intel AMT Access Control Realms that this IT administrator has access to. For IT administrators using Kerberos, each entry in the Kerberos ACL structure (depicted by each row in Figure 14.8) stores the Active Directory Group ID and the Intel AMT Access Control Realms that members of this group have access to. Groups (and individual users) in Active Directory are represented by their SID (Security Identifier). The Intel AMT ACL therefore just lists the SID, instead of the readable string name of the group. More details on SID in Active Directory and its use for group authentication are available in [8].

For a deeper insight into access control mechanisms, refer [12]. Role based access control mechanisms (check out [13]) are also relevant to this topic.

Trusted Time in Intel® AMT

Intel AMT uses a Protected Real Time Clock (PRTC) to provide a time value. Some example usages for the need of a trusted time base in Intel AMT are as follows

■ The logging application to log events inside Intel AMT with a time-stamp

■ The Certificate validation process

■ Kerberos ticket validation

■ Execution of time-driven policies, such as checking for updates on a weekly basis

The PRTC is separate from the regular system clock that prevents users or malicious programs running with user permissions from unauthorized modification of the system time. Such improper system time changes could cause inaccurate event log timestamps, missed certification validations, or loss of Kerberos synchronization.

The PRTC is connected to the RTC (Real Time Clock) power well, so the context of the PRTC is maintained throughout all system power states. Initial programming of time on the PRTC is needed only after the installation of a new RTC battery.

Furthermore, it is necessary to prevent attackers from using a rogue time source on the network. Middlemen must be prevented from making any modifications to configuration packets that are in transit along the wire and contain time values.

Intel AMT acquires trusted time from a remote ISV Management Console. Time synchronization commands are initiated by the ISV Management Console, either periodically or as part of the discovery mechanism. For synchronizing the time, the ISV Management Console initiates a mutually authenticated TLS session with the device. Once the TLS session is established, the ISV Management Console uses a WS-Management call to set the time. The ISV Management Console keeps accurate time using the

Network Time Protocol (NTP) by communicating with a NTP server, or by communicating with a Windows Domain Controller (if the Management Console is part of a Windows Domain).

Semantics that are similar to Simple Network Time Protocol/Network Time Protocol (SNTP/NTP – check out [14] and [15]) are used for calculating network latencies, resulting in high-accuracy time updates for more sensitive usage scenarios such as Kerberos. The protocol transactions are represented in Figure 14.9.

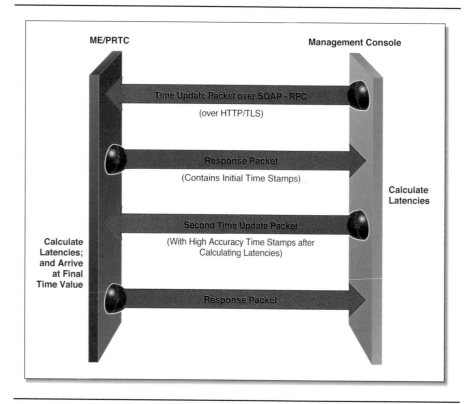

Figure 14.9 Time Sync Model for ME PRTC

If for some reason the time in the PRTC goes out of sync, a network sync of time using the aforementioned protocol is required to reset the time on the PRTC. In the event that network connectivity is not available or the internal firmware for time sync process is not functioning, a BIOS command protected with Intel AMT admin login is available to set the PRTC time locally. The BIOS command is primarily a recovery mechanism. It is a good idea for the ISV Management Console to periodically sync up the time of the PRTC.

Summary

In this chapter we discussed the various protections that Intel AMT offers to ensure that the bad guys are kept out, and the good guys are let in. Table below briefly captures the protection mechanisms. In the next chapter we will go into some of the more advanced security protection mechanisms built into Intel AMT.

Table 14.3 Security Protections in Intel® AMT

Protection Mechanism	Brief Description
Separate processing engine (Intel® ME)	Protects processes in the main Operating System from directly communicating with Intel® AMT
Separate memory for Intel ME	Protects processes in the main operating system from snooping into Intel ME memory
Flash region separation	Protects Intel AMT firmware and data from being snooped or overwritten by malicious entities
Firmware Signing	Prevents execution of arbitrary firmware on the Intel ME. Digital signature check ensures that only Intel-signed firmware executes on the Intel ME
Intel AMT BIOS password	Protects malicious entities from accessing the Intel AMT BIOS screen and changing the Intel AMT configuration settings
Intel AMT Authentication	Ensures that only authenticated entities can communicate with Intel AMT
HTTP Digest Authentication	Password based authentication to Intel AMT. Prevents password to be snooped on the wire. Also prevents BORE attacks, even if the same password is used on multiple Intel AMT systems
HTTP Negotiate (Kerberos) Authentication	Kerberos-based authentication to Intel AMT, integrated with Microsoft Active Directory Group permissions. Provides Single-Sign-On to Intel AMT, thereby making it scalable in the enterprise
TLS for on-the-wire security	Protects the communication between Intel AMT and the ISV management console. Someone snooping on the wire cannot read or modify the Intel AMT commands or responses. Also authenticates the machines on the two sides to each other.
Access Control	Separates the rights of one Intel AMT admin from another.
Secure Time	Protects the time value to be changed by a malicious entity in the main OS. Provides trusted time to other Intel AMT components such as certificate verification component, Kerberos component, etc.

Chapter 15

Advanced Security Mechanisms in Intel® Active Management Technology

Reason and free inquiry are the only effectual agents against error.
—Thomas Jefferson (1743–1826),
Notes on the State of Virginia

In this chapter we cover some of the security protections built into Intel® Active Management Technology (Intel AMT) that were not there in its first version, but were added in the later versions to make it more secure and resilient to attacks. These include some new hardware features as well as firmware features. The new hardware includes features such as a true random number generator, chipset key, and monotonic counters. The new firmware features include secure storage of sensitive data, measured launch of Intel AMT firmware and secure audit logging.

True Random Number Generator

Many cryptographic algorithms and mechanisms make use of random numbers, including several of the Intel AMT mechanisms described previously. The important feature of a random number generator (RNG) is its entropy. Entropy is the measurement of the inability of an external viewer to predict the next number that will be generated by the RNG, even if the viewer knows all the previously-generated random numbers by that generator. Many implementations use a pseudo-RNG (PRNG), a deterministic algorithm that produces the next random number based on the current generator's state. These algorithms maintain a high level of entropy, as long as the initial state (also called "the seed state") of the PRNG is not known [1]. For example, some PRNG implementations seed themselves according to the value of one of the platform clocks. This value is considered to be somewhat unpredictable (due to the high resolution of the clock), and therefore makes a reasonable seed for the PRNG that is suitable for applications requiring a moderate level of security. However, given that a large number of platforms power up at the same time, a time that may be known to within a few minutes or seconds, this could help a potential attacker to narrow down the possibilities and therefore crack the PRNG seed state, thereby predicting the next numbers generated by the PRNG. Conversely, an attacker could learn from the numbers generated by one hacked platform to break other platforms in the enterprise (known as a BORE attack: "Break Once, Run Everywhere").

Intel AMT hardware (beginning with Intel AMT 3.0) contains a true random number generator (TRNG) hardware device, as shown in Figure 15.1. The TRNG is based on two resistors that produce a thermal noise. The noise is amplified and provided as input to a frequency-modulated low-frequency oscillator. Combined with a high-frequency oscillator, a nearly-random bitstream is produced. A voltage regulator controls the above hardware components to avoid any bias based on voltage. In addition, a logic block attempts to correct the bitstream of any bias that may have been inserted (for example, due to the non-perfect duty cycle of the oscillator), by using a standard anti-bias correction algorithm.

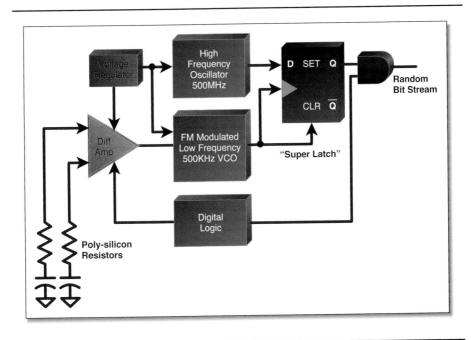

Figure 15.1 True Random Number Generator (TRNG) Hardware in Intel® AMT

One reason why it's not preferable to use this TRNG for Intel AMT usages (such as in TLS) as is, is that its takes relatively longer than a PRNG to generate random bits. In reality, Intel AMT uses a PRNG, whose state is occasionally reset, to initialize to a state generated by the TRNG. This creates a powerful high-quality RNG that is able to keep up with the high usage of random numbers in the Intel AMT subsystem.

Secure Storage of Sensitive Data: The Blob Service

As mentioned in Chapters 7 and 14, the Intel AMT nonvolatile flash memory contains the configuration data for Intel AMT, which stores some of the Intel AMT secrets. The flash controller prevents software applications and drivers running on the host operating system from accessing the flash part. However, an attacker may be able to steal a platform, pull out the flash part, and read its contents by using a flash reader. In this way, an attacker could secure a backdoor to the enterprise network by reading the secrets, or even modifying them before returning the flash part to the compromised system.

The blob service is a firmware mechanism that allows for protection of sensitive data on the flash part. The pieces of information protected by the blob service are called *blobs*. In this context, protection of a blob may take the following forms:

- ■ Encryption, to prevent the attacker from reading the content of the blob.

- ■ Integrity, to prevent the attacker from modifying the content of the blob.

- ■ Anti-replay protection, to prevent the attacker from reading an encrypted/integrity-protected blob (with a value known to the attacker), and later reusing it as-is while overriding a value unknown to the attacker.

Chipset Fuse Key

The Intel AMT hardware (beginning with Intel AMT 3.0) contains a key that is unique to each system, and it is known to the Intel AMT firmware only. This key is called the chipset fuse key. The chipset fuse key is actually a set of 128 fuses in the chipset. Each fuse can be blown or un-blown, corresponding to a 0 or 1 value. The status of each of the fuses (0 or 1) is determined at manufacturing. A random subset of the fuses is blown on the chipset manufacturing line, while the rest remain un-blown. Thus, a random unique value is created for each chipset. The 128-fuse set thus creates a 128-bit key.

Encryption of secrets is achieved by using standard encryption techniques, but the interesting feature is the key that is used for the encryption. The encryption key needs to be stored in some nonvolatile form, but the flash itself is obviously not a good place to store it (otherwise the attacker would first read this key from the flash and then use it to decrypt the rest of the protected data on the flash). Rather, the Intel AMT firmware derives an encryption key from the chipset fuse key, and uses this encryption key to encrypt the sensitive items being placed on the nonvolatile flash. A similar technique is used to generate the integrity key for the integrity part of the blob service. Since Intel AMT firmware is the only entity that has knowledge of the chipset fuse key, and therefore the encryption key and the integrity protection key, even if the attacker pulls out the flash part from the system and tries to read it directly, all he sees is encrypted and/or integrity protected data, depending on the protection put in place for a given data element.

Monotonic Counters

Beginning with Intel AMT 3.0, the Intel AMT hardware contains a few registers that implement simple counters. The counters are incremented by the firmware. Those registers are unique in the sense that they are powered by the platform coin battery (also known as the RTC battery, as it powers the platform real time clock). Therefore, the counters retain their value as long as the battery is functional; this is, typically in the range of a few years.

To implement anti-replay protection, the value of the counter is incremented, then appended to the blob before applying the integrity algorithm. When the blob is read by the firmware, the value of the counter in the blob is compared to the value in the register. If they match, only then is the value considered valid. As long as the counter register is not reset (either by wraparound of the counter or by the replacement of the coin battery), the value of the counter is unique and therefore the anti-replay is achieved.

The algorithm described here requires a separate hardware register for each blob that needs to be anti-replay protected. In fact we can take this method one step further. Only one blob (let us call it "the counter blob") in the system will be protected by one hardware counter only. But the counter blob can contain counter values for other blobs. Whenever an anti-replay protected blob is modified, its private counter is incremented; this means that the counter blob is modified, which requires the incrementing of the hardware counter. Therefore, the counter blob helps us reduce several counters to a single counter, maintained by the hardware and protected by the coin battery.

When the battery is replaced, the anti-replay protected blobs are invalidated. In some cases, this will require the user to reinsert some of the secrets protected by the anti-replay blob service.

Note that we assume that every anti-replay protected blob is also integrity protected. This assumption makes perfect sense—an anti-replay blob contains a unique value that prevents it from being replayed. If the blob is not integrity-protected, the unique value can be modified, and therefore the anti-replay quality is also lost.

Equipped with the aforementioned hardware tools (chipset fuse key and monotonic counter), the Intel AMT firmware offers a blob service to all of the other Intel AMT firmware modules. The blob service provides integrity protection, encryption, and anti-replay protection of data elements for storage on the flash. The firmware modules can decide the protections required depending on the security requirements of the data being protected.

A sample list of data blobs protected by Intel AMT by using the blob service is given in Table 15.1.

Table 15.1 Sample List of Data Blobs Protected by the Blob Service

Intel® AMT Data Structure	Integrity Protected	Encrypted	Anti-Replay Protected
Usernames and hashed passwords	Yes	No	No
Permissions, Access Control Lists	Yes	No	No
Certificates	Yes	No	No
Kerberos keys and attributes	Yes	Yes	No
Private portions of asymmetric key pairs	Yes	Yes	No
Integrated TPM secrets	Yes	Yes	Yes

Measured Launch of Intel® AMT Firmware

Someone not familiar with the concept of measured launch may ask "What's the meaning of measured launch, and why do we need it?" Let us begin by trying to answer this question. As a designer of Intel AMT, I would love to be able to say that Intel AMT is free of bugs—both design and implementation level bugs. But as you know, hardly any code is bug-free. Even some of the most critical systems such as airplane cockpit software or air-traffic control software have been known to have flaws. I remember a joke that went around a while back (probably still is making the rounds): a software engineer would never fly in an airplane if he knew that it was running the code written by him. Therefore, the entire computer industry depends on a perpetual cycle of bug-fixing and issuing updated software (also known as patches) on a regular basis that fixes the known flaws. With this mechanism we at least get rid of being vulnerable to known flaws (and hope that the fixes didn't introduce any new flaws!) But finding new vulnerabilities is not an easy task. Attackers (and researchers; who are the good guys) spend a lot of time understanding software via reverse engineering (and several other methods), and discover new flaws. The most common way software gets compromised is by being attacked by malware that makes use of known vulnerabilities in a system that was not updated with the latest updates. It is therefore a good idea to keep any software that you use updated with the latest updates, especially the security updates.

What's even worse is the inability to be able to know which version of the software is running. Bugs in the design or code make the software vulnerable to being exploited by malware. The first thing the smartest malware tries to do is to hide itself. One of the ways it could do so is by responding to any queries regarding the version number of the software as being the latest version. This could trick the software update mechanism into believing that the latest version of the software is already running, hence there is no need to update it.

One of the best known methods to render such an attack useless is to have a trusted piece of software take a measurement (that is, a cryptographic hash) of the software that is running (or about to be run) and compare the hash with a previously generated copy of the hash (or copy obtained via some trusted means) for a given version of the software. If the hashes do not match then we would know that the software version is not what it claims to be.

Now let us see how Intel AMT uses this concept to offer a measurement of the firmware that is running inside the chipset.

Intel® AMT Firmware Measurement

Software running on the host CPU (such as the BIOS or VMM loader or the host operating system) needs to be able to measure the Intel Management Engine (Intel ME) code before it starts executing. Intel AMT firmware measurement is a feature (available in Intel AMT 5.0 onwards) that provides the capability for the Intel AMT firmware to be measured (actually the entire Intel ME firmware; though referred to as Intel AMT firmware measurement throughout this chapter) into a register in the Intel ME that is directly readable (shadowed by hardware) by host software in the MEI PCI configuration space.

The other features in the chipset that come close to providing a functionality similar to firmware measurement are the signed firmware feature, and the ICH flash protection mechanism.

The signature verification on the signed firmware is done by the Intel ME (using the verification logic in the ROM code), and the measurement done during the signature verification process is not recorded anywhere in the platform for subsequent evaluation. Therefore, the host processor has no role to play in this verification, thereby leaving a host-based VMM loader or the BIOS with no capability to assess the validity of the firmware at any later point in time after platform power on. Therefore, host software cannot implement any policy enforcement to enforce certain system behavior depending on the evaluation of the Intel AMT firmware measurement.

The other problem with using just signed firmware images as an alternative to firmware measurement is that all images (belonging to a particular chipset generation) are valid on that chipset because they are signed by the Intel code signing private key (the corresponding public key hash being embedded in the ROM). Therefore, the existing firmware signature verification mechanism makes no distinction between the various versions of the firmware images that may have been produced by Intel for a given product generation/family.

The Intel AMT firmware measurement mechanism solves these issues by providing a direct mechanism for reading the firmware measurement by host-based software (such as BIOS, VMM loader, operating system, or OS agent), without imposing the burden of the knowledge of firmware address location or offsets in the flash on the host software. The architecture ensures by design that the measurement is always completed, recorded, and locked inside an Intel ME register before the firmware execution begins. Therefore, it is not possible to overwrite this measurement value after Intel AMT firmware execution begins. The overwrite protection is guaranteed by the hardware of the Intel ME. This measurement is also available throughout the time while the Intel ME is powered on. By definition, the measurement will be different for each firmware version, thereby giving the host a mechanism to read and validate the cryptographic measurement of the firmware image. So, even if there is a vulnerability (known or unknown) that somehow exists in the Intel AMT firmware, it is not possible for malware to exploit this vulnerability in a way such that it is able to modify the previously-recorded measurement value. The Intel AMT firmware measurement value is readable by the host software (such as BIOS, VMM loader, operating system, and so on) via the PCI configuration space of the Intel® Management Engine Interface (Intel MEI) device. (The Intel AMT processor is visible to the host OS as an Intel MEI PCI device.)

Security Audit Logs

Intel vPro™ technology creates a powerful tool for the network administrator to control the network entities. However, being in possession of a powerful tool comes with risks: the risk of erroneous use of this tool, and more importantly, the risk of malicious use of this tool. Rogue insiders are becoming a real threat to worldwide governments and enterprises, as demonstrated by a recent San Francisco network lockout [2].

A legitimate insider such as a network administrator already has very powerful credentials to access sources of business critical information in an enterprise. Unfortunately, if such administrators turn against the enterprise, they become rogue insiders, and prevention of malicious use of a privileged system is nearly impossible. However, the risk can still be mitigated by using deterrence mechanisms, and this is primarily where the Intel AMT auditing capability comes into play. This capability is available in Intel AMT 4.0 onwards.

The Intel AMT audit log shown in Figure 15.2 is an internal log that captures the administrator's operations in the system, and also captures unauthorized accesses to the system. When a security breach is discovered, the audit log can assist in tracking down the administrator (or the illegitimate user) that may have caused the breach.

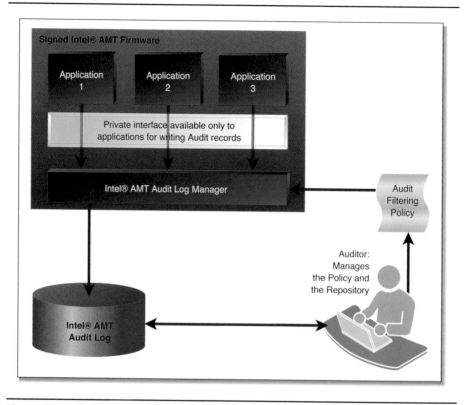

Figure 15.2 Intel® AMT Audit Log

The auditing capability cannot prevent system administrators from misusing the system, but it will prevent them from covering their tracks. The Intel AMT auditing subsystem allows an enterprise or the authorities to follow the steps of an administrator responsible for misusing the system, in a manner that is provable and undeniable. Having such a mechanism in place can deter an administrator from misusing the system in the first place.

The auditing capability also helps to provide a trail of attempts of unauthorized actions by unauthorized people or attackers, if the auditing policies have been so configured. However, this is not the primary use of the auditing subsystem, since it is assumed that the rest of the authentication and authorization mechanisms (as described in Chapter 14) would prohibit illegitimate people or attackers from performing actions within Intel AMT.

Separation of Duties

In an audited system, along with an administrator role, there is an auditor role. The auditor controls the audit log policies and contents. In many cases, an enterprise will outsource their auditing services to an impartial third-party company that provides auditing services. A separation of duties is required to create a true audited system, one that cannot be tampered with by the internal enterprise administrators. Intel AMT provides for the separation of duties by separating the roles of an administrator and auditor.

The separation of duties concept is adhered to in the credential mechanism embedded in the audit log subsystem. While the administrator might usually be omnipotent where the system is concerned, the audit log is outside of his or her realm. The administrator should not have the credentials to clear the log, modify the auditing policies, or modify the auditor's access credentials. The auditor, in turn, should only be given enough privileges to manage the audit log. Conversely, administrative operations in the system are typically out of the auditor's realm. This is the concept of *two person controls*. Thus, in order to compromise a network, and escape undetected, the administrator and auditor would have to collaborate.

The auditor role in Intel AMT is represented by an Access Control Realm called the Auditing Realm. Only the Auditor has access to this realm. Even the security administrator (the most power administrator in the Intel AMT subsystem) does not have access rights to the Auditing Realm. The Auditing Realm has commands that can export and clear the audit log and also to change audit logging policies and priorities. Any authorized administrator in the Intel AMT subsystem is allowed to read the audit log, since reading the log is not as sensitive as clearing it or changing the auditing policies.

Audit Log Records

A record in the audit log represents an administrative operation on the system. The record contains the following information:

■ Identifier of the operation being logged.

■ Access control credentials (username) that were used for the operation.

■ IP address of the management console that initiated the operation.

■ Timestamp of the operation.

■ Additional information specific to the operation, if applicable.

Posting an Event to the Log

For an enterprise to claim it maintains a security log, the sequence of records in the audit log must match what transpired in the system. This means that if the administrator initiated an operation that should be logged in the audit log according to the policy, and the log entry could not be written because the log was full (an extremely rare scenario, which as we explain later, we try to prevent from occurring at all costs), then the operation fails. When the log needs to be retrieved, the auditor can be certain that no auditable operations occurred in the system other than those written in the log.

Only Intel AMT applications (which are part of the Intel AMT signed firmware) can post events to the audit log. The Audit Log Manager inside the Audit Logging component exposes a private interface to Intel AMT firmware applications to post events to the log. This prevents any outside entity from posting to the audit log and thereby trying to corrupt its integrity.

All Intel AMT applications have been designed and developed to post events to the audit log when certain operations are perpetrated, if the audit logging function is turned on.

Auditing Policy

The auditing policy defines which administrative operations should be logged in the audit log. Operations can be defined in the policy as "critical" or "non-critical." Critical events will always be logged; if a critical operation occurs and the log is full, the operation will fail. Non-critical operations will be logged only if the log is at least 20 percent empty. When the log is nearly full and a non-critical operation occurs, the entry will not be logged and the operation will not fail. Non-critical operations are logged as space permits. The last 20 percent of the log is reserved for critical operations only.

The definition of the auditing policy is crucial to balance security with usability. When the auditor defines many frequent operations as critical, the log becomes full faster, thereby needing more frequent clearing and exporting by the auditor. On the other hand, only "critical" operations are truly audited in the foolproof sense described above.

The Audit Trail

Due to the limited capacity of the Intel AMT flash nonvolatile memory, and the usability concerns described earlier, the auditor needs to clear and export the log periodically. Before clearing the log, the auditor requests an audit trail. This is the current content of the log, signed by the firmware auditing service in a way that can later be verified by the auditor. The auditor can store the trail in long-term storage, such that if a breach occurs later, the old log can still be retrieved. The signature can attest to the fact that the logs have not been tampered with while in long-term storage. Figure 15.3 illustrates the structure of the audit log trail.

Two potential problems may arise with this approach. The first is the ability of the administrator deleting an entire signed trail from long-term storage. This issue may be addressed by adding an incremental counter to the signed trails. This allows the auditor to make sure that all signed logs are in place. In addition, the enterprise administrator should not have access to long-term storage, but a discussion of this issue is beyond the scope of this book.

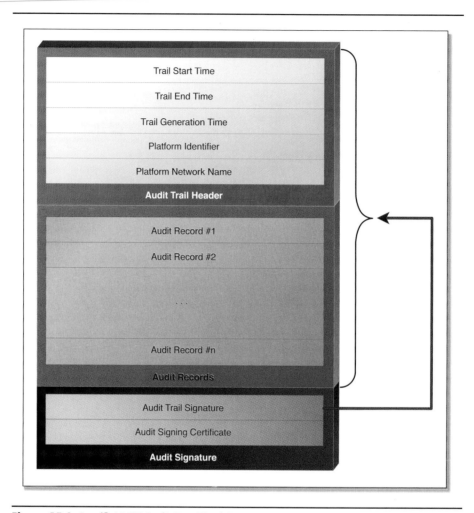

Figure 15.3 Intel® AMT Audit Log Trail Structure

A second issue that may arise from this approach is the revocation of the keying material used to sign the audit trail. It is recommended that the an additional signature be added to the auditing software by means of a temporal certificate being added to the trail before it is stored in long-term storage. When this certificate is replaced periodically, the logs in long-term storage should be re-signed. This adds another layer of authentication in case the keying material used to sign the audit trail is compromised or revoked.

This kind of an auditing system provides very robust protections against rogue-insider attacks.

Summary

In this chapter we saw how some of the more advanced security mechanisms help protect Intel AMT from attackers and malware. The true random number generator increases the security of several Intel AMT components such as higher quality session keys for TLS. The secure storage service helps to protect sensitive data on the Intel AMT nonvolatile memory from being stolen or changed by an attacker. The measured launch of Intel AMT provides assurance to an external entity that the Intel AMT firmware is indeed what it claims to be. Finally we saw how the security audit log deters insiders (such as IT technicians managing the enterprise networks) from misusing their access privileges and harming the system. It also helps to keep track of access violation attempts by adversaries who try to break in to the Intel AMT subsystem. All these security protections, along with those discussed in the previous chapter, ensure that Intel AMT is a well protected subsystem and very resilient to malware attacks.

Chapter **16**

Privacy Protection in Intel® Active Management Technology

The things most people want to know about are usually none of their business.

—George Bernard Shaw

In today's modern society, privacy is essentially someone's right to be left alone to mind their own business. More precisely, an individual's privacy is related to his or her willingness to reveal as much information or as little information about him- or herself to another individual. Privacy also relates to anonymity. If someone is private enough so as not to be noticed in public, then that person can be called anonymous. Unauthorized invasion of privacy is unwelcome in most cultures. Every time that there are moves to encroach upon people's right to privacy, it usually is met with resistance. This makes the topic of privacy a sensitive topic. In general, people are willing to sacrifice their privacy at the airports during body and baggage searches because it helps in providing security and safety during the travel. On the other hand, people in general resist attempts by the police to tap into their telephone lines without obtaining appropriate consent from the courts. The right to privacy and its protection in the technology world is an equally important and hotly debated topic.

Privacy in the World of Technology

Invasion of privacy has become a major problem in today's electronically dependent and highly connected world. On one hand we love the luxuries offered by our digital lifestyle and are more willing than ever to embrace digitization, thereby creating new paradigms for ourselves. On the other hand, these digital systems on which we entrust our lifestyle are not perfect. When these systems fail it bites us hard. It bites harder if these digital systems accidentally break or are purposely compromised such that an adversary is able to exploit the situation to his advantage, and against the individual.

Security and robustness of the digital systems play an important role in protecting the privacy of individuals and organizations. As an example, it would be disastrous if a major retailer's Web site database of customers' private information (such as their home address, phone number, credit card information, their shopping history, and so on) were to be accessed by a cyber-criminal. Or even worse, if a rogue insider (a disgruntled or ill-motivated employee) stole this information and misused it to even out a grudge, or make financial gains. To prevent such a disaster from ever happening, some online retailers invest a lot of resources to ensure that their systems are secure and robust, while their customers enjoy a rich online shopping experience.

In addition to building secure and robust systems, vendors of digital systems or services also need to make public claims about the privacy protections they offer to their customers. These are usually detailed in their privacy policy declarations that they adopt and commit themselves to. Another aspect that heavily influences privacy protection in digital systems is the user's (the customer or consumer of the product or service) choice and control of using various aspects of the product or service. For example, a customer may choose not to provide any credit card information to shop at Amazon.com. Instead he could send a check to Amazon.com for the purchase. The only drawback is that the order would not ship until the check is received and realized by Amazon.com. So in this case, the customer could trade the order fulfillment duration for privacy protection (of course, assuming that the check is not stolen). Therefore, privacy sensitive systems usually offer their users certain levels of choice and control regarding the nature and amount of information the user wishes to reveal. The level and quality of service the user receives varies accordingly.

> **Interesting Reading on Privacy**
>
> Here are some links to interesting privacy related Web sites
> - Electronic Privacy Information Center (www.epic.org)
> - Privacy.org (www.privacy.org)
> - Privacy Rights Clearinghouse (www.privacyrights.org)
> - TRUSTe Privacy (www.truste.org)

Privacy in the Workplace

Workplace privacy is usually a lesser-understood area by many employers and employees. The privacy laws and policies at the workplace vary by geography, country, and culture. For example, there is quite a significant difference between the policy adopted by the European Union (EU) employers and US employers. EU employers have to comply with the EU directive on the protection of privacy for individuals. Under this directive it is illegal for firms to monitor employees' e-mail messages or Internet traffic, or scan employees' computer for files or data without their consent. US employers on the other hand enjoy a more relaxed policy environment and many US firms monitor employees' e-mail messages and/or Internet traffic.

The employer is only one of many entities that can invade privacy of an individual, albeit the employer can do so very easily and stealthily. In large firms, there is usually a department or team that manages the computers and other IT infrastructure. Any ill motivated member of this team could misuse his legitimate access rights and invade employees' privacy by stealing their data files, or spying on their Web traffic or other supposedly personal information. Moving one step further, any employee in the firm not necessarily having legitimate access rights to employees' computers can also attempt to fish for his co-workers private information. The advantages such an employee has over a remote cyber-attacker is that he has physical access to several of these computers (presumably during quiet hours), and he knows enough about the security and networking setup in the firm to enable an attempt. Finally, remote cyber-attackers are always lurking around to steal private information such as credit card data, bank account passwords, and other sensitive data by luring users into visiting some Web sites, or into opening malicious email attachments, and so on. The scenario of remote cyber-attackers applies to all users of computers regardless of whether they are using employer-provided equipment or personal home equipment.

What Constitutes Private Information?

In the privacy policy and law terminology, PII (personally identifying information) is any piece of information that can potentially be used to uniquely identify or locate an individual. In the digital world, several such tidbits of information are available that can be exploited by cyber-criminals to steal the identity of the individual, which in turn can have significant financial consequences. Some examples of such pieces of PII are as follows.

- Name
- Date of birth
- Telephone number
- Street address
- E-mail address
- Social Security Number or National ID number (depending on country)
- Credit card information
- Bank account number

A web search on "personally identifying information" throws up a good list of Web sites that you can visit for more information.

The Legal Aspect of Privacy

As a result of the Internet boom, technology products have been the focus and target of privacy-related scrutiny. This is because today's technology makes it very easy to collect, store, and transmit PII. There are obvious advantages of this such as online loan applications and instant approvals (PII is transmitted over the wire), one-click shopping (the online shopping site remembers your credit card information), and so on. However, any lapse in securing the PII while it is in transit or being stored leads to PII leakage. Worse still, if word gets out of such a leak, especially to the press, it is usually very damaging to the reputation of the firm or agency, and puts the individuals (whose PII is leaked) at risk too. You may have read several such stories in the news about private information being lost or stolen from seemingly secure and protected environments. In some cases it is the negligence of IT personnel handling the information that causes the leaks. In other cases, bugs or design flaws in a product cause the leaks. The former is more often the case, but even in such scenarios, the products do come under the scrutiny of the press. And if the leak was a consequence of a flaw in the product, then such a product is bound to attract a lot of criticism from the press.

To steer away from such potentials breaches, several reputable vendors of products and services have established strong privacy policies and notices that they commit themselves to. Some examples are as follows.

- Intel Privacy Policy [1]
- Microsoft Online Privacy Notice [2]
- Amazon.com privacy notice [3]
- Privacy Policy for PayPal Services [4]

There are specific organizations (government funded and otherwise) that define guidelines and principles for organizations building technology products and services. The common theme of these guidelines is to ensure that organizations that deal with PII treat this information responsibly and respectfully. Some examples of such organizations are

- US Government's Export Portal (www.export.gov)
- Center for Democracy and Technology (www.cdt.org)
- Online Privacy Alliance (www.privacyalliance.org)

The U.S. Department of Commerce developed a "Safe Harbor" framework in consultation with the European Commission. This framework was developed to bridge the differences between privacy approaches and provide a streamlined means for U.S. organizations to comply with the European Commission's Directive on Data Protection[1]. The safe harbor Web site[2] is a rich repository of privacy related information. The overview page has a very good description of the safe harbor principles. They also maintain a good list of data privacy Web pages[3]. Intel is a participating organization of the safe harbor.

---

1   http://www.cdt.org/privacy/eudirective/EU_Directive_.html

2   http://www.export.gov/safeharbor/SH_Overview.asp

3   http://www.export.gov/safeharbor/SH_Privacy_Links.asp

The Online Privacy Alliance also has a well written set of guidelines for online privacy policies[4]. In particular, the CDT's set of privacy principles is very succinct and precise, reproduced here.

CDT: Privacy Basics

■ The Principle of Openness: The existence of record-keeping systems and databanks that contain personal data must be publicly known, along with a description of the main purpose and uses of the data.

■ The Principle of Individual Participation: Individuals should have a right to view all information that is collected about them; they must also be able to correct or remove data that is not timely, accurate relevant, or complete.

■ The Principle of Collection Limitation: There should exist limits to the collection of personal data; data should be collected by lawful and fair means and should be collected, where appropriate, with the knowledge or consent of the subject.

■ The Principle of Data Quality: Personal data should be relevant to the purposes for which it is collected and used; personal data should be accurate, complete, and timely.

■ The Principle of Finality: There should be limits to the use and disclosure of personal data; data should be used only for purposes specified at the time of collection; data should not be otherwise disclosed without the consent of the data subject or other legal authority.

■ The Principle of Security: Personal data should be protected by reasonable security safeguards against such risks as loss, unauthorized access, destruction, use, modification or disclosure.

■ The Principle of Accountability: Record keepers should be accountable for complying with fair information practices.

Source: CDT Privacy Basics
(http://www.cdt.org/privacy/guide/basic/generic.html)

---

4   http://www.privacyalliance.org/resources/ppguidelines.shtml

Importance of Privacy in Intel® AMT

Intel's products are designed to protect the end user's right to privacy, and Intel AMT is no exception. As you have read in earlier chapters, Intel AMT functionality allows IT technicians to remotely troubleshoot users' computer systems. Many of these capabilities have been available via software tools and applications that existed prior to the advent of Intel AMT. What makes Intel AMT particularly powerful is that it allows authorized IT technicians to remotely monitor and manage users' computers even if the user has turned off the computer. This makes Intel AMT a privacy-sensitive technology, especially if we consider scenarios where the privacy policies or laws prohibit the enterprise IT technicians from monitoring the user's usage of the computer. The following list recaps (from the previous chapters) some of the capabilities that Intel AMT offers to authorized IT administrators and technicians belonging to the organization, for managing the computers in a cost effective manner.

- Remotely power up and reboot the user's system for troubleshooting and repair

- Remotely access BIOS configuration screens on the user's system for fixing BIOS related problems

- Configure Intel AMT network traffic filters to protect the user's system from viruses and worms

- Verify that some of the critical applications on the user's system (such as antivirus software or personal firewall software) are properly running all the time

- Receive alerts generated by the Intel AMT firmware reporting events on the user's system that may require technical support

- Remotely troubleshoot the user's system by redirecting the boot process to a floppy disk, CD-ROM, or image located on the IT technician's system

- Allow software applications that have registered with the Intel AMT subsystem to store data on the Intel AMT nonvolatile flash memory. Authorized IT technicians can read this information remotely for purposes of software inventory collection and management.

■ Store private configuration data (such as network settings, access control lists, event and audit logs, and so on) that is necessary for proper functioning of the Intel AMT subsystem. Most of this data is remotely manageable by authorized IT technicians.

In some organizations that are highly privacy sensitive (that is, protective of the privacy of their employees from their own IT departments), these capabilities may be viewed as unsuitable. Going one step further, the fear of rogue administrators (who are legitimately entrusted with authority to use Intel AMT to manage the employees' computers) that try to spy on employees' computer activities is also very real. These rogue insiders could be motivated by any number of reasons, such as bearing a grudge against another employee, retaliation against poor performance reviews or salary increases, financial motives to steal valuable organizational secrets and sell to interested parties, or just having what they may perceive as some harmless fun.

Privacy Protection Mechanisms in Intel® AMT

In the design of Intel AMT we have taken several measures to protect the interests of end users and organizations from the privacy perspective. Intel AMT by its very nature is not a product that requires any PII for its operation. Obviously, Intel AMT does not need your date of birth, phone number, street address, or credit card information for its operation. It must also be equally obvious that Intel AMT does not store your bank account passwords, your email account passwords, and so on. Intel AMT works with information such as IP addresses, machine UUIDs, machine FQDNs, and the like. These pieces of information allow a network administrator to locate and connect to Intel AMT and perform computer management operations in a secure manner.

Intel AMT has several built in mechanisms to ensure that computer management happens securely and only by authorized IT administrators belonging to the organization's IT departments. It also provides several options that offer choices and control to IT administrators and end-users of the computers for opting in or opting out of various capabilities. It also ensures that the data stored by Intel AMT is protected from unauthorized access. Mechanisms are also available to protect against attacks by rouge administrators. Intel also collaborates with its ecosystem partners (such as OEMs and ISVs) to offer privacy protections in Intel AMT-related components that are built by them.

Opt-in and Opt-out

Intel AMT has opt-in and opt-out settings for the whole subsystem as well as individually for several features. The IT administrator or the end-user can turn Intel Management Engine (Intel ME) and/or Intel AMT on or off from the Intel Management Engine BIOS Extensions (Intel MEBX) screen in the system BIOS. Similarly, some of the Intel AMT features can also be turned on or off such as IDE-Redirection (IDE-R), Serial over LAN (SoL) and Firmware Updates. These options are provided to offer the principle of choice and participation to users of computers with Intel vPro™ technology. Figures 16.1 through 16.6 show the Intel MEBX screens that demonstrate these options.

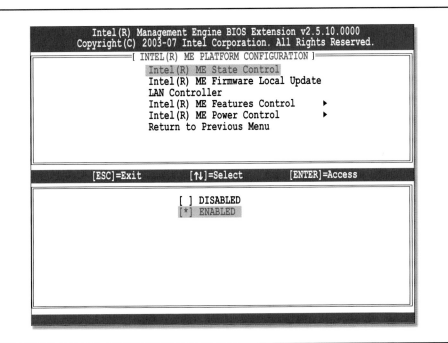

Figure 16.1 Intel® MEBX Option to Enable or Disable Intel® ME

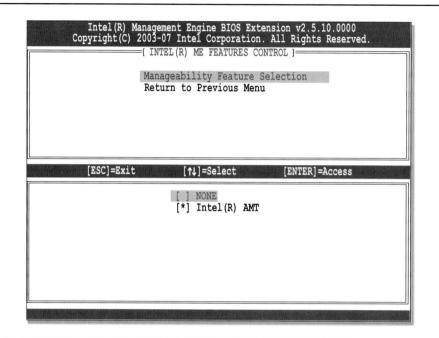

Figure 16.2 Intel® MEBX Option to Enable or Disable Intel® AMT

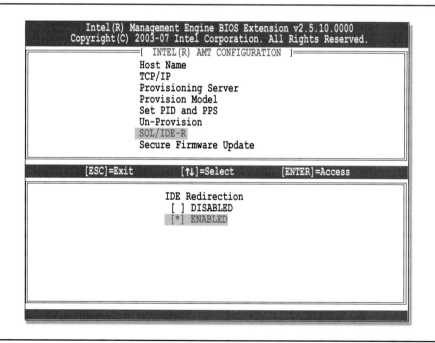

Figure 16.3 Intel® MEBX Option to Enable or Disable IDE-Redirection

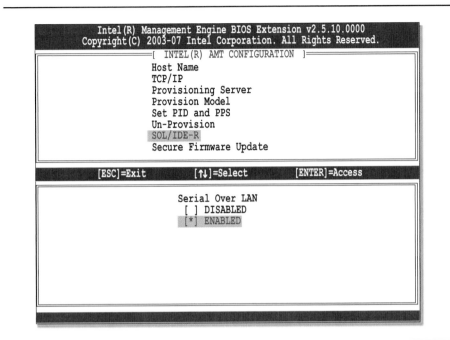

Figure 16.4 Intel® MEBX Option to Enable or Disable Serial over LAN

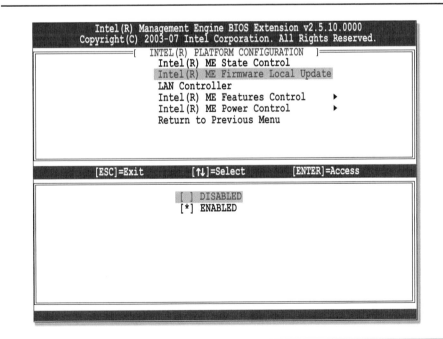

Figure 16.5 Intel® MEBX Option to Enable or Disable Local Firmware Update

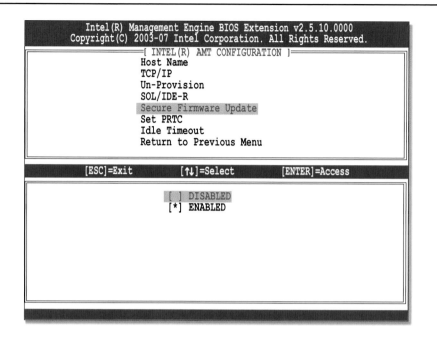

Figure 16.6 Intel® MEBX Option to Enable or Disable Secure Firmware Update

One particularly relevant distinction is end-user choice versus IT administrator choice. End-user in this context is the actual person using the vPro computer. As mentioned earlier, some organizations want to give their end-users the final right to their privacy (even when working on the computers belonging to the organization). In such cases the end-user may go into the Intel MEBX screen of the system BIOS and opt out of Intel AMT capability or some specific features depending upon his or her choice. In such case, the remote IT administrator cannot change the end-user preferences. The Intel MEBX configuration setting overrides the setting configured by the remote IT administrator. Of course, the remote IT administrator can change the settings in the Intel MEBX if he or she knows the end user's BIOS and Intel MEBX passwords, but we expect end-users to keep these passwords confidential.

Secure Local Configuration

The end-user configuration of some Intel AMT settings (such as enabling or disabling Intel AMT or certain features in it) is not possible to do from the host operating system. This is because host software is susceptible to attacks from viruses and malware, and we do not want such malicious programs to modify the configuration settings. If modification of configuration settings is allowed to happen from the host operating system, then Intel AMT has no way to find out whether the configuration is being modified by a malicious program or a legitimate end-user. Malicious programs can then make configuration modifications silently without requiring any end-user input or intervention. This is a very undesirable scenario. So we need to look for another mechanism that is more secure to allow the end-user to interact with Intel AMT to modify the configuration settings. The other piece of software that executes on the computer that the end-user can interact with is the system BIOS. Viruses that attack the BIOS are far rarer than viruses that attack popular operating systems, such as Windows. Therefore Intel AMT uses the BIOS (that is, the Intel MEBX, as shown in the Figures 16.1 through 16.6) as the interface to allow the end-user to modify privacy related Intel AMT configuration settings. The Intel MEBX–based interface inherently enforces the physical presence of an end user to interact with it, and one that has knowledge of the Intel MEBX authentication password. This largely eliminates the possibility of a silent and remote exploit by a malicious program. Examples are the same as illustrated in the screens shown in Figures 16.1 through 16.6.

End User Notification

Intel AMT's activity within the user's computer and within the communication network is largely invisible to the user. As a result, the end user has little knowledge whether his or her computer is being managed and monitored by another entity—the IT administrator. From a privacy standpoint, the impact of such a mode of operation might range from an uncomfortable feeling for the end user to something more significant. Therefore, Intel developed a host software-based notification mechanism (an application icon in the system tray) that explicitly made the end-user aware that Intel AMT is available within the platform, and some other information regarding its status.

The main functionality of the tray icon application is to give Intel AMT status to the end user of the computer with Intel vPro technology. This icon application is available for the most popular versions of Windows and Linux (Windows XP, Windows Vista, Red Hat Linux, and Novell SuSE Linux). On Windows, the system tray icon application adheres to Microsoft's guidelines for system tray icons. The system tray icon supports notifications of events via notification bubbles. Apart from the status, the system tray icon includes an option to initiate a remote connection from Intel AMT to the enterprise management console upon user's request. Figure 16.7 shows the Intel AMT system tray icon on a Windows-based computer with Intel vPro technology.

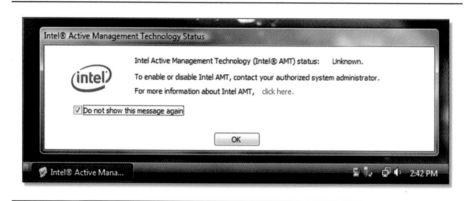

Figure 16.7 Intel® AMT System Tray Icon Application

The tray icon application communicates with Intel AMT firmware using the host interface commands exposed by the firmware. The tray icon obtains the following pieces of information from the Intel AMT firmware and reports it to the end user:

■ Whether Intel AMT was detected in the firmware or not

■ If detected, the Intel AMT firmware version number

■ Whether Intel AMT is enabled or disabled

■ Whether Intel AMT is configured or not

■ Whether Intel AMT is configured in enterprise mode or SMB mode

■ Whether web-based user interface is enabled or disabled

Upon double clicking the system tray icon application, a window opens up that shows some more details including a link to an Internet site where more information can be obtained on Intel vPro technology and Intel AMT.

Private Data Storage Protection

Intel AMT stores sensitive pieces of information such as key material, access control lists, certificates, profiles and policies, logs, and so on. This information is stored in a private region of the nonvolatile flash memory that is accessible only to the Intel AMT subsystem and not to the host operating system. Therefore any malicious program that may be running on the host cannot access this data. However, if an attacker were to gain physical access to the computer (such as by stealing it at the airport), the attacker could use a flash memory reader to access the physical flash memory device on the computer's motherboard and read all the data on it—including the data stored in the private region. To protect against such a severe class of attacks, Intel AMT encrypts the most sensitive pieces of data stored on the flash memory using a special hardware key that is embedded deep inside the chipset manufactured by Intel. It is practically impossible to get to these hardware keys. Therefore the most sensitive data stored on the flash memory by Intel AMT is protected against very severe forms of attack. Intel AMT integrity protects some pieces of data as well. Table 16.1 lists some such pieces of data (please note that this may not be a complete list, as there may be some product changes from the time of this writing).

Table 16.1 An illustrative list of Intel® AMT data structures that is encrypted and integrity protected while being stored on the nonvolatile flash memory device

Intel® AMT Data Structure	Encrypted	Integrity Protected
Usernames and hashed passwords	No	Yes
Permissions, Access Control Lists	No	Yes
Network Security Settings	No	Yes
Certificates	No	Yes
Intel® AMT Configuration settings and parameters	No	Yes
Admin authentication password	Yes	Yes
Configuration passphrases	Yes	Yes
Kerberos keys and attributes	Yes	Yes
Private portions of asymmetric key pairs	Yes	Yes

When an Intel AMT subsystem is decommissioned (that is, when an IT administrator takes the computer out of daily use and readies it for removal from service), all the private data stored on the flash memory device is erased and the contents are restored to their original factory default values. The technical details of this storage protection are available in Chapter 15.

Secure Communication of Information

Intel AMT uses strong authentication (Kerberos or HTTP Digest password based authentication), authorization (HTTP realm–based authorization) and session security (TLS using AES 128- or 256-bit security) mechanisms to protect the communication traffic. More details of these aspects are available in Chapter 14.

Mitigating the Rogue Administrator

Intel AMT has the capability to log the actions of the IT administrator. Intel AMT builds in the notion of dual-person controls by separating the duties of the IT administrator and the IT auditor. The IT auditor is the person who monitors the actions of the IT administrator and ensures that the actions did not represent any purposeful malicious intent. Therefore, to be able to do harmful and malicious actions within an Intel AMT subsystem and escape undetected, the IT administrator and IT auditor must collude. This requirement of dual-person control inherently increases the security of the system and provides a sufficient level of deterrence to the IT administrator from performing intentionally malicious actions. And if the IT administrator does perform malicious actions, the IT auditor can furnish sufficient evidence (in the form of audit logs) to be able to prosecute the corrupt IT administrator. More technical details on the audit logging mechanism in Intel AMT are available in Chapter 15.

Summary

In this chapter we learned the basics of privacy sensitivities in the technology world, some of the initiatives related to protecting online privacy and privacy guidelines and best practices. We also briefly discussed the privacy sensitive capabilities of Intel AMT, and discussed why privacy is so important to Intel AMT. Finally we covered the various mechanisms put in place within the design of Intel AMT to adhere to the online privacy guidelines and best practices, and how Intel AMT offers a high level of privacy protection to its users.

Chapter 17

Deploying and Configuring Intel® Active Management Technology

There is no stigma attached to recognizing a bad decision in time to install a better one.

—Laurence J. Peter (1919–1988)

Intel® Active Management Technology (Intel AMT) is an interactive subsystem that responds to various kinds of inputs. Most hardware or software products need some kind of initialization or setup before becoming operational. Intel Active Management Technology is no different in this regard. The IT administrator of the Intel AMT computers needs to properly configure Intel AMT according to his IT environment so that he derives maximum benefit from deploying this technology. Intel AMT offers a wide choice of options and tools to set up and configure it, catering to various usage scenarios and needs. The goal of this chapter is to help you understand the various scenarios that are supported for configuring Intel AMT, the technical details of the options that are available for configuration, and the tools that Intel offers to do the configuration. This chapter does not provide a step-by-step guide to configuring Intel AMT, nor does it provide exhaustive lists of configuration parameters or settings and their descriptions. Please refer to Intel AMT manuals for such information. Instead this chapter dives into the design aspects of Intel AMT setup and configuration.

What Is Setup and Configuration for Intel® AMT?

Intel AMT requires some information about the network and IT environment in which it needs to operate. This includes parameters like network domain name, IP address, DNS information, 802.1x information and credentials, Wi-Fi[†] settings, Active Directory credentials, administrator passwords, permissions, and so on. Intel AMT also needs to be initialized with various policies and settings that control how Intel AMT behaves, such as System Defense policies, power policies, and Agent Presence policies.

The IT administrator of Intel AMT needs to configure these settings, policies and parameters. Only then will Intel AMT be able to operate correctly and as expected. For example, let us consider the scenario of a wireless router that many of you might have configured in your homes. A wireless router is similar to Intel AMT in some respects such as both are embedded devices, both are connected to wired/wireless networks, both need to be managed (remotely, in most cases) by an administrator of some sort, and both provide services to some end users. Any wireless router provides various configuration settings that you (as an administrator of the router device) can set according to your needs, such as setting an administrative password, setting up an IP address, DHCP and an IP address pool, enabling/disabling security settings (such as WEP or WPA), port filtering/firewall configuration, and so on. Once this is done, your router operates based on your settings and ensures that your home network works the way you wanted. Analogously, Intel AMT needs to be configured for it to work in your networking environment as you expect. However, the scenarios in which Intel AMT operates are obviously very different from wireless routers, so it would be a mistake to take this analogy too far. The following section describes the various scenarios in which Intel AMT may need to be configured. Subsequent sections describe how Intel AMT gets configured in each of these scenarios.

Deployment Scenarios

Intel AMT is a product that can be used by businesses of any size—Fortune 500 enterprises, large businesses, or small and medium businesses. Our consideration of a small business is one that has less than 100 employees; a medium business is one that has 100 to 1000 employees; and anything over 1000 employees is a large business. Each of these classes of businesses may have a different set of requirements for how they would like to configure Intel AMT. In order to have a broad and general deployment capability, Intel AMT needs to work well in each of these deployment scenarios. Following are just some of the examples of deployment scenarios for Intel AMT.

- A large enterprise may have a strong need to do a fully automated configuration of Intel AMT, but is willing to bear some costs associated with it.

- A small enterprise may be extremely cost conscious, but may be willing to compensate for this by doing a few manual steps.

- A large business may have several branch locations but a centralized IT administration organization. Such an organization may prefer to opt for a fully remote configuration of Intel AMT because it may be too expensive to send a technician to each computer to configure Intel AMT. Such an organization may already have or be willing to deploy some central servers and tools to achieve remote configuration.

- A one-person IT department of a small business (all of it located in one building) may find it totally acceptable to walk up to every computer in the building to configure and turn on Intel AMT, perhaps on a weekend.

Factors to Consider

The examples above demonstrate that several factors could influence the option that an IT department chooses to configure Intel AMT. These could be the cost of resources (tools, additional hardware/software), geographical distribution, the number of machines that need to be configured, the security and trust the IT department places in the infrastructure used for configuration, and so on. These factors govern various configuration options that businesses choose, such as who configures Intel AMT, where is it configured, and when is it configured. Let's look at some of these below.

Who Can Configure Intel® AMT?

Of course, the main control or authority in configuration of Intel AMT resides with the IT administrator of the computer. But the IT administrator may have the original equipment manufacturer (OEM) configure Intel AMT with some initial parameters that are specific to his enterprise, such as the domain name of the enterprise. The OEM may offer such customization options for a group of computers being shipped to that organization. This would require the customer to specify the customization details to the OEM at the time of placing the order. These customized parameters would be stored on the flash device in the computers. If the OEM does not do any customization of configuration parameters, then the IT administrator may do some initial configuration personally by turning on each computer and doing some manual operations on Intel AMT (via the BIOS screens). It is also possible that Intel AMT gets configured in a fully automated way without any particular configuration being done on it beforehand. Lastly, the end user of the computer could also configure Intel AMT in a plain vanilla manner (with reduced capabilities and functionality), without using any special tools or resources. The IT department may weigh several considerations before asking the OEM to configure Intel AMT parameters, such as additional administrative or operational costs involved, or the willingness of the IT department to share any information about its infrastructure with the OEM.

Where Can Intel® AMT Be Configured?

As described above, some initial customer-specific custom configuration of Intel AMT can occur at the OEM's factory, at the time the computer is being manufactured. Alternatively, the organization can buy off-the-shelf computers from the OEM and do the configuration at their own end. Within the organization, the IT departments may do some or the entire Intel AMT configuration themselves before handing over the computers to employees (end users). Or the computers may be shipped directly to the employees, without getting routed to the IT department. In such case, the configuration of Intel AMT would happen at the employee's location, albeit under IT controlled processes and over the intranet of the organization. This is called *remote configuration*. This scenario applies, for example, to organizations having several branch locations without dedicated IT staff being present at each location. Conversely, a well staffed IT department may choose to configure Intel AMT at a specific IT location (such as an IT depot) so that any manual configuration operations (as opted by the IT administrators) can be performed by the IT personnel and not depend on the end users to do the same. This is called *one-touch configuration.*

When Can Intel® AMT Be Configured?

It is possible to configure Intel AMT on a bare-metal computer (a computer that has no operating system installed on it). Such configuration occurs solely over the out-of-band (OOB) network channel. This scenario may occur when an IT department does Intel AMT configuration before loading an operating system image on the computer, soon after receiving the computer shipments from the OEM. This is called *bare-metal configuration.* On the other hand, IT departments may configure Intel AMT some time after they have rolled out the computers to their employees (for example, several months later). In such a scenario, the configuration of Intel AMT would require some assistance from the host operating system to trigger the configuration process, albeit still via the IT controlled processes. This is called *delayed configuration.* Delayed configuration may happen if an IT department is not yet ready to turn on Intel AMT (for various business or technical reasons, such as when the IT department is still conducting pilot tests, or waiting to hire a team that will turn on Intel AMT), but would like its employees to start using the new computers soon after they arrive.

Many possible scenarios need to be covered for successful deployment of Intel AMT. The next few sections describe the various configuration methods that are available in Intel AMT, and how these methods can be effectively used to cater to all of the aforementioned scenarios.

Intel® AMT Setup and Configuration Overview

Intel AMT configuration is done using a configuration server (Enterprise Configuration), or using a browser over a web-based interface. The web-based interface is usually used for pilot projects or small businesses. Large sized (even medium sized) enterprises will usually prefer to use the configuration server mechanism. The configuration server is available as part of ISV management suites, such as those available from Microsoft (Microsoft† System Center Configuration Manager), Symantec (Symantec† Notification Server), and LANDesk† (LANDesk Management Suite). The configuration server establishes a secure connection with Intel AMT and then downloads the configuration data into Intel AMT. The protocols for setting up the secure connection are described in subsequent sections.

Intel® AMT Web-based Configuration

Intel AMT is designed to provide a web-based configuration method for small businesses or for pilot projects in enterprises that want to try out the capabilities of Intel AMT. The beauty of the web-based configuration method is that it does not depend on any third-party software. However, since the configuration process requires manual operation on each individual Intel AMT computer, it is not scalable beyond a few machines (otherwise an IT technician would have to spend several sleepless nights performing the same operations over and over again on different computers).

In the web-based configuration method, the initial configuration of Intel AMT is performed through a specialized BIOS module, available on Intel AMT systems, called the Intel Manageability Engine BIOS Extensions (Intel MEBX). An administrator brings up the Intel MEBX screen by going into the computer's BIOS, and configures various settings in Intel MEBX such as a password, and some network settings. Sample Intel MEBX screens are shown in Figure 17.1 and 17.2. Using the network settings configured in Intel MEBX, the administrator now connects to the Intel AMT subsystem over the network using a browser, and configures it from the browser interface (much like you would configure your home networking router by connecting your browser to the router).

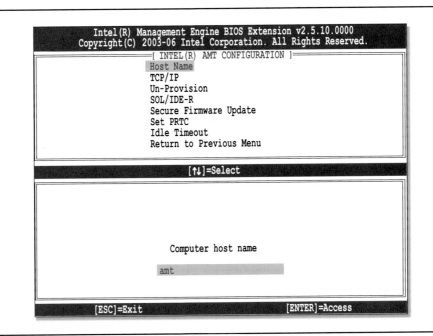

Figure 17.1 Intel® MEBX Screen for Setting Up the Host Name for Web-based Configuration

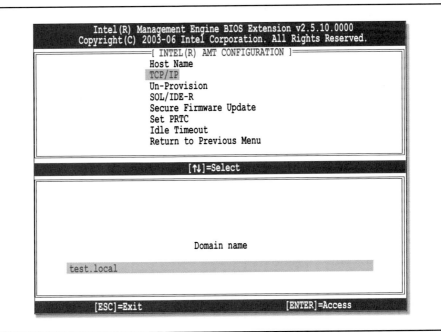

Figure 17.2 Intel® MEBX Screen for Setting Up the Domain for Web-based Configuration

Figure 17.3 shows a sample of the Intel AMT Web page for configuring the various settings in Intel AMT. This Web page is obtained by a web browser after it successfully connected to the Intel AMT subsystem. Note that the default port number used by the Intel AMT subsystem for this web-based configuration interface is 16992.

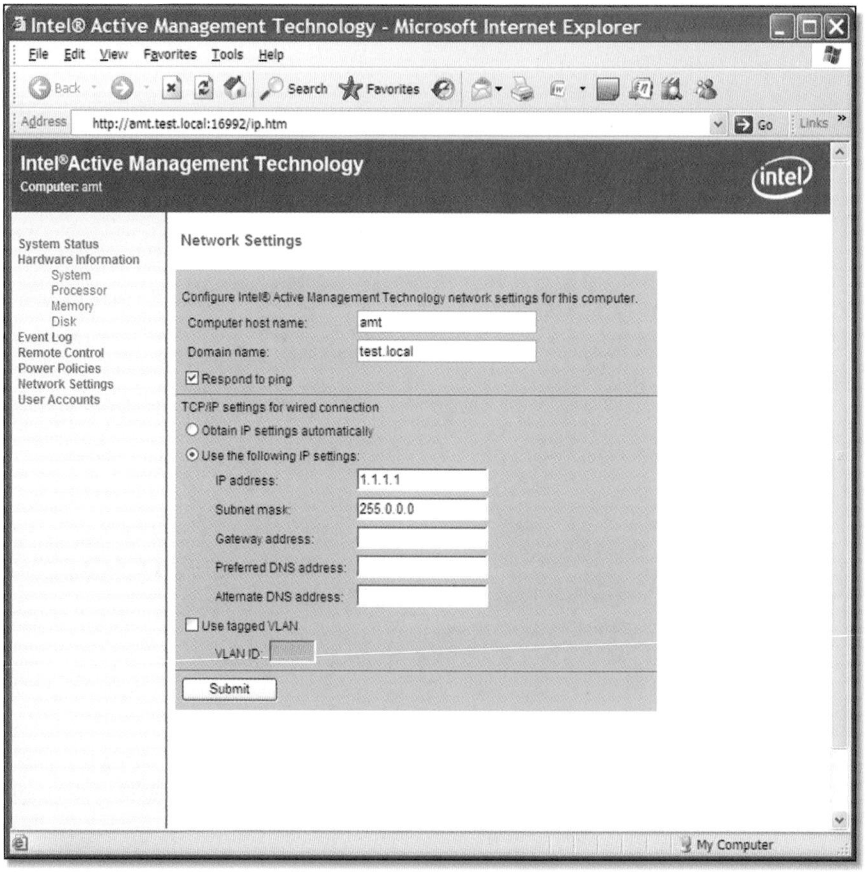

Figure 17.3 Intel® AMT Web-based Configuration

A step-by-step procedure to configure Intel AMT using this mechanism is given in the Appendix A.

Intel® AMT Enterprise Configuration

Configuration of Intel AMT in the enterprise environment is fundamentally based on two protocols, the pre-shared key (symmetric key) based TLS protocol and the asymmetric key based TLS protocol. Certain attributes and properties of these protocols can be adjusted to achieve varying levels of security and configurability. We will cover all these methods in detail in the sections below.

However, before we go into the details of the aforementioned protocols, it is important to note that Intel AMT does not support pure host-based configuration. That is, a piece of software running on the operating system of the Intel AMT computer cannot alone set up and configure Intel AMT without any other authentication or security checks. Even though host based configuration may appear to be a very simple and straightforward approach to configure Intel AMT, it comes with its own risks and issues. If this configuration mechanism were allowed, a virus or malware in the operating system could configure Intel AMT too, causing adverse security consequences for the enterprise. So, as we will see in the mechanisms described below, Intel AMT requires more trust establishment to be able to proceed with the configuration rather than just the mere presence of a piece of software in the operating system environment of the Intel AMT computer. Before the advent of Intel AMT, manageability technologies such as the Alert Specification Format (ASF) and Wired for Management (WfM) were configured through the host operating system. For example, configuration of Intel's ASF management controller was performed through a Windows Management Instrumentation (WMI) provider on the locally installed Microsoft Windows OS. This could be used by any software application to configure ASF, specify ASF policies, and designate remote management servers. From a security perspective, even the malware applications located on the host operating system could exploit the capabilities provided by ASF. However, since those capabilities were limited to alerts and remote power-up/power-down operations, the consequences of such misuse were typically low, as was the overall vulnerability of the system. Intel AMT offers much stronger protections to the enterprise IT departments, including the capability to boot systems from a remotely-situated media and to share data between local and remote software agents. With this in mind and with the ongoing rise in malware vulnerability incidents, Intel AMT requires a more resilient configuration method that can protect against such malware.

Pre-Shared Key TLS based Configuration Protocol

The pre-shared key (PSK) based TLS protocol is based on the TLS-PSK RFC (RFC #4279). This RFC specifies a mechanism by which two parties can establish a secure channel of communication between themselves. See the gray side box for a quick overview of the TLS-PSK protocol.

TLS-PSK Protocol Overview

The TLS-PSK protocol is a mechanism for two interested parties to set up a secure channel of communication between them. The two parties start out by sharing a secret. They then use this secret to derive a TLS pre-master secret. This pre-master secret is then used to encrypt all the data between the two parties. There are several cryptographic algorithms that can be used to encrypt the traffic such as AES, RC4, and so on.

Some of the popular TLS-PSK cipher suites are as follows:

■ TLS_PSK_WITH_RC4_128_SHA

■ TLS_PSK_WITH_AES_128_CBC_SHA

■ TLS_PSK_WITH_AES_256_CBC_SHA

As long as no one else besides the two parties involved on either side of the connection knows the shared secret, they cannot compute the pre-master secret, and hence cannot decrypt the communication.

The TLS-PSK protocol is essentially a modification of the asymmetric key based TLS protocol. In TLS PSK, several of the messages are not required. The overview of the protocol is depicted in Figure 17.4, with respect to the asymmetric key based TLS protocol. The messages that are struck through show the messages from the asymmetric protocol not required in TLS PSK.

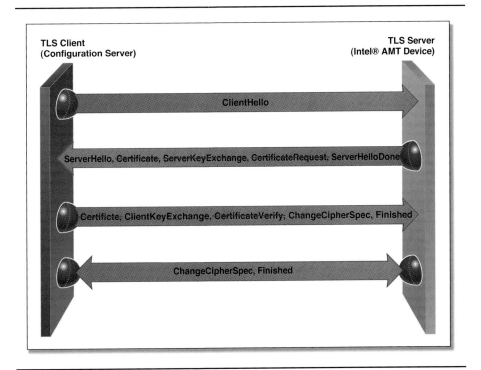

Figure 17.4 TLS-PSK Protocol Flow

In the case of Intel AMT, the two parties interested in setting up a secured communication channel are the Intel AMT subsystem and the Intel AMT Configuration Server (also simply referred to as the configuration server). Intel AMT acts as the TLS server, and the configuration server acts as the TLS client. The starting assumption of the TLS-PSK protocol is that both parties must already share a secret. In our context, we call this shared secret a *provisioning passphrase* (PPS). There is also an associated identifier with each PPS called the Provisioning ID (PID). How the configuration server and Intel AMT get to agree upon this shared secret is the subject of the rest of this section. After the secret sharing has been accomplished, the configuration server and Intel AMT set up a TLS-PSK based secure session between them. Per the TLS-PSK RFC, Intel AMT sends the PID as the "PSK_Identity_hint" value within the TLS handshake, allowing the configuration server to locate the matching PPS value and use it in the session establishment of the TLS session. Once the TLS session has been established, the configuration server proceeds with the configuration of the Intel AMT device with the enterprise-specific information. This is described in the section on configuring enterprise data, later in this chapter.

The PID and PPS

The PID and PPS are strings of characters comprising capital letters A–Z and numbers 0–9. The PID is 8 characters long and PPS is 32 characters long. The reason for restricting the PID and PPS to capital letters was to reduce manual errors in entering the values. By including small letters, the entropy of the PPS could have been increased by a huge amount, or possibly the length of the PPS could have been reduced. But we decided to trade off these benefits in favor of avoiding errors during manual entry. In addition to this, every fourth character of the PID and PPS is a check-character, that is, it indicates whether the previous three characters were typed correctly or not.

```
PID: KRM8-6D6Y

PPS: G6HH-VD5R-DFP2-INJ9-XV6C-KA6E-J27Z-2V15
```

This enables any software that uses a PID and PPS to immediately detect whether these values are properly formed or not.

A Note on the Security Strength of PPS

The PPS is a 32-character value, with each charater having 36 possible values (A–Z and 0–9). But out of the 32 characters, only 24 characters comprise the true secret value. The remaining 8 characters are derived characters (remember every fourth character is a check character). Therefore the total number of uniquely possible provisioning passphrases are $36\wedge24$. This translates to approximately 125 bits of security.

PID/PPS Sharing Techniques

Intel AMT provides several ways to achieve the sharing of PID and PPS between the configuration server and the Intel AMT susbsystem, as described below.

Manual Entry of the PID/PPS Pair

The PID/PPS pair can be manually entered into the Intel AMT subsystem via a BIOS interface screen of the Intel Management Engine (Intel ME) called the Intel Management Engine BIOS Extension (Intel MEBX). The same PID/PPS pair is entered into the configuration server. The configuration server is expected to expose interfaces to allow entering the PID/PPS. For example this could be a manual interface like a GUI dialog, or a programmatic/scripting interface for automated entry. Alternately, the configuration server could be designed to generate a list of PID/PPS pairs and allow the IT technician to print the list. The IT technician would then go from machine to machine entering a PID/PPS entering a PID/PPS value from this list one by one via the Intel MEBX interface on each Intel AMT machine.

Automated Entry of PID/PPS into Intel® AMT

As you can imagine, manual entry of PID/PPS into Intel AMT machines via the Intel MEBX interface is not a very scalable over more than a small number of machines. To overcome this problem the Intel MEBX has a special capability to detect if a USB thumb drive is plugged into the computer and can read PID/PPS pairs from the USB thumb drive.

The first step in this method is for the IT technician to go to the configuration server and select the option of generating data and loading it on a USB thumb drive. The configuration server generates a list of PID/PPS pairs, formats the records in the appropriate format that would be readable by Intel MEBX, and loads them onto the USB thumb drive that was inserted into the configuration server machine. Next, the technician goes to each Intel AMT machine, plugs the USB thumb drive into it, and powers it on. As soon as the machine boots and the Intel MEBX logic executes, it detects that a USB thumb drive is available. The Intel MEBX logic also detects that the USB thumb drive has a list of PID/PPS pairs loaded in it in the expected format. The Intel MEBX then reads the first available PID/PPS pair and stores that information into the Intel AMT nonvolatile flash memory. It also marks that PID/PPS pair as "unavailable." Then the Intel MEBX deletes the PPS value from the USB thumb drive. This is done so that if the USB thumb drive is lost and falls into the wrong hands, then the attacker does not get access to the PPS values already configured into Intel AMT machines. After working for a few seconds, the computer will automatically reboot or prompt for reboot. This automated method offers increased convenience and scalability in the act of configuring the PID/PPS pair relative to the manual method.

However, some very large or complex IT departments may find even this mechanism inconvenient to use. There could be several reasons for this. Some of them may be as follows:

■ The enterprise is so large, complex, and scattered that it is impractical for a number of IT technicians to go to every Intel AMT machine, plug in a USB thumb drive, power it on and then power it off.

■ For some enterprises, the cost of staffing this group of IT technicians may itself be a prohibitive option.

■ An enterprise has the practice of shipping newly purchased computers directly to end-user locations without even opening the cardboard packaging. The end user is expected to open the box, take out the computer, plug it into the power socket, plug in the network cable, and start using it. This leaves no opportunity with the IT department to touch the computer before it reaches the end user.

To overcome this obstacle there is yet another way to share the PID/PPS pair that involves the OEM (such as Dell, HP, and so on). However, in reality, this manufacturer could be a supplier to the OEM, or a supplier to the supplier to the OEM. The process of computer manufacturing is fairly complex and involves multiple parties that form a manufacturing chain. To keep things simple, we will group all of these parties into a single category that we call the OEM.

Configuration of PID/PPS by the OEM

The OEM can configure a PID/PPS pair into an Intel AMT computer at the time of manufacturing it, and then ship this computer to the customer along with the PID/PPS using some transmission mechanism such as sending an e-mail message to the customer, printing the PID/PPS pair on a paper and enclosing it in the computer packaging, or storing it on a CD-ROM and packaging the media along with the computer. The customer or the IT technician that receives this computer enters this PID/PPS pair into the configuration server. The OEM uses special low-level software tools that execute on the computer manufacturing line to configure the PID/PPS into the Intel AMT computer.

The above description is meant to explain the technical theory of operation. Of course, it may not be practical for an OEM to configure a PID/PPS for a customer buying a single computer. This method makes more sense when a large enterprise customer orders a fairly substantial number (say, a few hundred or more) machines from an OEM, and negotiates with the OEM to configure the PID/PPS pairs on the computers on the OEM manufacturing line. This saves the effort on part of the customer to configure the PID/PPS into the machines and instead transfers that responsibility to the OEM. We will not go into the economics of this negotiation. Some OEMs may charge the customer for configuring PID/PPS pairs into the machines, while some other OEMs may work in the cost into the overall price without charging an additional amount for this. Customers should discuss these options with their OEMs. For a large order, the OEM may be willing to e-mail a list of the configured PID/PPS pairs to the customer, or send a CD-ROM to the customer.

It is more secure if every machine is configured with a unique PID/PPS pair, however in some scenarios the customer and OEM may negotiate that all machines for that customer's order would be configured with the same PID/PPS pair. This method reduces the number of PID/PPS pairs to be managed and hence may be seen as a case of increased convenience obtained by sacrificing the security aspect. Security is significantly lowered in this case because if an attacker breaks into the hardware of one machine in that lot of machines, and if he knows that all other machines have the same PID/PPS pair, then the security of all the machines is compromised. The benefit to the OEM is that it does not have to configure a unique PID/PPS on each machine. This makes the manufacturing process simpler. The OEM could create a common configuration image for the whole lot, and configure all machines in that lot with the same image without doing anything different from machine to machine. The transmission of the PID/PPS also becomes simpler since only a single pair needs to be sent to the customer instead of a long list.

In all of the OEM configuration mechanisms mentioned above (whether unique PID/PPS pairs are programmed, or a common pair is programmed across several machines), it is important to note that the communication of the PID/PPS pair(s) to the customer must happen in a secure manner. For example, sending the pair(s) over unencrypted e-mail is not advisable. Some better alternatives could be encrypted e-mail, sending a courier/mail with the list in a disk or CD-ROM, and so on. The customer and the OEM should negotiate a secure mechanism that is acceptable for them.

The previous sections described how the pre-shared (symmetric) key based configuration happens for Intel AMT machines. The next few sections describe public (asymmetric) key based configuration mechanisms. In asymmetric key based mechanisms we will see how remote configuration is achieved and yet maintaining protections from attacks.

Asymmetric Key TLS based Configuration Protocol

The asymmetric key based configuration protocol for Intel AMT is the protocol to achieve Remote Configuration. It is based on the TLS standard (RFC #4346), using mutual authentication. This TLS standard specifies a protocol by which two parties can set up a secure channel of communication between themselves using RSA key pairs established by each of them beforehand. There is no need to pre-share any secret such as PID/PPS pairs between the two parties. This is the biggest advantage of this mechanism—no mechanisms need be devised to share secrets, as was the case in the previous protocol, which also was its biggest hurdle. See the gray box below for a quick overview of the RSA key pair based TLS protocol.

The asymmetric key based configuration protocol for Intel AMT is available in several flavors that differ very slightly from each other. We will cover the most general flavor first to get a good grounding into its behavior. Then we will cover the differences across various flavors.

TLS Protocol Overview

The TLS protocol is a mechanism for two interested parties to set up a secure channel of communication between them. Unlike TLS-PSK, the two parties do not have to share a secret. Each party (at least one of them) possesses a private key and a public key certificate. The private key and public key share a mathematical relationship between themselves. The public key of each party is known to the other party. One of the parties uses the other party's public key to send a shared secret. In this manner the two parties end up negotiating a pre-master secret. This pre-master secret is then used to encrypt all the data between the two parties. Several cryptographic algorithms can be used to encrypt the traffic such as AES and RC4.

Some of the popular TLS cipher suites are as follows:

- TLS_RSA_WITH_RC4_128_SHA
- TLS_RSA_WITH_AES_128_CBC_SHA
- TLS_RSA_WITH_AES_256_CBC_SHA

As long as no one else other than the individual holding the private key knows that private key, they cannot compute the pre-master secret, and hence cannot decrypt the communication.

The overview of the protocol is depicted in Figure 14.5.

As you know by now, the two parties interested in setting up a secure channel in our case are the Intel AMT machine and the configuration server. Intel AMT acts a TLS server and the configuration server acts as the TLS client. Since we will depend on mutually authenticated TLS, both parties require a RSA private key and public key certificate. On one hand, Intel AMT generates a 2048-bit modulus based RSA key pair early during its lifetime (when the machine was first boots and the Intel ME begins execution), creates a self-signed X.509v3 certificate for this key pair, and stores the certificate and private key in the nonvolatile flash memory associated with Intel AMT. On the other hand, the configuration server uses standard mechanisms to generate a 2048-bit modulus based RSA key pair and obtain a certificate for the public key from a partner commercial Certification Authority (CA). Intel has partnered with some of the leading CAs to streamline the process for obtaining certificates for Intel AMT configuration. The partner CAs at the time of this writing are Verisign, Comodo, Godaddy, and Starfield. Please check the latest Intel AMT documentation for the most current list of partner CAs. The IT administrator obtaining a certificate from one of these commercial partner CAs will have to pay some fee for the certificate.

One important point to note is that the self-signed certificate generated by Intel AMT is not important to establish the authenticity of Intel AMT to the configuration server. Some internal design considerations in Intel AMT caused us to designate the configuration server as the TLS client and Intel AMT as the configuration server. The TLS protocol mandates that the TLS server must have a certificate. Hence Intel AMT uses the self-signed certificate only to provide confidentiality of the TLS channel. The authentication of the configuration server is established by the involvement of the certificate belonging to the configuration server. Remember, the main intent of securing the configuration channel is to ensure that a legitimate configuration server configures the Intel AMT subsystem. Therefore, the TLS protocol's main intent is to verify the identity of the configuration server. An optional mechanism (based on a One Time Password) exists to verify the identity and authenticity of the Intel AMT subsystem, which we will cover later on.

Another important aspect of Intel AMT configuration using asymmetric key based TLS protocol is that the Intel AMT firmware image comes pre-configured with cryptographic hashes (SHA1 hashes) of the root certificates of partner CAs. We will refer to these hashes as *certificate hashes* (or cert hash in short) in the rest of this chapter. Since these cert hashes are part of the firmware image, they provide a pre-configured and strong root of trust (that is anchored in hardware) for verifying configuration server certificates. The only reason why we chose to store a hash of the root certificate and not the entire root certificate itself is to save storage space on the nonvolatile flash memory. A full certificate could run into a couple of kilobytes of space, whereas a SHA1 hash of the certificate requires just 20 bytes for storage.

With this much preparation at both ends, we can now dive into the actual mechanics of the configuration protocol. To begin with, the configuration server and Intel AMT initiate the establishment of a TLS session between them. The following checks are done by Intel AMT to ascertain the authenticity of the configuration server as described in the sections below.

- Certificate chain validation
- Configuration server identity validation
- Certificate usage validation

Certificate Chain Validation

During the TLS session establishment, since Intel AMT offers a self-signed certificate, the configuration server cannot verify it. So the configuration server skips the verification of the self-signed certificate. Remember, we will not use the self-signed certificate for establishing trust anyway. The configuration server must send the entire certificate chain (including the root certificate) to Intel AMT during the TLS handshake. Since the configuration server certificate is signed by a CA whose root cert hash is already available to Intel AMT, Intel AMT can verify the entire certificate chain, first by ensuring that the root certificate is authentic (by calculating its hash and comparing it with the one stored in the firmware image). Subsequently Intel AMT verifies the rest of the certificates in the certificate chain following the validation procedures described in Section 6.1 of RFC 5280.

Now Intel AMT knows that the certificate chain is valid. It still does not know, however, whether the FQDN of the configuration server is something it should trust or not. For instance, if the Intel AMT machine actually belongs in a enterprise called foo.com, how does Intel AMT know that it should not get configured by a configuration server that presents a certificate with an FQDN of say, hacker.com? Remember, the legitimate owner of the domain hacker.com can get a legitimate certificate from a commercial CA for hacker.com. But we don't want this certificate to be used to configure machines in foo.com. Let us fix this problem by doing the configuration server's identity validation.

Configuration Server Identity Validation

To verify the authenticity of the FQDN presented in the configuration server certificate, Intel AMT obtains the DNS domain (the DNS suffix of FQDNs of machines in that DNS domain) of the network it is in by querying the DHCP server with option 15. Per the DHCP options RFC (RFC #2132), this option specifies the domain name that client should use when resolving hostnames via the Domain Name System. If in a particular network configuration, the

DHCP infrastructure does not support option 15, then this mechanism of configuration will not be available.

Now the attacker cannot use his certificate belonging to hacker.com to configure Intel AMT machines in the foo.com network because the DHCP and DNS information revealed by the network to Intel AMT will indicate the network DNS suffix as foo.com and not hacker.com. So we have made the job of the attacker more difficult. Now the attacker must also attack and defeat the DNS and DHCP infrastructure of the enterprise before it can attack Intel AMT configuration. This is a very significant barrier for the attacker to overcome.

Certificate Usage Validation

A potential problem still exists that needs to be fixed. An attacker can try to find a weakly protected certificate and private key somewhere else on the enterprise network that has a FQDN value that belongs to the enterprise. Then the attacker does not have to defeat the DNS and DHCP infrastructure. He would simply use this stolen certificate and private key and use it as an Intel AMT configuration certificate and private key. As an example, a weakly protected certificate and private key could be available in some old web server that someone hosted in the intranet, and later discarded.

Intel AMT first confirms that the certificate includes both "TLS Client" and "TLS Server" roles. This guarantees that the CA issuing the certificate has verified that the certificate applicant is associated with the name appearing in the CN field, as is the case for standard TLS certificates used on the Internet. Then Intel AMT also checks a particular qualifier in the certificate. This qualifier specifically denotes that this certificate is meant for Intel AMT configuration. Intel AMT will not accept any certificate that does not have this qualifier. So now the stolen certificate just became useless. We do not expect any old web server certificate to have this newly defined qualifier, thereby rendering any such old certificates unusable for purposes of Intel AMT configuration. When an IT administrator requests a certificate from a partner CA for Intel AMT configuration, he must explicitly require this qualifier, otherwise the certificate won't be usable for Intel AMT configuration. The CA would not add this qualifier for any other certificates (such as simple web server certificates). The qualifier can be of one of two types in any given Intel AMT configuration certificate.

- A well defined usage OID. This OID is defined and registered as an OID to denote Intel AMT configuration certificate. The OID value is 2.16.840.1.113741.1.2.3.

- A well known string in the OU field. The string is "Intel(R) AMT Setup Certificate".

Figure 17.5 shows two sample Intel AMT certificates with these qualifiers. The one on the left is issued by Comodo with the Enhanced Key Usage OID (highlighted). The one on the right is issued by Verisign with the well-known string in the OU field (highlighted).

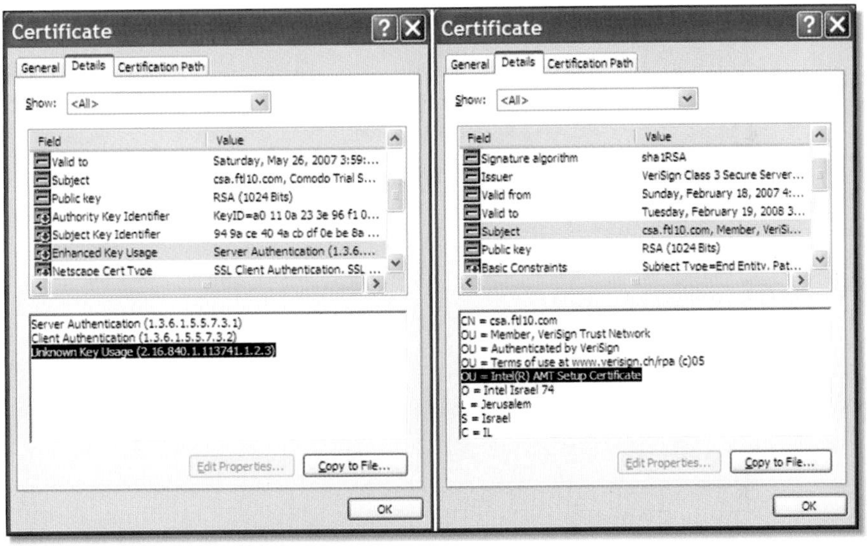

Figure 17.5 Intel® AMT Configuration Server Certificates with the Special Qualifiers

More Security Protections for Remote Configuration

Let us make the job of the attacker even harder. Let us assume that the attacker has successfully defeated the DNS and DHCP infrastructure of the enterprise. By the way, if this happens, then the enterprise is in deep trouble anyway, with or without Intel AMT in the picture. But since this book is about Intel AMT, we will not speculate how else could the attacker harm the enterprise. We will restrict our focus to Intel AMT only.

Configuration Enabling from a host OS based ISV agent When Intel AMT is in the unconfigured state, it keeps its out-of-band (OOB) network interface closed1. So an attacker cannot even communicate with Intel AMT, let alone attempt to configure it with illegitimate means. So even a compromised DNS and DHCP infrastructure does no harm to Intel AMT at this point. The only way for Intel AMT to open up its OOB network interface is for a software agent on the local host OS of the Intel AMT machine to tell Intel AMT to open its OOB interface. A software agent sends this command to Intel AMT via the local host to the Intel Management Engine (Intel ME) communication channel called Intel Management Engine Interface (Intel MEI), which we have covered in Chapter 7. So, to add to the attacker's woes, in addition to defeating all of the above barriers, he now also has to somehow sneak in a malicious software agent on all the Intel AMT machines. This malicious agent must escape undetected by the anti-virus and anti-spyware software on the host OS of the machine. This is therefore not an easy attack point either.

In the normal scenario, the IT management consoles and agents need to be augmented to push a script or piece of software (such as, for instance, an ISV agent) on the local host OS from a centralized IT management console that issues the command to Intel AMT to open up its OOB network interface and starting the configuration process.

One Time Password Another thing that the ISV agent (as discussed in the previous section) does is that it sets a one time password (OTP) into Intel AMT via the MEI. This is called an OTP because this password is never used later on after the configuration process is over. The OTP is recommended to be unique for every Intel AMT computer. During the actual configuration process over the OOB network interface, the Intel AMT subsystem needs to return this OTP to the configuration server as a proof that this is the same Intel AMT subsystem that the configuration server wants to be configured. The OTP flow from the ISV management server to the ISV agent, to the Intel AMT subsystem, to the configuration server, and back to the ISV management server helps to establish the chain of trust at the management server side, especially that the entity being configured is the same one that the management server wanted to configure.

---

1   Some Intel AMT will keep the out-of-band interface open for a few hours after first power own. Check OEM manuals for details.

If you notice carefully, so far there has been no need to manually touch the Intel AMT machine at all, either by the OEM or by the IT technician. All the operations above were based on communication between Intel AMT and a remotely placed configuration server on the network. All the technician had to do was to purchase an Intel AMT configuration certificate from a partner CA and install it into the configuration server. Also, the technician had to send a software update to the Intel AMT machines (via already defined software update mechanisms) that would send a command to Intel AMT to open its OOB interface. We call this mechanism of Intel AMT configuration Remote Configuration.

One Touch Enhancements to Remote Configuration

The barriers offered by remote configuration are significantly high for the attacker to break or circumvent. But, believe me, some enterprises are extremely cautious regarding the security of their IT infrastructure. Or, some enterprises have IT policies that they need to comply with, and the Remote Configuration protocol needs to be further enhanced to comply with those policies. For such enterprises, the security of the configuration protocol can be further strengthened so long as they are willing to touch the Intel AMT machines and configure some parameters into the Intel AMT subsystem. The mechanisms to configure these parameters via a one-touch operation still remain the same as described earlier, namely:

■ Manually via the Intel MEBX interface

■ In a automated manner by using a USB thumb drive via the Intel MEBX interface

■ By negotiating with the OEM to configure the parameters at the time of manufacturing the machine

The following two aspects are optional and further increase security by requiring a touch to the Intel AMT computer.

Enterprise Root CA   Suppose an enterprise policy disallows trusting a commercial CA for root of trust. The policy only allows for enterprise's own root of trust. To solve this problem, Intel AMT allows the use of an enterprise CA root of trust instead of trusting a partner commercial CA such as Verisign. The enterprise IT manager can decide to place the cert hash of the enterprise root certificate in the nonvolatile flash memory of the Intel AMT subsystem (using one of the aforementioned one-touch operations). If this cert hash is placed in the nonvolatile flash and the pre-configured commercial CA cert hashes are marked disabled, then Intel AMT will use only this cert hash for purposes of verifying configuration server certificates. The configuration server will then have to use a certificate issued by this enterprise CA, instead of any other CA. This mechanism completely cuts off an attacker from being able to attack the configuration process of Intel AMT because the attacker needs to have access to the CA infrastructure of the enterprise, which is usually a very heavily guarded asset.

Trusted Pre-Configured DNS Suffix Now suppose that an enterprise finds it acceptable to trust a partner commercial CA, but it does not trust its own DNS and DHCP infrastructure to be very secure. This could happen for many reasons, such as outsourced management (or management by contractors) of DNS infrastructure, or shared DNS infrastructure across sister organizations of a larger parent enterprise. Or possibly the DNS domains are so disorganized that relying on DNS domain suffixes obtained from DHCP option 15 is not practical. Or maybe that DHCP option 15 is not supported in a given environment. How does Intel AMT verify the domain suffix to compare against the FQDN in the certificate? To overcome this problem, Intel AMT allows a domain suffix to be configured into the nonvolatile flash memory of the Intel AMT subsystem (using one of the aforementioned one-touch operations). If this domain suffix is configured into the nonvolatile flash, then Intel AMT does not use DHCP option 15 to learn the network's domain suffix. Instead it uses the domain suffix configured using the one-touch operation for validating the FQDN in the configuration server certificate.

Remote Configuration Protocol Summarized

Armed with the understanding from previous sections, let us look at the protocols used for remote configuration of Intel AMT. We break down the protocol into two phases as shown in Figures 17.6 and 17.7.

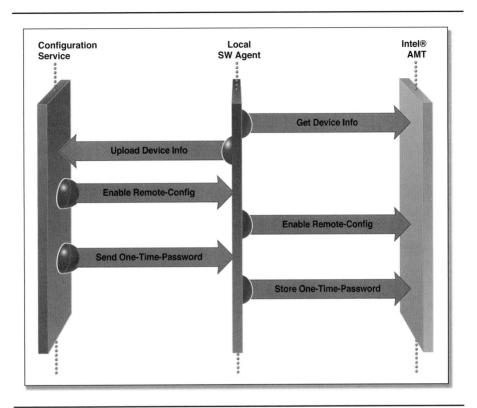

Figure 17.6 Phase 1 of Intel® AMT Remote Configuration

Remote Configuration: Phase 1

To start with, Intel AMT is unconfigured, its network interface is disabled, effectively disabling any remote configuration attempts; and its MEI is enabled. In Phase 1, a local host ISV software agent detects the state of Intel AMT by using the MEI, and then can upload device information to the configuration server. The information includes the firmware version, the installed root certificate hashes, and whether the device is configured to operate in PSK or Asymmetric Key provisioning mode. In this scenario we assume it is the latter.

Next, the configuration server instructs the agent to enable remote configuration of Intel AMT, and it provides the agent with the OTP. Once Intel AMT enables remote configuration and stores the OTP into Intel

AMT, it enters Phase 2 of the protocol. In phase 2 the configuration server communicates directly with Intel AMT via the OOB channel, as shown in Figure 17.7.

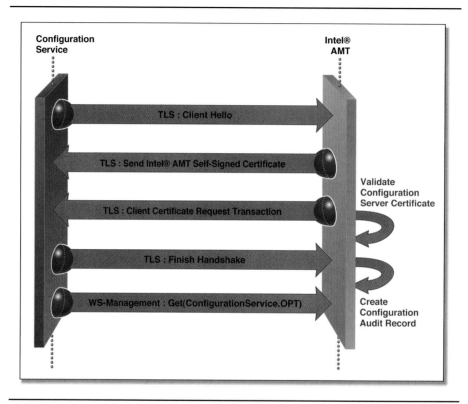

Figure 17.7 Phase 2 of Intel® AMT Remote Configuration

Remote Configuration: Phase 2

In Phase 2 of the configuration flow, the configuration server and Intel AMT establish a TLS session between them. This phase commences when the configuration server opens a TLS session with the Intel AMT device. As part of the TLS handshake, Intel AMT sends its self-signed certificate. The configuration server skips the verification of the self-signed certificate. However, the server requires the public key embedded in it to successfully complete the TLS handshake with Intel AMT. Next, the configuration server sends the entire TLS certificate chain (including the root certificate) to Intel AMT. Intel AMT performs validation of the configuration server by validating the information provided in the certificate chain. The validation includes validating the following aspects as discussed earlier.

■ Mandatory: Certificate chain validation

■ Mandatory: Configuration server identity validation

■ Mandatory: Certificate usage validation

■ Optional: Validation of the certificate chain rooted in the enterprise root CA

■ Optional: Validation of the server identity against a trusted pre-configured DNS suffix

The TLS session is now established.

Once the TLS connection is established, the configuration server requests the OTP from Intel AMT. The configuration server validates the OTP against the one it had stored for this Intel AMT device. If the two match, the session setup is completed, and the configuration server proceeds with the configuration of the Intel AMT device with the enterprise specific information.

Configuring Enterprise Data

The configuration of the Intel AMT device entails downloading a bundle of enterprise specific information (such as access control policies, wireless profiles, and security parameters) that allows the Intel AMT functionality to operate properly within the enterprise environment. Some of the pieces of information that are downloaded into Intel AMT as part of the configuration process are as follows. This is not a complete list however.

■ Network policies (TCP/IP settings, DNS settings, and so on)

■ Active Directory policies (Kerberos settings, master key, and so on)

■ Current Time (for PRTC)

■ Wireless profiles

■ 802.1x profiles

■ TLS settings (enabled/disabled, private keys and certificates, cipher selection, and so on)

- Administrator usernames, passwords (HTTP digest), access control list
- Audit Log policies, auditor authentication credentials

Intel AMT leverages the CIM of the DMTF to represent the various configuration settings that are communicated to Intel AMT. This configuration is done over the WS-Management protocol. Certain configuration properties of Intel AMT utilize DMTF's management profiles mandated by DASH. For example, local user-account management and authorization are based on DMTF's Simple Identity Management and Role Based Authorization profiles. The Intel AMT SDK provides a complete list of supported management profiles.

Configuration Audit Record

Once the Intel AMT device establishes trust with the configuration server, it creates a configuration audit record, recording the configuration TLS certificate details and additional parameters. This record is subsequently locked down to prevent any further modifications, but it is still available for being read via the local MEI interface as well as through the Intel AMT network interface. Since the record is "read-only" it allows policy enforcement applications to detect occurrences of un-authorized configuration and use of Intel AMT systems.

Bare-Metal Configuration

The scenario described earlier in the chapter is called the "Delayed Configuration" scenario, and the assumption is that the Intel AMT configuration process takes place once the host OS is already deployed. Recall that Phase 1 for the previously mentioned configuration method required a software agent to enable the network interface of the Intel AMT system and provide discovery information back to the configuration server.

Bare-metal configuration is another configuration capability of Intel AMT that allows configuration prior to OS installation. In fact one key usage of bare-metal configuration is to push down an OS installation or image to the platform by using Intel AMT remote boot operations. Naturally, this step can only take place after Intel AMT has been configured.

Both Pre-Shared Key and Asymmetric Key methods can be utilized for bare-metal configuration. Intel provided the system manufacturers with the capability to designate in manufacturing a "bare-metal timer," typically limited to 24 hours, in which Intel AMT enables its network interface. This allows a configuration server to configure a device without the need for the software agent trigger, required in Phase I of the "Delayed Configuration" model. Bare-metal configuration is enabled from the initial boot of the system and for the accumulated system up-time duration, specified by the bare-metal timer. After this duration, Intel AMT disables its network interface. To configure Intel AMT from this point onward, a delayed configuration method must be used. Figure 17.8 is a sequence diagram depicting Phase 1 for bare-metal configuration. In order to use bare-metal configuration, an alias for the configuration server address is registered on the relevant DNS servers in the enterprise. This allows Intel AMT to discover the IP address of the configuration server by querying the DNS server.

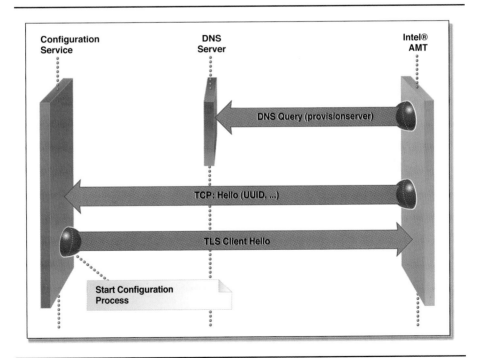

Figure 17.8 Bare-Metal Configuration of Intel® AMT

During the bare-metal time window, Intel AMT tries to acquire a DHCP IP address, detect the DNS server address, and use that address to query for the designated configuration server. Intel AMT uses a concatenation of a predefined host name "provisionserver" and the DNS suffix it has learned, to query DNS for an IP address. Intel AMT sends a notification to the configuration server, depicted in Figure 17.8 as a "Hello" message. The Hello message is TCP-based and provides the configuration server with the platform's additional information that can assist in completing the configuration process. As long as the bare-metal time window has not elapsed, the configuration server can initiate a TLS session with Intel AMT (by using either the PSK or the Asymmetric Key method), and complete the configuration process.

Summary

In this chapter we discussed the various scenarios that are supported for configuring Intel AMT, the various mechanisms and protocols available for configuration of Intel AMT, and we outlined the various options and parameters that can be adjusted to make the tradeoffs between security, cost, and convenience. One of the aspects of Intel AMT configuration that we want to reiterate here is that Intel AMT offers a wide selection of configuration options, catering to almost every type of customer, ranging from a small home business to a Fortune 500 enterprise. At one end of the spectrum, it is possible to configure Intel AMT in a matter of minutes, and get it up and running on a test machine. At the other end of the spectrum, it is possible to configure a vast array of Intel AMT machines in a large enterprise, without even physically touching those machines once (remote configuration); moreover, they can be configured in such a way that the process is trusted and secure, and not vulnerable to being attacked or snooped by malware or other prying eyes. Several optional parameters can further increase the security strength of the remote configuration process. It is also possible to remotely configure Intel AMT on a bare metal computer (that is, a computer with no operating system installed).

Chapter 18

Developing Solutions for Intel® Active Management Technology

Goto, n.: A programming tool that exists to allow structured programmers to complain about unstructured programmers.

—Ray Simard

In this chapter, we cover the development and architecture decisions involved in building Intel® vPro™ technology solutions. Individuals, software vendors, and organizations can all decide to build their very own software that makes use of Intel Active Management Technology (Intel AMT), or add Intel AMT support onto existing software. In all cases, there are a set of common decisions that can have a large impact the cost, feature set and level of integration or the final product.

As with all technologies, developers face a learning curve to get up to speed and ready to build new software, so we want look at all of the options first, before starting work on software development.

Complete Reuse

For many people just getting started with Intel vPro technology, having deployed just a few computers so far and considering adding Intel vPro support to an existing software, probably the easiest way to go is to take in existing software practically as-is. Intel provides the open source Manage-ability Developer Tool Kit (DTK), which includes many sample tools that work with Intel vPro technology. Two of the tools in the DTK are especially made for integration into existing software. These are the Manageability Commander Tool and the Manageability Terminal Tool. Both of these can be invoked from the command line to manage a targeted computer:

```
"Manageability Commander Tool.exe" -h:<hostname>
-u:<username> -p:<passwork> [-tls]
```

This command line will invoke the Commander tool to manage a single computer with Intel vPro technology. The user interface is simplified a little because only one computer is managed. The user can't, for example, add or remove a computer. It is pretty easy to add an option to launch the Commander tool for another software package, and when doing it this way, the list of managed computers and credentials is not kept in the Commander tool, but rather by the calling software. As a simple first solution, existing management software should add the option to invoke the Commander tool when the user selects a computer with Intel vPro technology.

All of the software in the Manageability DTK is provided as open source. As a result, developers can freely change or re-brand the code to best suit their needs.

The Commander tool can deal with most of the Intel AMT features including support for Serial-over-LAN and IDE-Redirect. Invoking directly the Commander tool is by far the fastest way to add Intel vPro support to existing software. It is limited to running on Microsoft Windows using the .NET framework, but otherwise performs rather well.

Supporting Serial-over-LAN

Another tool in the DTK with the approximately the same launch options as the Commander tool is the Manageability Terminal.

```
"ManageabilityTerminalTool.exe" -h:<hostname>
-u:<username> -p:<password> -t:(title)
```

The Terminal tool can be launched to target a computer. The calling software can also optionally specify the title of the window that is displayed on top of the terminal. This way to launch the terminal tool also allows the terminal to support remote control and IDE-Redirect. This is by far the easiest way to add Serial-over-LAN support into an existing application.

Selecting a Terminal

There are other approaches to supporting serial-over-LAN. Some vendors have opted to use existing terminals such as Putty, Microsoft Telnet, or Microsoft Hyperterm, which is included with Microsoft Windows XP and optionally available on Microsoft Vista as a supplemental download. In order to do this in the past, software solutions would use the IMRSDK.dll to connect to a managed computer and forward the traffic back and forth to a local TCP socket. As a result we have the traffic flow shown in Figure 18.1.

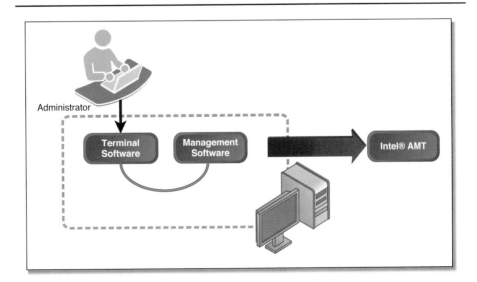

Figure 18.1 Management Software Traffic Flow When Using Separate Terminal Software

At this point, any VT100 terminal software could be used as long as it's capable of connecting to a local TCP port. One example is to invoke the Microsoft Windows Telnet tool like this:

```
Telnet.exe localhost 12345
```

Where `12345` is the local port on which the management software is listening. Even the Manageability Terminal Tool included in the DTK can be used in this role since it can also be invoked just like the Microsoft Telnet tool.

```
"ManageabilityTerminalTool.exe" <hostname> <port> (window title)
```

Developers will have to build the IMRSDK.dll to TCP replay on their own and the Intel AMT SDK can help. Once completed, this solution as the benefit of running on Linux. Developers must be advised that just any terminal will not do; terminals should support 25 display lines. Many terminals intended for modem usages support only 24 lines. Also, telnet applications don't make good VT100 terminals; they are somewhat compatible with VT100, but it's not perfect. Putty for example supports both Telnet and RAW modes, and the RAW mode would be preferable.

It's also important to note that the IMRSDK library is only provided in binary form with no source code for Microsoft Windows and Linux, in both 32-bit and 64-bit versions. Developers must make sure that this library can run on their platform before starting to build a terminal solution.

In general, redirecting traffic to an existing terminal is not really a great solution, it's probably best to use the DTK terminal if possible because it's custom built for Intel vPro. Also, the DTK's terminal will support F1 to F12 keys for various BIOS, and so on. So it's generally more user friendly.

Another option is to use the terminal control that is in the DTK. This Microsoft .NET control can be dropped into an existing .NET application, giving great compatibility while letting developers have flexibility about how it can be best integrated into an existing application. The terminal control can be added to an existing form, making the resulting application more integrated.

If a developer opts to build his own terminal from the ground up, it's generally recommended to take a look at the DTK's terminal as a starting point. Developers can learn from it and use it to avoid many time consuming mistakes.

Selecting a Software Stack

On a practical level, developers will have to select a software stack for their Intel vPro development or build their own. Figure 18.2 shows three commonly used Intel AMT source bases.

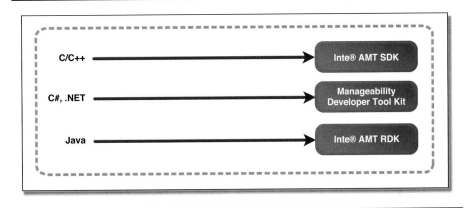

Figure 18.2 Available Development Stacks for Various Programming Languages

Figure 18.2 is a bit of an oversimplification. All developers, regardless of the programming language they use, should get to know the Intel AMT SDK since it's the official reference for everything else. Both the Manageability Tool Kit and the Intel AMT RDK where built with the Intel AMT SDK as the starting point.

In general, if the target software is Microsoft .NET–based, developers should look at the DTK's Manageability Stack.dll. It includes wrapper classes for practically all of the Intel AMT features with many DTK tools service as samples on top of this stack.

For C/C++ software development, developers will likely have to start from the Intel AMT SDK. This SDK provides detailed documentation but all samples are very low level and so, much work has to be done to use all of the features. Still, it's the basis for all other Intel vPro software and is the official software development kit for Intel AMT in addition to being the most up-to-date with latest platform features.

For Java development, Intel provides the Reference Developer Kit (RDK). This Java reference code is not maintained as much as the SDK and DTK, but it still serves as a good start for Java developers. Even if the RDK is Java, it won't run on all platforms since it does make native calls to IMRSDK for Serial-over-LAN and IDE-Redirect support.

Selecting a WS-Management Stack

Developers using the Manageability Developer Tool Kit will find that it includes its own C# built WS-Management stack that was custom made to work with Intel AMT. For developers not using the DTK's code, there are two other well known solutions for supporting WS-Management. Figure 18.3 shows the WS-Management stacks that are commonly available.

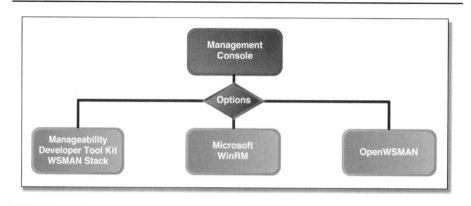

Figure 18.3 Management Consoles Have a Choice of Three WS-Management Stacks

In the Manageability Developer Tool Kit, the WS-Management stack is fully written in C# and works on top of the HTTP client that is built into .NET. Since it's built with Intel vPro in mind, it works very well, but does not claim to be a general purpose WS-Management stack. It is also built to be fast and work correctly with the Intel vPro Enabled Gateway. For developers using .NET, this is clearly the WS-Management stack that is recommended.

Starting with Microsoft Vista, Microsoft includes a WS-Management stack with the operating system. Microsoft WinRM can also be installed as a freely available package on Microsoft.com. All of the Intel AMT SDK samples based on WS-Management use WinRM and so, the Intel AMT SDK provides plenty of sample code for using WinRM. Even the C# samples in the SDK use WinRM, and so work differently from the C# code in the DTK. Microsoft WinRM is widely used but has a few major disadvantages:

Microsoft WinRM must be configured in advance. When using Microsoft WinRM, the user must first configure and start WinRM. Instructions on how to do this are included in the Intel AMT SDK.

Microsoft Windows XP users must download and install an extra package. If not automated, this can be a time-consuming process.

WinRM is also slow. Because each WS-Management call required a new HTTP connection, making many consecutive WS-Management calls can be rather slow. OpenWSMAN and the DTK WS-Management stack don't have this problem and users will notice a significant improvement in call performance.

WinRM can't ignore un-trusted certificates. It is sometimes useful to connect to a TLS enabled Intel AMT computer even if the certificate on the Intel AMT computer is not trusted by the console. For example, this is practical if the certificate must be renewed.

Lastly, this stack may not work well with Intel vPro Enabled Gateway. Because the developer can't setup a different proxy for each HTTP session, instead it must be set system-wide, possibly disrupting other applications on the same computer.

For all these reasons, even if WinRM is heavily used with all of the Intel AMT SDK samples, it is a stack that should be avoided when possible.

Lastly, OpenWSMAN is likely the best solution for C/C++ developers. It's available at no cost, it's well supported, and it works well with Intel AMT.

Other WS-Management stacks are available for JAVA and other languages. In the case of Java, the Intel AMT RDK does not support WS-Management, only SOAP and so does not yet use a WS-Management stack of its own.

Using the WS-Management Translator

Since Intel AMT started out using SOAP and is moving over to WS-Management, new manageability solutions should focus on providing excellent support through WS-Management. Still, Intel AMT enabled computers before version 3.0 do not have support for WS-Management and to help with backward compatibility, Intel provides a freely available WS-Management translator that allows WS-Management–only solutions to communicate with SOAP-only Intel AMT computers.

Except for developers using the Management Developer Tool Kit, which supports both WS-Management and SOAP in the same stack, all other developers should consider focusing on WS-Management support first, with native SOAP support second or using the WS-Management translator for legacy support.

Using the Manageability DTK Stack

The Manageability Developer Tool Kit (DTK) is more than a set of reference tools; it also includes a usable Microsoft .NET stack built in C#. The DTK stack has many benefits such as automatic detection of TLS and WS-Management and support for all versions of Intel AMT, all the way back to Intel AMT 1.0.

The DTK includes two major DLLs that most of the DTK tools make use of:

Manageability Stack.dll Includes all of the .NET classes needed to connect to and manage an Intel AMT computer. The stack supports all of the features demonstrated by all the tools and supports remote and local (LMS) connection, TLS support, WS-Management support and much more. This stack contains only one user visible form for debugging. Any application built on top of this stack can cause the stack to show this debug form, making it easier to see what the stack is doing.

Manageability Controls.dll In the DTK, all common Intel AMT forms are located in this controls DLL. This includes the VT100 terminal, and common forms for editing certificates, circuit breakers, and much more. Because most of these controls have a look and feel that is unique to the DTK, many developers may opt to use the DTK stack as-is, but change the forms from the Manageability Controls.dll to best match their own application. Probably by far the most popular control in this DLL is the VT100 terminal, one of the only terminals custom built specifically for Intel AMT serial-over-LAN.

A really good way to get started with the DTK stack is to take a look at the ManageabilityCmd.exe sample that is available as part of the DTK's source code. The code sample is about two pages long and demonstrates the basics of how to use the stack to connect to an Intel AMT computer and perform management commands on it.

```
// In the main method
AmtSystem computer =
  new AmtSystem(hostname, 16992, username, password,
false, true);
computer.AutoFetchCache = false;
computer.OnStateChanged +=
  new AmtSystem.ObjectStateHandler(SystemStateChangedHandl
er);
computer.Connect();


// Event sing method
private static void SystemStateChangedHandler(AmtSystem
computer)
{
    switch (computer.State)
    {
        case AmtSystemObjState.Connecting:
            Console.Out.WriteLine("Connecting.");
            break;
        case AmtSystemObjState.Disconnected:
            Console.Out.WriteLine("Disconnected.");
            break;
        case AmtSystemObjState.Connected:
            Console.Out.WriteLine("Connected.");
            break;
    }
}
```

In this code sample, an object of class `AmtSystem` is created and setup for managing a target hostname with a given username and password. The specified port "16992" indicates that this computer is probably not setup with TLS, but the stack may automatically change the port to 16993 if TLS is detected.

The `AutoFetchCache` property is set to false so that the stack does not start to load up all of the settings of the computer upon connection. If set to true, the stack will pre-load all of the computer's settings making subsequent calls to get Intel AMT parameters much faster. This caching feature was added to the DTK stack to speed up user interfaces.

Finally, the Connect and Disconnect methods can be called on the `AmtSystem` object to connect and disconnect from the Intel AMT computer. Since calls are made over HTTP, the stack's concept of connection is really made up, at any given time the stack many not be truly connected to the computer, but the concept of connection was created for simplicity. Both Connect() and Disconnect() methods on the stack are non-blocking and will return immediately. An application must catch the state change event to get notified of the connection.

At any time, the DTK stack will update the connection state from "disconnected" to "connecting" to "connected" and back to "disconnected" by updating the `State` property and firing the `OnStateChanged` event. Figure 18.4 shows the possible transitions between these states. Only when an object is in "Connected" state can management operations be called.

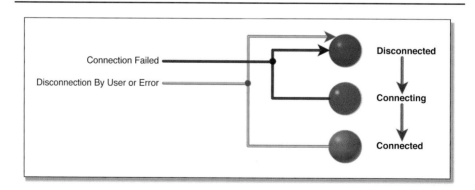

Figure 18.4 Connection State of the Manageability DTK Stack

Using the connection and state system of the DTK stack, an application can easily keep track of the state of each connection. It's generally recommended in this model to call Connect() or Disconnect() and only update the user interface once the state of the object as changed and the event is fired. This way, a user interface only needs to update at a single place in the code.

Manageability Stack Services

Once the DTK stack is in connected state, it's time to perform management operations. To do this, the stack offers a set of sub-objects, each representing a set of features, as shown in Table 18.1.

Table 18.1 DTK C# Sub-objects for Performing Management Operations when the DTK Stack Is in the Connected State

Info	SecurityAdmin
Remote	CircuitBreaker
Network	Wireless
Assets	NetworkAccessControl
Events	NetworkAccessControlAdmin
Redirection	RemoteAccessAdmin
Storage	NetworkTime
Watchdog	AuditLog
WatchdogLocal	

Once connected, a developer can simple use any of these services by calling methods like this:

```
computer.Assets.GetBios();
computer.CircuitBreaker.GetCircuitBreakerFilters();
computer.Redirection.GetIderSessionLog();
computer.Storage.GetStorageAttributes();
computer.Wireless.GetWirelessCapabilities();
computer.Watchdog.GetAgents();
```

These are only some of the many methods that can be called on services. There is one important point to remember: if a service is not available on a given computer, the service object will be null. For example on Intel AMT 1.0, there is no support for Circuit Breakers (Intel® System Defense) and so the "CircuitBreaker" services will be null. As a precaution, a developer can perform a test:

```
if (computer.CircuitBreaker != null)
{
    // Supported
    computer.CircuitBreaker.GetCircuitBreakerFilters();
}
else
{
    // Not supported
}
```

Another good example of this test is when the DTK stack is connected locally via LMS, in this case, most of the services are not available but some services are uniquely available when connected locally.

```
if (computer.Watchdog != null)
{
    // Remote connection
    computer.Watchdog.GetAgents();
}
if (computer.WatchdogLocal != null)
{
    // Local connection
    computer.WatchdogLocal.GetWatchdogs();
}
```

In this example, the stack can be connected locally or remotely and in both cases, one of the two services will usually be accessible. Speaking of connecting the stack locally using LMS, the DTK stack is built to attempt to automatically detect local connections, so this code will work:

```
// In the main method
AmtSystem computer =
  new AmtSystem("localhost", 16992, username, password,
false, true);
computer.LocalConnection = true;
computer.Connect();
```

The "localhost" string will cause the stack to connect to the local LMS and will automatically detect that only local services are present and functional. We can optionally set the LocalConnection property to true ahead of invoking the Connect() method, this will give a hint to the stack that a local connection is expected and accelerate the connection process. We can check local connectivity after connection with the following code:

```
if (computer.LocalConnection == true)
{
    // Local LMS connection
}
else
{
    // Remote network connection
}
```

There is one other case where giving a hint to the stack prior to connection can significantly accelerate the speed of connection. This is when we expect to connect to the TLS enabled Intel AMT computer.

```
// In the main method
AmtSystem computer =
    new AmtSystem(hostname, 16993, username, password,
false, true);
computer.UseTls = true;
computer.Connect();
```

In this case, both the port and the UseTls property are used to give hints to the stack that a TLS connection is expected. After connection is established, both Port and UseTls properties can be read again to see what value was actually used. If the TLS setting is not correct, the stack will automatically try again but there is usually a 5- to 10-second penalty for the detection process to occur.

Developers building their own Intel AMT stack may be interested in the process of auto-detecting Intel AMT Version, TLS, LMS and WS-Management. There is no formal way to do this and Intel AMT was certainly not designed to make the process easy. The "TryConnect()" method in AmtSystem.cs performs this nearly magical task. Care was taken for this process to work even as early back as Intel AMT 1.0 and so the methodology will seem very odd.

Once connected, the version of Intel AMT is located in the `CoreVersion` property of the `AmtSystem` object. This value is really the first piece of data the stack attempts to retrieve from Intel AMT after which it will adapt itself to work correctly.

Certificate Operations

Developers will notice quickly that it is important to be able to operate on certificates in order to provision or use many of the features of Intel AMT. When building the DTK, it became important to create, sign, validate, and conduct other certificate operations. The DTK stack provides a class called `CertificateOperations` that contains only static methods. These methods use the OpenSSL executable and some built-in Microsoft .NET methods to perform these operations.

With Microsoft .NET 2.0, there is not built-in support for a certificate authority. In addition, with Intel AMT 1.0 and 2.0, pushing a certificate into Intel AMT involved a bit of magic. While it's beyond the scope of this book to go into details, developers should look at the `CertificateOperations` class for insight into how the DTK handles certificates.

The DTK stack also makes heavy use of the Microsoft Windows personal certificate store. If Intel AMT is set up to use mutual-authentication, the DTK stack will automatically try each certificate with the correct usage flags in the personal certificate store in trying to connect to an Intel AMT computer.

Kerberos Support

Starting with Intel AMT 2.0, Intel AMT has support for Kerberos user authentication. Some provisioning tools support it and the DTK stack is capable of logging into an Intel AMT computer with Kerberos. This feature is somewhat hidden. To log using the current account, just leave the username and password blank:

```
// In the main method
AmtSystem computer =
  new AmtSystem(hostname, 16993, "", "", false, true);
computer.UseTls = true;
computer.Connect();
```

The stack also supports using any Kerberos username and password, simply add a "\" in the username with the format "domain\username" like:

```
// In the main method
AmtSystem computer =
  new AmtSystem(hostname, 16993, "domain\user", "pass",
false, true);
computer.UseTls = true;
computer.Connect();
```

The presence of the "\" in the username field will automatically cause the DTK stack to use Kerberos authentication. One word of warning about using Kerberos and Serial-over-LAN and IDE Redirect: because of a limitation in the IMRSDK.dll which does not allow the Kerberos credentials to be passed into the library, Kerberos will only work with the locally logged-in user. Leaving both username and password blank will make Serial-over-LAN and IDE-Redirect work since both the stack and IMRSDK will use the local user account.

Summary

Before starting a new software project, or before adding Intel vPro support to an existing project, important decisions must be taken. Considering the programming language, type of solution and cost, many options are available. This chapter covered much of the high level information needed to make proper design decisions.

We also covered the basics of using the Manageability Developer Tool Kit stack, a community-supported open source stack that is available freely to developers.

Chapter 19

Support for WS-Management and CIM Profiles

If there is anything the nonconformist hates worse than a conformist, it's another nonconformist who doesn't conform to the prevailing standard of nonconformity.

—Bill Vaughan

In Chapter 3 we looked at Common Information Model (CIM) and WS-Management standards. We also discussed several CIM profiles that are defined within the DMTF under the DASH initiative umbrella. In this chapter, we will discuss the native support built into Intel® Active Management Technology (Intel AMT) to support the CIM data model and DASH profiles.

WS-Management Support in Intel® AMT

Intel AMT supports the following standard WS-Management specifications available from DMTF:

- DSP0226: Web Services for Management, version 1.0.0
- DSP0227: WS-Management CIM Binding Specification, version 1.0.0b
- DSP0230: WS-CIM Mapping Specification, version 1.0.0

In Chapter 3, we looked at some of the protocol flows for WS-Management. Intel AMT supports most of the WS-Management key operations, which include Get, Put, Create, Delete, Enumerate and event subscription and delivery. For the data that is accessed using WS-Management, Intel AMT uses the CIM data model. The profiles that are supported by Intel AMT are described in this chapter.

From a WS-Management protocol perspective, there are a few things that need to be kept in mind specific to an Intel AMT implementation.

Return Value from Put Operations

Intel AMT does not return the representation of an object after a Put operation. The client should invoke another Get request to get the new representation. However, if the Put request includes a read/write property, and the Intel AMT device does not return a fault, the client can assume that the value of any changed fields has been updated to the requested value

Enumeration Support

The WS-Enumeration specification indicates that enumeration is a three-part operation: An initial `wsen:Enumerate` is issued to establish the enumeration context and `wsen:Pull` operations are used to iterate over the result set. When the enumeration iterator is no longer required and not yet exhausted, a `wsen:Release` is issued to release the enumerator and associated resources.

Intel AMT allocates a resource that is reserved for the client during the enumeration period. The enumeration flow (enumerate, pull, release) should be completed within 30 seconds. If the enumeration flow does not complete after 30 seconds, the enumeration context may be purged for the use of other clients requesting to enumerate a resource.

Intel AMT Release 3.0 supports a maximum of three concurrent enumeration flows.

Envelope Size

WS-Management protocol defines an optional `<wsman:MaxEnvelopeSize>` tag in the SOAP header that specifies the client's request to limit the length of the response size. Intel AMT requires that if clients specify a maximum response size limitation, then the value for the tag must be at least 50000. If a client specifies a lower value, then it might receive a corresponding WS-Management fault according to the WS-Management specification.

OptionSet Support

Intel AMT does not support the WS-Management Options. If the WS-Management Header OptionSet element is passed with `soap:mustUnderstand=true`, a soap fault element with a fault code of `MustUnderstand` will be returned.

Using Create and Put with Read-Only Properties

When using the Create and Put operations, all `Key` or `Required` properties must be passed. Notice that not all fields of a class are writable; for example, the `CreationClassName` property is never writable in Intel AMT.

Properties that are read-only and are passed in the Create or Put operations will be ignored, and Intel AMT fills its own value for them. Any schema-compliant value may be passed for these properties.

Specifically, this means the client must pass all keys, whether they are read-only or writable; read-only keys will be ignored, but must nevertheless be passed.

Whitespace in XML Elements

Intel AMT treats any information within a simple XML element tag as the tag's value. Numeric fields may contain whitespaces; however, string and string-based elements containing any whitespace, including heading or trailing whitespaces, will be treated as though the whitespaces are part of the field's value.

Class Namespace Usage

Intel AMT implements standard DMTF CIM classes as well as CIM classes specific to Intel AMT.

Classes whose name begins with CIM_ are provided by the DMTF. The exact versions are documented in Intel AMT's class reference documentation. The namespace prefix and ResourceURI prefix that should be used to access these classes is

```
http://schemas.dmtf.org/wbem/wscim/1/cim-schema/2+/
```

For example, CIM_ComputerSystem will belong to the namespace

```
http://schemas.dmtf.org/wbem/wscim/1/cim-schema/2+/CIM_
ComputerSystem.xsd
```

and this is also its ResourceURI.

Classes whose names begin with AMT_ are provided by Intel Corporation. Their namespace prefix is

```
http://intel.com/wbem/wscim/1/amt-schema/1/
```

Currently, the Intel-specific schema is not published as XSD on the Web. Therefore the above namespace prefix can only be used for identification purposes. The schema is provided in the Intel AMT SDK.

Following sections go into more discussions of the data model and CIM classes supported by Intel AMT.

Intel® AMT Data Model

Intel AMT capabilities are exposed by a set of CIM classes that are organized into profiles. Intel AMT supports standard profiles as defined by DMTF. In addition, certain capabilities, for which there are no standard profiles (or none existed at the time of product development), Intel AMT implements extended CIM profiles with its own vendor-defined classes.

DASH Profiles

Here we will review the DASH profiles that are supported by Intel AMT. These profiles are listed in the DMTF DSP0232 (DASH Implementation Requirements) document. Each of the profile is then defined in detail in a separate profile document, also available from DMTF.

The focus here is not to list each and every CIM class and properties that are supported by Intel AMT. Instead, we will focus on the platform capabilities that can be used when a specific profile is used.

Profile Registration

The Profile Registration profile is used to find out what other profiles are implemented by the Intel AMT system. Enumerating all instances of class `CIM_RegisteredProfile` returns the number of instances that corresponds to the supported DASH profiles. Within those instances `RegisteredName` property gives the ASCII string that provides the name of the registered profile. Thus, a management application can programmatically discover the supported capabilities using this profile.

Base Desktop and Mobile

This mandatory DASH profile describes the managed desktop or mobile computer system that contains Intel AMT. Other CIM classes are mostly associated to the main computer system. The central class of this profile is `CIM_ComputerSystem`. Enumerating this class provides an instance of the class that refers to the desktop or mobile system that Intel AMT subsystem is managing. Within this class instance, the following properties are useful:

■ *Dedicated* – This is an enumerated integer, with the value 32 corresponding to a Desktop system, and the value of 33 corresponding to a Mobile system. Any Intel AMT implementation will have one of these values. Other values are not used.

■ *Name* – This string property has the DNS hostname of the system.

■ *EnabledState* – This enumerated integer represents the state of the system. In Intel AMT systems, this property can have three possible values. The value of 2 (enabled) represents that the system is in S0 state, i.e. it is fully powered up. The value of 3 (disabled) represents that the system is in S5 state, i.e. it is powered off. The value of 5 (Not Applicable) is used for all other power states.

Boot Control

The DASH Boot Control profile defines classes and mechanisms for temporarily overriding the boot flow configured in the managed system, as well as permanently changing this configuration. Intel AMT only supports single-use boot configurations that are used to temporarily override the boot flow configured in the managed system on the next boot cycle.

The `ChangeBootOrder()` method in the `CIM_BootConfigSetting` can be called to specify the boot order on next boot. Console application must first discover the existing boot sources on a specific platform by enumerating `CIM_BootSourceSetting` and reading the values of the property `StructuredBootString`. Some of the allowed values are Floppy, Hard-Disk, CD/DVD, Network, PCMCIA, and USB. The existing order can be discovered as well.

Intel AMT provides extension to the DASH Boot Control profile by additional classes that allow further discovery of capabilities and allow additional controls. See "Intel AMT Boot Extensions" below.

Power State Management

The Power State Management profile allows a management console to discover the power management capabilities of the Intel AMT system and perform power control operations on the system. `CIM_PowerManagementCapabilities` class can be enumerated to discover what power states (such as S0, S1, S2, S3, S4, S5 and so on) are supported, and in what ways those could be changed.

`CIM_PowerManagementService` has a method `RequestPowerStateChange()`, which is used for power control operations, such as power on, power off, or reset operations. When `RequestPowerStateChange()` causes a boot cycle, the operation of the boot cycle can be controlled using the boot control classes described in the Boot profile above.

The `EnabledState` property in the `CIM_PowerManagementService` is another useful property that indicates the current power state of the Intel AMT managed system. This provides more granular information than the `EnabledState` property in the `CIM_ComputerSystem` described earlier.

CPU

The CPU profile provides information about the processors in the computer system. The `CIM_Processor` class from this profile can be enumerated to find out how many logical processors are present in the system. For each processor, information such as processor model, family, stepping, clock speed, and status are available. Several management applications use this information to identify the system processing power and other processor capabilities.

FAN

The Fan profile is a very simple profile. Using this profile, a management console can query `CIM_Fan` instances to find out how many cooling fans are present on the system, and what their health state is (running okay or stopped).

Physical Asset

The Physical Asset profile is used to identify the hardware asset information about the system. This profile has several classes that identify different physical components of the platform. The classes from this profile are associated to corresponding logical elements via `CIM_Realizes` association. For example, to get the physical asset information about a Processor package, one must find out the `CIM_Chip` instance that is associated to `CIM_Processor` using `CIM_Realizes` association. Once, the appropriate `CIM_Chip` instance is found, the properties such as Manufacturer, Model, and Version can be found. It can also be found if the chip is a field replaceable unit (FRU) or not.

`CIM_PhysicalMemory`, which is also part of this profile, can be used to identify the memory type, speed, capacity, manufacturer, serial number, and part number.

`CIM_ComputerSystemPackage` has a PlatformGUID, which is typically used by a number of management consoles to uniquely identify a specific computer on the network.

`CIM_Chassis` has the asset tag information, which is programmed by enterprise IT to keep track of the computer asset.

Power Supply

The Power Supply profile is another fairly straightforward profile. A management console can query the instances of CIM_PowerSupply to get information of the power supply such as total output power and health state.

Record Log

The Record Log profile is used by Intel AMT to expose the event log entries that is maintained by Intel AMT in the NVRAM. CIM_LogEntry provides a standard way to enumerate these log entries. CIM_RecordLog aggregates all these log entries and provides administration functions such discovering total size of the log, and a function to clear the log.

Sensors

The Sensors profile allows Intel AMT to expose the voltage or temperature sensors information to a management console. The sensors describe the possible states and current state of the sensor. Current health state of the sensors is also available.

Software Inventory

The Software Inventory profile is used by Intel AMT to describe the identification and version information about the Intel AMT firmware itself.

System Memory

The System Memory profile is used to find out the amount of memory installed and available to the OS on the managed system. The central class of this profile is CIM_Memory. It has properties such as BlockSize and NumberOfBlocks that can be used to compute memory on the system. A management console can also query if the memory is read-only, writable, persistent, or volatile.

Simple Identity Management

The Simple Identity Management profile can be used to create or modify a user account on Intel AMT. The central class for this profile is `CIM_AccountManagementService`. The `CreateAccount` method can be called to create a new user. New user account information is passed using `CIM_Account` as a template. The `CIM_Account.UserID` field is used to identify a new user; Intel AMT ignores `CIM_Account.Name`.

An existing user account can be updated using a Put operation for `CIM_Account`. In this operation, the `Name` field is used to update the entry and the `UserID` field is ignored.

Role-based Authorization

The ability to manage and configure roles for a managed system is represented by the `CIM_RoleBasedAuthorizationService` instance. The `CIM_RoleBasedAuthorizationService` class is the central class of the profile and, through extrinsic methods, serves as the interface for a client to request deletion and modification of existing roles, creation of new roles, and assignment of roles to security principals. The authorized roles on a managed system are represented through instances of `CIM_Role`. Rights granted to a security principal through membership in a role are represented by instances of `CIM_Privilege` that are associated with the instance of `CIM_Role` through the `CIM_MemberOfCollection` association.

The `ActivitiesSupported`, `ActivityQualifiersSupported`, and `QualifierFormatsSupported` properties of the Associated Privilege Management Capability represents the full list of supported activities of the privilege. Note that the `ActivityQualifiersSupported` field identifies the Realms supported in a particular release of Intel AMT. Each realm has a short string associated with it. These strings are used to grant a user access to one or more realms or to see which privileges a user has. See, for example, `CIM_Privilege.ActivityQualifiers`. Table 19.1 lists the realm abbreviations.

Table 19.1 Realm Abbreviations

Realm	Abbreviation
PTAdministrationRealm	ADMIN
NetworkTimeRealm	NETT
HardwareAssetRealm	HAI
RemoteControlRealm	RC
EventManagerRealm	EVTMGR
LocalUN	LOCAPP
EventLogReaderRealm	EVTLOG
StorageAdminRealm	STORA
StorageRealm	STOR
RedirectionRealm	REDIR
AgentPresenceLocalRealm	AGPL
AgentPresenceRemoteRealm	AGPR
CircuitBreakerRealm	CB
GeneralInfoRealm	INFO
FirmwareUpdateRealm	FWUPD
EIT	EIT
EndpointAccessControlRealm	EAC
EndpointAccessControlAdminRealm	EACADM
SecurityAuditLogRealm (Added in Release 4.0)	AUDIT
UserAccessControlRealm (Added in Release 4.0)	UAC
Reserved	RESERVED

Indications Profile

Intel AMT supports the Indications profile for subscriptions and delivery of WS-Management events. `CIM_FilterCollection`, `CIM_FilterCollectionSubscription`, and `CIM_ListenerDestinationWSManagement` are key classes of this profile implemented by Intel AMT.

Each instance of `CIM_FilterCollection` in Intel AMT is a filter that passes a predefined set of events. There are six instances of `CIM_FilterCollection`, defined using the following strings:

- "Intel(r) AMT:FW ProgressEvents"
- "Intel(r) AMT:User"
- "Intel(r) AMT:All"
- "Intel(r) AMT:Platform"
- "Intel(r) AMT:CorePlatform"
- "Intel(r) AMT:Features"

To subscribe for notification of events, a user specifies an instance of `CIM_FilterCollection` to define the desired subset of events. A `CIM_ListenerDestinationWSManagement` instance is created for each valid subscription request, as well as an instance of `CIM_FilterCollectionSubscription` as an association between the instance of `CIM_FilterCollection` mentioned in the subscription request and the newly created instance of `CIM_ListenerDestinationWSManagement`.

The number of subscriptions is limited to six. Attempting to create more than six subscriptions without unsubscribing from one of them will fail.

Intel® AMT Extension Profiles

Following are the data profiles that are extensions to the standard CIM. The list discussed here is not exhaustive of all Intel AMT profiles. Since the profiles are being added constantly to Intel AMT implementation, it is advised that reader refers to the SDK for the most current list.

Intel® AMT Boot extensions

Intel AMT provides extension to the DASH Boot Control profile by providing additional classes that allow further discovery of capabilities and allow additional controls.

The `AMT_BootCapabilities` class instance can be retrieved to discover a number of important capabilities about what is available or not available on the Intel AMT system. Each of these is represented by a Boolean property in the `AMT_BootCapabilities` class, including those listed in Table 19.2

Table 19.2 AMT_BootCapabilities Class Properties

Property	Description
IDER	Indicates whether the platform supports IDE Redirection
SOL	Indicates whether the platform supports Serial Over Lan
BIOSReflash	Indicates whether the platform supports update (reflash) of the BIOS upon boot.
BIOSSetup	Indicates whether the platform supports system automatically entering into BIOS Setup upon reboot
BIOSPause	Indicates whether the platform supports pausing the BIOS upon reboot
ForcePXEBoot	Indicates whether the platform supports forcing of PXE Boot (network boot)
ForceHardDriveBoot	Indicates whether the platform supports forcing of boot from the Hard Drive
ForceHardDriveSafeModeBoot	Indicates whether the platform supports forcing of Hard Drive Safe Mode Boot
ForceDiagnosticBoot	Indicates whether the platform supports forcing of a Diagnostic Boot
ForceCDorDVDBoot	Indicates whether the platform supports forcing of CD or DVD Boot
VerbosityScreenBlank	Indicates whether the platform supports a BIOS blank screen (no messages) on next reboot
PowerButtonLock	Indicates whether the platform supports locking the Power Button
ResetButtonLock	Indicates whether the platform supports locking the Reset Button

Table 19.2 AMT_BootCapabilities Class Properties *(continued)*

KeyboardLock	Indicates whether the platform supports locking the Keyboard
SleepButtonLock	Indicates whether the platform supports locking the Sleep Button =
UserPasswordBypass	Indicates whether the platform supports bypassing the password in next reboot
ForcedProgressEvents	Indicates whether the platform forces the BIOS progress events to be reported
VerbosityVerbose	Indicates whether the platform supports verbose messages from BIOS at the next boot
VerbosityQuiet	Indicates whether the platform supports minimal amount (quiet) of messages on the console at the next boot
ConfigurationDataReset	Indicates whether the platform supports all configuration data reset at next boot

AMT_BootSettingsData is another class that affects the flags that are to be used on the next system boot, as described in Table 19.3.

Table 19.3 AMT_BootSettingsData Class Properties

Property	Description
UseSOL	When True, Serial over LAN is used on the next boot cycle.
UseSafeMode	When a Hard-drive boot source is chosen (using CIM_BootConfigSetting) and this property is set to True, the Intel® AMT firmware will boot the platform in safe mode.
ReflashBIOS	When True, the Intel AMT firmware reflashes the BIOS on the next boot cycle.
BIOSSetup	When True, the Intel AMT firmware forces the platform BIOS to enter the CMOS Setup screen on the next boot cycle.
BIOSPause	When True, the BIOS pauses for user input on the next boot cycle.
LockPowerButton	When True, the Intel AMT firmware disables the power button operation for the system, normally until the next boot cycle.
LockResetButton	When True, the Intel AMT firmware disables the reset button operation for the system, normally until the next boot cycle.
LockKeyboard	When True, the Intel AMT firmware disallows keyboard activity during its boot process.
LockSleepButton	When True, the Intel AMT firmware disables the sleep button operation for the system, normally until the next boot cycle.
UserPasswordBypass	When True, the Intel AMT firmware boots the system and bypasses any user or boot password that might be set in the system.
ForcedProgressEvents	When True, the Intel AMT firmware transmits all progress PET events to the alert-sending device.
FirmwareVerbosity	When set to a nonzero value, controls the amount of information the managed system writes to its local display.
ConfigurationDataReset	When True, the Intel AMT firmware forces BIOS to reset its non-volatile configuration data to the managed system's Setup defaults prior to booting the system.
IDERBootDevice	Specifies the device to use when UseIDER is set.
UseIDER	When True, IDER session is started on the next boot cycle.
BootMediaIndex	This property identifies the boot-media index for the managed platform (when a boot source is set using the CIM_BootConfigSetting.ChangeBootOrder method)

Agent Presence

The Agent Presence Profile allows management of Agent Presence capability configuration.

The `AMT_AgentPresenceCapabilities` class provides the discovery of how many maximum agents can be monitored, how many maximum actions can be taken and what is the minimum guaranteed actions that will always be executed when an event occurs.

`AMT_AgentPresenceWatchdog` is an extension of standard `CIM_watchdog` class. This class is instantiated for each agent that is being monitored by Intel AMT. The description of the agent that is being monitored is available in the `MonitoredEntityDescription` property. This class provides a number of methods. The `RegisterAgent()` method is issued by applications that wish to start reporting their running state. The `AssertPresence()` method is issued periodically by applications to report their running state. The `AssertShutdown()` method is issued by applications to report their termination state. The `AddAction()` method adds an action to the application watchdog. `DeleteAllActions()` removes all actions associated with the watchdog.

A few additional classes are used for configuration of actions and policies.

Event Management and User Notifications

These profiles allow management of event log entries and configurations of Platform Event Traps (PETs), filters, and trap destinations.

`AMT_EventLogEntry` expands `CIM_LogEntry` (described in the standard Record Log Profile above) and provides a specific format of the log entries, which includes fields like EventSeverity, EventType, SensorNumber and EventData among a lot of other useful information.

`AMT_EventSubscriber` classes provide the data structures to store information about the event subscribers. An instance is created for every new subscriber.

`AMT_PETCapabilities` and `AMT_PETFilterSetting` classes are used to configure PET capabilities and filters to appropriate generate PETs on specific events.

Firmware Update Status

Intel AMT uses `CIM_SoftwareInstallationService` to provide the mechanism to update the Intel AMT firmware. The `CIM_ConcreteJob` class is instantiated when the firmware update process is started. This can be used to find out the status of the firmware update.

Redirection

`AMT_RedirectionService` provides description and management of IDE redirection and Serial over LAN (SoL) capabilities for the Intel AMT subsystem. The capabilities provided are primarily discovering that the capability exist and enable/disable it, if needed.

Service Processor

In the case of Intel AMT, the service processor represents the Intel AMT subsystem. The Service Processor profile defines the minimum top-level object model needed to define a service processor subsystem within a managed computer system. Other profiles add additional management objects to this model to provide non-volatile storage, network outbreak containment, firmware update, and other capabilities supported by Intel AMT.

The profile consists of a single instance of `CIM_ComputerSystem` representing the management processor subsystem within a managed computer system. The service processor is associated with the `CIM_ComputerSystem` instance that represents the managed system via the `CIM_SystemComponent` association, according to the Service Processor profile.

Setup and Configuration

`AMT_SetupAndConfigurationService` provides the description and control of setup and configuration capabilities in Intel AMT. This service has the properties that define Intel AMT provisioning mode, provisioning state, a flag indicating if Zero Touch Configuration is enabled. This service has a number of methods that provide provisioning and unprovisioning operations.

System BIOS

`CIM_BIOSElement` provides information about the system BIOS. It includes information such as manufacturer, version, and release date.

System Defense Profile

This profile allows configuration and management of System Defense policies and actions. `AMT_SystemDefenseService` is the central class of this profile, although most of the useful data is in the classes associated to it. The `AMT_GeneralSystemDefenseCapabilities` class provides information about number of supported policies and filters. `AMT_Network-Filter` and `AMT_IPHeaderFilter` provide configuration of filters. There are a few other classes that provide system defense statistics. The classes in this profile are closely interrelated, and the reader is advised to refer to Intel AMT SDK for details.

Third Party Data Storage

The management of Third Party Data Storage is provided using this profile. This profile consists of two services, `AMT_ThirdPartyDataStorageAdmin-istrationService` and `AMT_ThirdPartyDataStorageService`. Both of these services have a number of extrinsic methods. The administration service enables administrators to reconfigure the global parameters that govern allocation and use of third-party nonvolatile storage. It also enables to retrieve various management data, and perform management actions. The storage service provides limited nonvolatile storage services to third-party software applications running either on the local computer system host processor or on a remote system. Third party applications primarily use this interface.

Time Synchronization

The Time Synchronization profile defines classes and mechanisms for retrieving the local time from the Intel AMT device and synchronizing the device's internal clock with an external clock. The central class of this profile is `AMT_TimeSynchronizationService`, which has an extrinsic method `GetLowAccuracy-TimeSynch()` to read Intel AMT's internal clock, and another method `SetHighAccuracy-TimeSynch()` to synchronize the Intel AMT device's internal clock with an external clock.

Summary

Intel AMT supports a number of CIM data profiles that can be easily accessed by a management console that uses WS-Management and CIM profiles for managing the systems on the network. For the management consoles that do not yet incorporate WS-Management natively, Intel AMT SDK provides a higher level library that can be used as a higher level of abstraction.

Epilogue

It is better to know some of the questions than all of the answers.
— James Thurber (1894–1961)

We trust that this book provided you with enough details about platform management in general and Intel® Active Management Technology (Intel AMT) in particular to get you started using modern management practices. Since we probably left you with a few questions as well, please go to this book's companion Web page at http://www.intel.com/intelpress/iamt for live reference links, a digital edition of the book, and links to the authors' blogs.

In the initial chapters of the book we described the general manageability concepts and reviewed various solutions and technologies from a historical perspective. We also defined the basic components that make a computer a manageable one.

We reviewed various standards and technologies both from a historical perspective as well as current state of the art management technologies, such as CIM and WS-Management.

These standards are used by Intel Active Management Technology, which is a capability of platforms with Intel® vPro™ technology. Computers with Intel vPro Technology provide manageability, security, and energy efficiency using technologies such as Intel AMT, Intel® Virtualization Technology (Intel

VT), and Intel® Trusted Execution Technology (Intel TXT). A number of ingredients in the platforms, such as CPU, chipset, LAN, and BIOS, work together to provide a computing platform geared to enterprise and small business usages.

For a major part of the book we focused on Intel AMT and the ingredients that are specifically used in delivering this capability.

We looked at how Intel AMT provides a number of capabilities that allow discovery, healing, and protection of the platform and resources. These capabilities can be accessed using local or network interfaces in a secure manner. We reviewed how these capabilities are used to solve end user problems.

In Chapter 7, we drilled down into the components that make up Intel AMT. This included the hardware components such as the Intel Management Engine (Intel ME) inside the chipset, the nonvolatile storage, memory, network controller, and so on. Then we described the firmware components such as the Intel ME kernel, common services, and firmware applications. We also discussed some details of the software components that reside on the host OS of the computer that has Intel AMT, as well as components that reside on management consoles on computers remotely located over the network.

Chapter 8–10 discussed in detail the Discover, Heal, and Protect pillars of Intel AMT functionality. In Chapter 8, "Discovery of Platforms and Information," we discussed how to scan for Intel AMT computers on the network, connect, and gather inventory and discovery data from the Intel AMT computer. In Chapter 9, "Healing the Platforms," we covered IDE redirection and Serial-over-LAN, two of the most powerful features of Intel AMT and two features that allow an administrator to take action over a remote computer to diagnose and fix problems. Chapter 10, "Protecting the Platforms," covered the System Defense and heuristic filters that can be used without the need of any specialized software running on each computer. Agent presence support can be added to mission critical software to help monitor their correct operation and make sure to take appropriate action if it is not the case.

In order to realize the full potential of out-of-band manageability, it is important to look at different mechanism to reach an Intel AMT system. Connectivity to Intel AMT is as easy as connecting to any normal web server on the Internet. As with any web server, security considerations are very important. Intel AMT provides very robust authentication and privacy, along with an extra layer of protection when the computer is connected on a foreign network.

Intel® Fast Call for Help allows access from outside the firewall and makes Intel AMT not only a great hardware-based manageability solution but is sometimes the only one that can be deployed and that will truly work.

In Chapter 13, we got hands-on experience with Intel AMT covering two of the main features of Intel AMT: Serial-over-LAN and Intel System Defense. The Manageability Developer Tool Kit (DTK) was introduced, which is a good starting point for people experimenting with Intel AMT for the first time or wanting to check the state of Intel AMT in the field. Users are encouraged to play around with Commander and Outpost. An extended user's guide and many tutorial videos are available on the Manageability Developer Tool Kit Web site, the links for which can be found in the References section.

In Chapters 14–16, we discussed in detail the security and privacy protection mechanisms that are available in Intel AMT.

In Chapter 17 we discussed the various scenarios that are supported for configuring Intel AMT, the various mechanisms and protocols available for configuration of Intel AMT, and we outlined the various options and parameters that can be adjusted to make the tradeoffs between security, cost, and convenience.

Chapter 18 gets into some advanced usages and development of applications using the Developer Toolkit.

We finished the book by circling back in Chapter 19 to standards and discussing the standard interfaces and profiles supported by Intel AMT.

We hope you enjoyed the book and benefited from it.

—Arvind, Purushottam, and Ylian

Appendix

Quick Intel® AMT Setup

This appendix is a quick setup guide for getting the hands-on experience with a new system enabled with Intel® vPro™ technology. This is not intended to provide enterprise class setup and provisioning details, but more of a single system setup that you can perform and start to get a feel of Intel Active Management Technology (Intel AMT) functionality in just a few minutes. A second system with a network and Internet browser is needed to connect to the Intel AMT system.

Identify If You Have an Intel® AMT System

You may have received your system from one of several system vendors, and might have asked for a system with Intel vPro technology, which will have fully functional Intel AMT. However, if you received your system through indirect channels, such as your company having bought the system and provided it to you, and you do not know if your system has Intel AMT capability, the first step is to boot the system and look for Intel AMT setup boot screen.

On motherboards that come from Intel[1], Intel AMT setup is performed within the BIOS, which is accessed by pressing the F2 key at boot time. For most other vendors, Intel AMT setup occurs using the Intel® Management

---

1   For a complete list of Intel motherboards and specifications: http://support.intel.com/support/motherboards

Engine BIOS Extension (Intel MEBX) and can be accessed using Ctrl-P key combination at boot time.

Intel Motherboards

Entering the BIOS is usually done by pressing the F2 key at boot time. Try this a few times while the system is booting. You have to be quick and intercept the boot process before the control is passed to the operating system.

Once in the BIOS setup screen, look for "Intel AMT". If you have such a screen as shown in Figure A.1, your system has Intel AMT, and you can continue with the short setup steps below. While at the BIOS screen, make sure to enable Intel AMT or Intel MEBX so that when you reboot, you can enter into the appropriate setup screens. Within a few minutes you will be interacting with Intel AMT.

Most Other Motherboards

For most other vendors, Intel AMT setup is accomplished using the Intel ME BIOS Extension (Intel MEBX). Users must enter this screen, shown in Figure A.2, by pressing Ctrl-P at some point in the boot sequence. Intel MEBX is active just after the BIOS boot screen and usually appears along with other BIOS extensions such as LAN and RAID extensions.

Even if Intel MEBX is used to set up Intel AMT, many vendors still have some BIOS-specific Intel AMT settings in the BIOS. Some consultation of vendor manuals may be required.

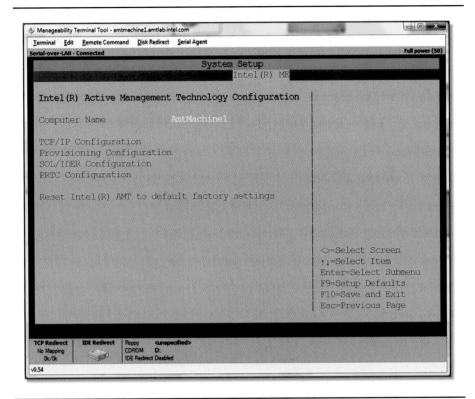

Figure A.1   Sample Intel® AMT Setup Screen within the Intel BIOS

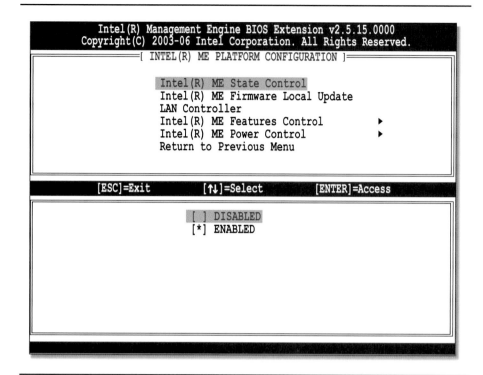

Figure A.2 Intel MEBX Screen for Intel® AMT 2.5

Setting Up the Intel® AMT System

To set up the Intel AMT System, follow these steps:

1. Connect the Intel AMT system to a power outlet. This is necessary because some of the Intel AMT capabilities maybe disabled on battery power. Reset the system to a fresh boot.

2. At the system reboot, enter the BIOS or Intel MEBX to get into Intel AMT setup, as described in previous section.

3. You will be asked to enter the password, and forced to change it. Default factory password is "admin". Change this to a strong password such as: "Amt%1234". Intel AMT will never be enabled unless the password is changed.

4. Select ME Configuration. Verify that the following are set correctly:
   - ME State Control = Enabled
   - ME Features Control -> Manageability Feature Selection is set to "Intel AMT"

5. Select ME Power Control -> ME ON in Host Sleep States, and at the menu selection, pick ON in S0, S3/AC, S4-S5/AC

6. Select AMT Configuration, and go to TCP/IP setup. Configure the static IP address as follows:

   IP Address: 192.168.1.20

7. Subnet Mask: 255.255.255.0

8. Save the configuration.

Configure a Browser to Connect

To configure a browser to connect, follow these steps:

1. Select a system that you can connect to the Intel AMT system using an Ethernet cable. Go to the network settings of this system and configure[2] the IP address. Assign a static IP address

   IP Address: 192.168.1.21

   Subnet Mask: 255.255.255.0

2. Now, connect this system to the Intel AMT system using an Ethernet cable.

3. Open a command prompt, and try pinging the Intel AMT system.

   ping 192.168.1.20

   You should get a ping response.

---

2 Network configuration is specific to the operating system. For example, on Windows XP, the network configuration screen can be reached by selecting Start Menu→Control Panel→Network Connections→Local Area Connection. Once on this screen, selecting Internet Protocol (TCP/IP) and clicking on Properties will get you to the IP configuration screen.

Connect and Explore

Now you are ready to start a web browser.

1. Point the web browser to the address

   http://192.168.1.20:16992

2. When prompted for username/password, type *admin* for username and *Amt%1234* as the password, as shown in Figure A.3.

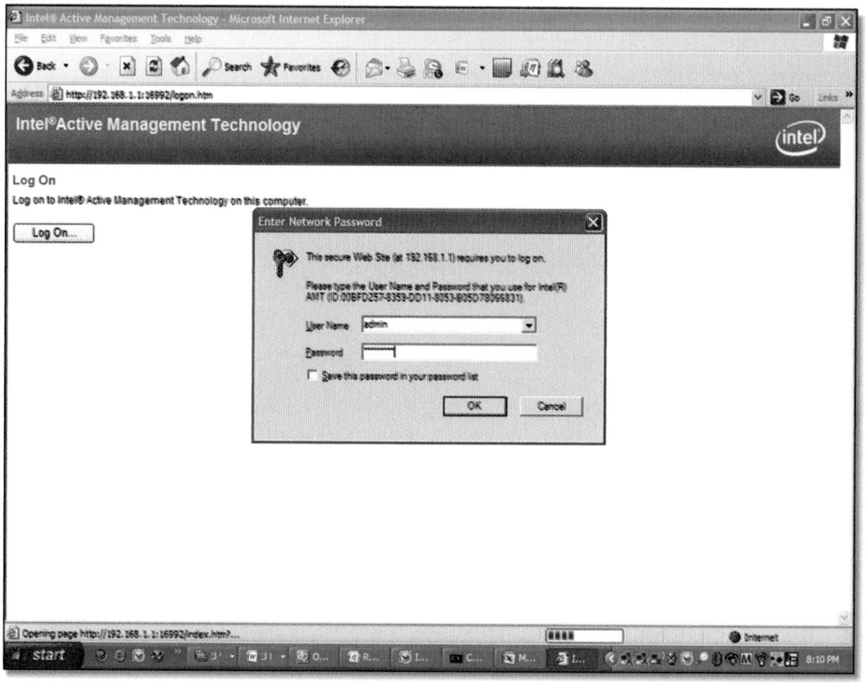

Figure A.3   Intel® AMT Web Browser Login Screen

You are now connected, as shown in Figure A.4

3. Try rebooting the system by going to the Remote Control task from the list items in the menu shown in Figure A.5.

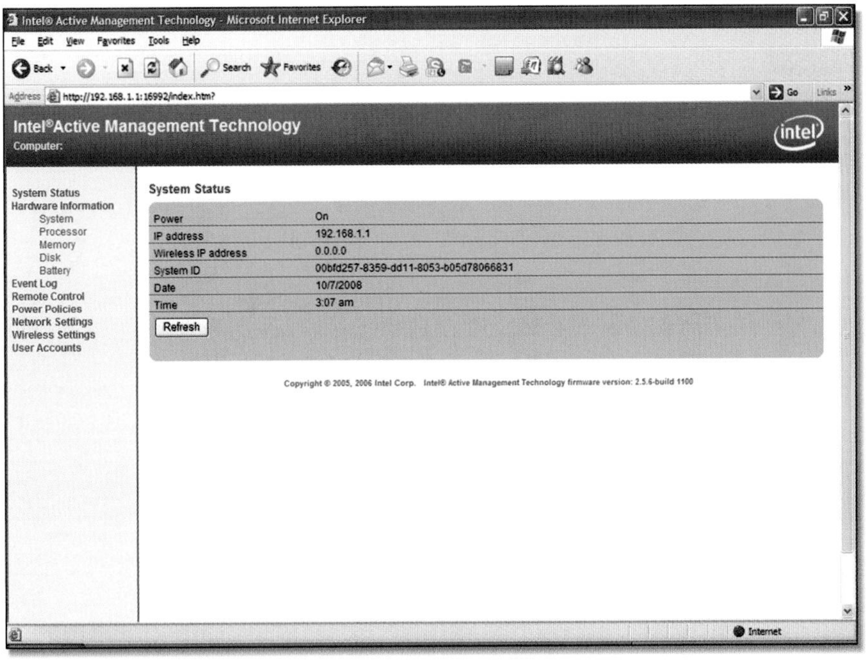

Figure A.4   Intel® AMT Web Browser Screen

Figure A.5 Remote Power Control Using Intel® AMT Web Browser Screen

Notes

When entering the BIOS or Intel MEBX configuration screens, it's important to note that the keyboard will work only in US standard layout, regardless of the keyboard that is connected to the computer. As a result, if a French or British keyboard is connected, the keys typed in don't always give the expected result. For example, the hash key # is different on a US English and on British or French keyboards.

This can lead users to type a different password in BIOS or Intel MEBX (not layout aware) and the web browser (layout aware), even if the same keys are pressed.

One trick is to go to the computer name field in the BIOS or Intel MEBX and type in your password and watch the result on the screen.

Summary

So, there you have it. Now that you have done a basic exploration, you can set up dynamic IP addressing using DHCP and connect using your standard IP configuration in your home or office setup. You can further explore wireless access, secure access using HTTPS, access outside of the firewall and a number of other configuration options. These details can be found in other chapters of the book. Chapters 11–13 and Chapter 17 in particular provide a lot of insights into accessing, configuring, and using Intel AMT.

References

This section contains the links to various reference materials that are relevant to the content in specific chapters. To access this section online and have the convenience of clicking through the links, please go to this book's companion Web page at http://www.intel.com/intelpress/iamt. Before you can access the contents of this section online, you will be asked to first register your book. To complete the registration, find its serial number printed on your book's last page, enter it, and you will automatically be taken to the companion Web page. In addition to the live links provided in this section, you will also find a digital edition of your book in Portable Document Format (PDF) on the companion Web page. (Note: A cookie will be stored on your computer indicating you have registered your book and subsequently, you will be taken to the actual Web page and will not be asked to register again.)

Chapter 2: History of Manageability

1. An excellent reference site for Simple Network Management Protocol (SNMP)

   http://www.snmplink.org/

2. Original SNMP RFC 1157

   http://www.ietf.org/rfc/rfc1157.txt

3. SNMP MIB-II

   http://www.ietf.org/rfc/rfc1213.txt

4. Distributed Management Task Force (DMTF)

   http://www.dmtf.org/

5. Desktop Management Interface (DMI) Information

   http://www.dmtf.org/standards/dmi/

6. Wired for Management (WFM) Specifications

   http://www.intel.com/design/archives/wfm/

7. Preboot Execution Environment (PXE) Specification

   http://download.intel.com/design/archives/wfm/downloads/pxespec.pdf

8. Intelligent Platform Management Interface (IPMI)

   http://www.intel.com/design/servers/ipmi/

9. Alert Standard Format (ASF)

   http://www.dmtf.org/standards/asf/

10. Common Information Model (CIM)

    http://www.dmtf.org/standards/cim/

11. Web Based Enterprise Management (WBEM)

    http://www.dmtf.org/standards/wbem/

Chapter 3: Manageability Standards

1. Common Information Model (CIM)

   http://www.dmtf.org/standards/cim/

2. DMTF Management Profiles

   http://www.dmtf.org/standards/profiles/

3. Web Based Enterprise Management (WBEM)

   http://www.dmtf.org/standards/wbem/

4. Web Services for Management (WS-Management)

   http://www.dmtf.org/standards/wsman/

5. Web Services Specifications used by WS-Management

   http://www.w3.org/Submission/ws-addressing/

   http://www.w3.org/Submission/WS-Transfer/

   http://www.w3.org/Submission/WS-Enumeration/

   http://www.w3.org/Submission/WS-Eventing/

   http://www.w3.org/TR/soap/

6. System Management Architecture for Server Hardware (SMASH)

   http://www.dmtf.org/initiatives/smash_initiative/

7. Desktop and Mobile Architecture for System Hardware (DASH)

   http://www.dmtf.org/initiatives/dash_initiative/

8. DMTF Technologies Diagram (Reproduced in Figure 3.14 with permission from DMTF)

   http://www.dmtf.org/standards/stackmap/

Chapter 4: Overview of Intel® vPro™ Technology

1. Intel® vPro™ Technology

   http://www.intel.com/technology/vpro/

2. A number of articles on Intel® vPro™ in *Intel Technology Journal*

   http://www.intel.com/technology/itj/index.htm?iid=tech_vpro_rhc_itj

3. Intel® Virtualization Technology

   http://www.intel.com/technology/virtualization/

4. Intel® Trusted Execution Technology

   http://www.intel.com/technology/security/

5. Intel® Active Management Technology

   http://www.intel.com/technology/platform-technology/intel-amt/

Chapter 5: Intel® AMT Overview

1. Intel Active Management Technology (Intel AMT)

   http://www.intel.com/technology/platform-technology/intel-amt/

2. Intel AMT Software Development Kit

   http://www.intel.com/software/amt-dtk

3. Intel AMT SDK – Start Here Guide

   http://software.intel.com/en-us/articles/intel-active-management-technology-intel-amt-software-development-kit-sdk-start-here-guide/

Chapter 7: The Components of Intel® AMT

1. Advanced Configuration and Power Interface (ACPI)

   http://www.acpi.info/

2. Intel® Core™ i7 Processor

   http://www.intel.com/products/processor/corei7/index.htm

   http://en.wikipedia.org/wiki/Intel_Core_3

3. Intel® Microarchitecture

   http://www.intel.com/technology/architecture-silicon/next-gen/index.htm

4. Intel® Active Management Technology

   http://www.intel.com/technology/platform-technology/intel-amt/

5. Intel® Management Engine BIOS Extension (Intel® MEBx)

   http://www.intel.com/support/motherboards/desktop/sb/CS-029882.htm

6. Intel AMT on Wikipedia

   http://en.wikipedia.org/wiki/Intel_Active_Management_Technology

   http://en.wikipedia.org/wiki/Intel_AMT_versions

7. *Dynamics of a Trusted Platform; A building block approach* by David Grawrock. (Hillsboro, OR: Intel Press, 2009 ISBN 13: 978-1-934053-17-1)

8. *Applied Virtualization Technology: Usage models for IT professionals and software developers* by Sean Campbell and Michael Jeronimo. (Hillsboro, OR: Intel Press, 2006 ISBN 13: 978-0-976483-23-6)

Chapter 11: Connecting and Communicating with Intel® AMT

1. RFC 2617: HTTP Authentication: Basic and Digest Access Authentication

   http://www.ietf.org/rfc/rfc2617.txt

2. RFC 4120: The Kerberos Network Authentication Service

   http://www.ietf.org/rfc/rfc4120.txt

Chapter 12: Internet Platform Management

1. STunnel open source application

   http://www.stunnel.org/

2. Apache Web Server

   http://www.apache.org/

3. Openwsman

   http://www.openwsman.org

4. WS-Management v1.1 from Microsoft Download site

   http://www.microsoft.com/Downloads/details.aspx?FamilyID=845289ca-16cc-4c73-8934-dd46b5ed1d33&displaylang=en

Chapter 13: Intel® AMT in Small and Medium-sized Business

1. Intel AMT Software Development Kit

   http://www.intel.com/software/amt-dtk

Chapter 14: Securing Intel® AMT from Attacks

1. *Network Security: Private Communication in a Public World* (2nd Edition) by Charlie Kaufman, Radia Perlman, Mike Speciner. (Upper Saddle River, NJ: Prentice Hall, 2003 ISBN 13: 978-0130460-19-6)

2. Kerberos: The Network Authentication Protocol

   http://web.mit.edu/kerberos/

3. Kerberos Papers and Documentation

   http://web.mit.edu/kerberos/papers.html

4. Designing an Authentication System: a Dialogue in Four Scenes

   http://web.mit.edu/kerberos/dialogue.html

5. HTTP-Based Cross-Platform Authentication via the Negotiate Protocol

   http://msdn.microsoft.com/en-us/library/ms995329.aspx

6. Microsoft Kerberos

   http://msdn.microsoft.com/en-us/library/aa378747.aspx

7. Windows 2000 Kerberos Authentication

   http://technet.microsoft.com/en-us/library/bb742431.aspx

8. Utilizing the Windows 2000 Authorization Data in Kerberos Tickets for Access Control to Resources

   http://msdn.microsoft.com/en-us/library/aa302203.aspx

9. Code Signing

   http://en.wikipedia.org/wiki/Code_signing

10. Transport Layer Security – RFC 2246

    http://www.ietf.org/rfc/rfc2246.txt

11. TLS Extensions – RFC 3546

    http://www.ietf.org/rfc/rfc3546.txt

12. Access Control Lists

    http://en.wikipedia.org/wiki/Access_control_list

13. Role Based Access Control

    http://en.wikipedia.org/wiki/Role-based_access_control

14. Network Time Protocol

    http://www.ntp.org

    http://www.ietf.org/rfc/rfc1305.txt

15. Simple Network Time Protocol

    http://www.ietf.org/rfc/rfc2030.txt

16. HTTP Digest – RFC 2617

    http://www.ietf.org/rfc/rfc2617.txt

Chapter 15: Advanced Security Mechanisms in Intel® AMT

1. Pseudo Random Number Generators

   http://en.wikipedia.org/wiki/Pseudorandom_number_generator

2. "S.F. Officials Locked Out of Computer Network," *San Francisco Chronicle*, July 14, 2008.

   http://www.sfgate.com/cgi-bin/article.cgi?f=/c/a/2008/07/14/BAOS11P1M5.DTL&tsp=1

3. Pseudorandom Bits and Sequences (Handbook of Applied Cryptography, Chapter 5)

   http://www.cacr.math.uwaterloo.ca/hac/

4. The Intel Random Number Generator – Benjamin Jun and Paul Kocher

   http://download.intel.com/design/chipsets/rng/CRIwp.pdf

5. TCG Architecture Overview

   https://www.trustedcomputinggroup.org/specs/PCClient

6. TCG EFI Platform Specification

   https://www.trustedcomputinggroup.org/specs/PCClient

7. Advanced Security Features of Intel® vPro™ Technology

   http://www.intel.com/technology/itj/2008/v12i4/10-paper/1-abstract.htm

8. Intel® Trusted Execution Technology

   http://www.intel.com/technology/security/

9. Windows Event Logging

   http://technet.microsoft.com/en-us/library/bb726966.aspx

10. Introduction to XDAS – Security Audit Services

    http://www.opengroup.org/security/das/xdas_int.htm

Chapter 16: Privacy Protection in Intel® AMT

1. Intel® Online Privacy Notice Summary

   http://www.intel.com/sites/sitewide/en_US/privacy/privacy.htm

2. Microsoft Online Privacy Notice Highlights

   http://privacy.microsoft.com/en-us/default.mspx

3. Amazon.com Privacy Notice

   http://www.amazon.com/gp/help/customer/display.html?nodeId=468496

4. Privacy Policy for PayPal Services

   http://www.paypal.com/cgi-bin/webscr?cmd=p/gen/ua/policy_privacy-outside

5. Electronic Privacy Information Center

   http://www.epic.org

6. Privacy.org

   http://www.privacy.org

7. Privacy Rights Clearinghouse

   http://www.privacyrights.org

8. TRUSTe Privacy

http://www.truste.org

9. Directive of the European Parliament on the protection of individuals with regard to the processing of personal data and on the free movement of such data

http://www.cdt.org/privacy/eudirective/EU_Directive_.html

10. Safe Harbor Overview

http://www.export.gov/safeharbor/SH_Overview.asp

11. Safe Harbor Data Privacy

http://www.export.gov/safeharbor/SH_Privacy_Links.asp

12. International Security Trust and Privacy Alliance

http://www.istpa.org/

13. Online Privacy Alliance

http://en.wikipedia.org/wiki/Online_Privacy_Alliance

14. AMT 4.0 - Intel Management & Security Status Icon

http://www.youtube.com/watch?v=2bF6PJZ4f2Y

Chapter 17: Deploying and Configuring Intel® AMT

1. "Simple Identity Management Profile, DSP1034, Version 1.0.0." July 2008

2. "Role Based Authorization Profile. *DSP1039*, Version 1.0.0a." October 2006.

3. Intel AMT Software Development Kit

http://www.intel.com/software/amt-dtk

4. Configuring Intel Active Management Technology

http://www.intel.com/technology/itj/2008/v12i4/6-paper/1-abstract.htm

5. Pre-Shared Key Ciphersuites for Transport Layer Security (TLS)

http://www.ietf.org/rfc/rfc4279.txt

6. Pre-Shared Key (PSK) Ciphersuites with NULL Encryption for Transport Layer Security (TLS)

   http://www.ietf.org/rfc/rfc4785.txt

7. DMTF. "Alert Standard Format Specification (ASF)." DSP0136. April 2003.

8. Intel Corporation. "Wired for Management Baseline, Version 2.0." December 1998.

9. "ITU-T Recommendation X.509 (2005) | ISO/IEC 9594-8:2005." Information Technology-Open Systems Interconnection-The Directory: Public-key and attribute certificate frameworks.

10. DHCP Options and BOOTP Vendor Extensions – RFC 2132

    http://www.ietf.org/rfc/rfc2132.txt

Chapter 18: Developing Solutions for Intel® AMT

1. Windows Remote Management (WinRM)

   http://msdn.microsoft.com/en-us/library/aa384426(VS.85).aspx

2. Intel® WS-Management Translator

   http://software.intel.com/en-us/articles/intel-ws-management-translator/

3. Intel® Active Management Technology Reference Design Kit (RDK)

   http://software.intel.com/en-us/articles/intel-active-management-technology-reference-design-kit-rdk-utility-application-package/

4. Openwsman

   http://www.openwsman.org/

5. Kerberos: The Network Authentication Protocol

   http://web.mit.edu/Kerberos/

Chapter 19: Support for WS-Management and CIM Profiles

1. DSP0226: Web Services for Management (WS Management)

    http://www.dmtf.org/standards/published_documents/
    DSP0226_1.0.0.pdf

2. DSP0227: WS-Management CIM Binding Specification

    http://www.dmtf.org/standards/published_documents/DSP0227.pdf

3. DSP0230: WS-CIM Mapping Specification

    http://www.dmtf.org/standards/published_documents/DSP0230.pdf

4. DSP0232: DASH Implementation Requirements

    http://www.dmtf.org/standards/published_documents/
    DSP0232_1.1.0.pdf

5. DMTF Management Profiles

    http://www.dmtf.org/standards/profiles/

Index

Continuing Education is Essential

It's a challenge we all face – keeping pace with constant change in information technology. Whether our formal training was recent or long ago, we must all find time to keep ourselves educated and up to date in spite of the daily time pressures of our profession.

Intel produces technical books to help the industry learn about the latest technologies. The focus of these publications spans the basic motivation and origin for a technology through its practical application.

Right books, right time, from the experts

These technical books are planned to synchronize with roadmaps for technology and platforms, in order to give the industry a head-start. They provide new insights, in an engineer-to-engineer voice, from named experts. Sharing proven insights and design methods is intended to make it more practical for you to embrace the latest technology with greater design freedom and reduced risks.

I encourage you to take full advantage of Intel Press books as a way to dive deeper into the latest technologies, as you plan and develop your next generation products. They are an essential tool for every practicing engineer or programmer. I hope you will make them a part of your continuing education tool box.

Sincerely,

Justin Rattner
Senior Fellow and Chief Technology Officer
Intel Corporation

Turn the page to learn about titles
from Intel Press for system developers

Dynamics of a Trusted Platform
A Building Block Approach
By David Grawrock
ISBN 978-1-934053-08-9

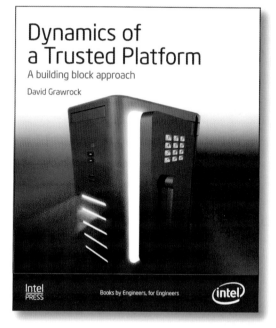

In Dynamics of a Trusted Platform David Grawrock has updated his highly popular Intel Safer Computing Initiative with new topics covering the latest developments in secure computing. The reader is introduced to the concept of Trusted Computing and the building block approach to designing security into PC platforms. The Intel® Trusted Execution Technology† (Intel® TXT) is one of those building blocks that can be used to create a trusted platform by integrating new security features and capabilities into the processor, chipset, and other platform components.

"The chapters on Anatomy of an Attack and System Protection present useful, practical information that will help familiarize a person with the impacts of protection (or lack thereof) of system components and resources. Treatment of the topic of measurement is particularly useful for system designers and programmers." - *Amy C Nelson, Dell, Inc*

"David finds analogies in everyday life to clearly explain many of the concepts in this book. I would highly recommended Dynamics of a Trusted Platform for researchers, architects, and designers who are serious about trusted computing." - *Dr. Sigrid Gürgens Fraunhofer Institute for Secure Information Technology (SIT)*

"The opportunity now exists to start building trusted systems, making this book very timely. It would be foolhardy to start without a thorough understanding of the concepts; and this is what Dynamics of a Trusted Platform gives you. The building blocks described here are certainly able to imbue the infrastructure with a higher level of trustworthiness, and we may all look forward to the many benefits flowing from that." - *Andrew Martin Director, Oxford University Software Engineering Centre*

Applied Virtualization Technology

Usage Models for IT Professionals and Software Developers

By Sean Campbell and Michael Jeronimo
ISBN 978-0-976483-26-6

Server and desktop virtualization is one of the more significant technologies to impact computing in the last few years, promising the benefits of infrastructure consolidation, lower costs, increased security, ease of management, and greater employee productivity.

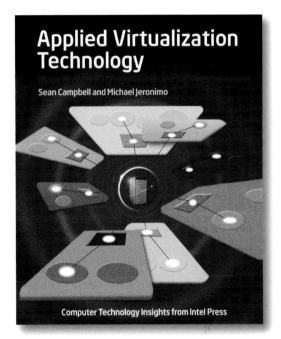

Using virtualization technology, one computer system can operate as multiple "virtual" systems. The convergence of affordable, powerful platforms and robust scalable virtualization solutions is spurring many technologists to examine the broad range of uses for virtualization. In addition, a set of processor and I/O enhancements to Intel server and client platforms, known as Intel® Virtualization Technology (Intel® VT), can further improve the performance and robustness of current software virtualization solutions.

This book takes a user-centered view and describes virtualization usage models for IT professionals, software developers, and software quality assurance staff. The book helps you plan the introduction of virtualization solutions into your environment and thereby reap the benefits of this emerging technology.

Highlights include
- The challenges of current virtualization solutions
- In-depth examination of three software-based virtualization products
- Usage models that enable greater IT agility and cost savings
- Usage models for enhancing software development and QA environments
- Maximizing utilization and increasing flexibility of computing resources
- Reaping the security benefits of computer virtualization
- Distribution and deployment strategies for virtualization solutions

Energy Efficiency for Information Technology

How to Reduce Power Consumption in Servers and Data Centers
By David Grawrock
ISBN 978-1-934053-08-9

Minimizing power consumption is one of the primary technical challenges that today's IT organizations face. In Energy Efficiency for Information Technology, Lauri Minas and Brad Ellison point out, that the overall consumption of electrical power by data centers can be reduced by understanding the several sources of power consumption and minimizing each one. Drawing on their engineering experience within Intel Corporation and with the industry, they break down power consumption into its constituent parts and explain each in a bottom-up fashion. With energy consumption well defined, Minas and Ellison systematically provide guidance for minimizing each draw on electrical power.

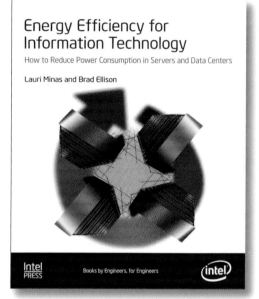

"Throughout my global travels, I hear increasing concern for the issues of power consumption by data centers, both due to the costs and also harm to the planet. *Energy Efficiency for Information Technology* addresses a critical issue for IT suppliers and consumers alike." Vernon Turner, Senior Vice President & General Manager, Enterprise Computing, Network, Consumer, and Infrastructure, IDC

"In *Energy Efficiency for Information Technology* Minas and Ellison underscore the magnitude of increases in power consumption, they systematically suggest ways to minimize consumption and provide checklists and assessments tables that are particularly useful to gather or summarize the right information for the planning. This is a multidimensional book that addresses a serious challenge to IT departments around the globe."
YY Chow, Managing Director, Systems and Securities Services, Mitsubishi-UFJ Securities

"*Energy Efficiency for Information Technology* is a remarkable compilation of cutting-edge technical knowledge for addressing the critical issue of power and cooling in data centers. It shows how your data center can compute more but cost less, while also reducing energy use and environmental impacts".
Jonathan Koomey, Ph.D., Project Scientist, Lawrence Berkeley National Laboratory

"Lauri Minas and Brad Ellison have written an important book that explains how diligent IT professionals can maximize the productivity of their data centers while minimizing power costs. These Intel engineers speak from experience and with authority. Anyone seriously interested in the greening of IT should read *Energy Efficiency for Information Technology*." Lorie Wigle, President, Climate Servers Computing Initiative.

Service Oriented Architecture Demystified

A pragmatic approach to SOA for the IT executives

By Girish Juneja, Blake Dournaee, Joe Natoli, and Steve Birkel

ISBN 978-1-934053-02-7

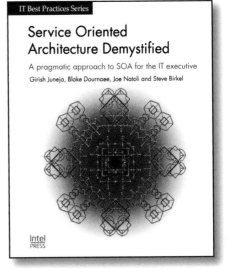

The authors of this definitive book on SOA debunk the myths and demonstrate through examples from different vertical industries how a "crawl, walk, run" approach to deployment of SOA in an IT environment can lead to a successful return on investment.

One popular argument states that SOA is not a technology per se, but that it stands alone and can be implemented using a wide range of technologies. The authors believe that this definition, while attractive and elegant, doesn't necessarily pass pragmatic muster.

Service Oriented Architecture Demystified describes both the technical and organizational impacts of adopting SOA and the pursuant challenges. The authors demonstrate through real life deployments why and how different industry sectors are adopting SOA, the challenges they face, the advantages they have realized, and how they have (or have not) addressed the issues emerging from their adoption of SOA. This book strikes a careful balance between describing SOA as an enabler of business processes and presenting SOA as a blueprint for the design of software systems in general. Throughout the book, the authors attempt to cater to both technical and organizational viewpoints, and show how both are very different in terms of why SOA is useful. The IT software architect sees SOA as a business process enabler and the CTO sees SOA as a technology trend with powerful paradigms for software development and software integration.

SOA can be characterized in terms of different vertical markets. For each such market, achieving SOA means something different and involves different transformational shifts. The vertical markets covered include healthcare, government, manufacturing, finance, and telecommunications. SOA considerations are quite different across these vertical markets, and in some cases, the required organizational shifts and technology shifts are highly divergent and context dependent.

Whether you are a CTO, CIO, IT manager, or IT architect, this book provides you with the means to analyze the readiness of your internal IT organization and with technologies to adopt a service oriented approach to IT.

The Business Value of Virtual Service Oriented Grids

Strategic Insights for Enterprise Decision Makers

By Enrique Castro-leon, Jackson He, Mark Chang and Parviz Peiravi
ISBN 978-1-934053-10-2

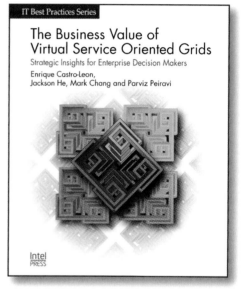

"In this book the authors track the trends, create new rules based on new realities, and establish new market models. With virtual service-oriented grids, the sky is the limit," writes Wei-jen Lee, a University of Texas – Arlington professor, about *The Business Value of Virtual Service Oriented Grids*, a new book published by Intel. The application of service-oriented architecture (SOA) for business will interest application developers looking for the latest advances in technology and ideas on how to utilize those advances to keep up in a global economy. *The Business Value of Virtual Service Oriented Grids* provides a framework that describes how the convergence of three well-known technologies are defining a new information technology model that will fundamentally change the way we do business. The first step, say the authors, is the development of new applications for the consumer market. However, even bigger is the development of new applications in a federated fashion using services modules called *servicelets*. These federated or composite applications can be built in a fraction of the time it takes to develop traditional applications. This new environment will lower the bar for applications development, opening opportunities for thousands of smaller players worldwide.

"We live in exponential times. . . . The economy is now thoroughly global. The Internet has replaced many of the middle layers of business, has enabled many to work from home or from a small company, and is revolutionizing the retail industries." writes Portland State University professor Gerald Sheble.

"The advent of SOA is going to impact information processing and computer services on a scale not previously envisioned." The speed-up in application development and integration will accelerate the deployment of IT capabilities, which in turn will have a consequential effect on the organization's business agility. Corporate decision makers will enjoy the ability to pick and choose among capital and operations expenses to suit their organization's business goals. The book describes the business trends within which this convergence is taking place and provides insight on how these changes can affect your business. It clearly explains the interplay between technology, architectural considerations, and standards with illustrative examples. Finally, the book tells you how your organization can benefit from *servicelets*, alerts you about integration pitfalls, and describes approaches for putting together your technology adoption strategy for building your virtual SOA environment using *servicelets*.

About Intel Press

Intel Press is the authoritative source of timely, technical books
to help software and hardware developers speed up their development
process. We collaborate only with leading industry experts to deliver
reliable, first-to-market information about the latest
technologies, processes, and strategies.

Our products are planned with the help of many people in the developer
community and we encourage you to consider becoming a customer advisor.
If you would like to help us and gain additional advance insight to the latest
technologies, we encourage you to consider the Intel Press Customer
Advisor Program. You can register here:

www.intel.com/intelpress/register.htm

For information about bulk orders or corporate sales, please send e-mail to:
bulkbooksales@intel.com

Other Developer Resources from Intel

At these Web sites you can also find valuable technical information and
resources for developers:

www.intel.com/technology/rr	Recommended reading list for books of interest to developers
www.intel.com/technology/itj	Intel Technology Journal
developer.intel.com	General information for developers
www.intel.com/software	content, tools, training, and the Intel Early Access Program for software developers
www.intel.com/software/products	Programming tools to help you develop high-performance applications
www.intel.com/netcomms	Solutions and resources for networking and communications
www.intel.com/idf	Worldwide technical conference, the Intel Developer Forum

6175-0137-9508-8522

If serial number is missing, please send an
e-mail to Intel Press at intelpress@intel.com